Latin American Political Economy in the Age of Neoliberal Reform

Theoretical and Comparative
Perspectives for the 1990s

North·South Center
UNIVERSITY OF MIAMI

Latin American Political Economy in the Age of Neoliberal Reform

Theoretical and Comparative
Perspectives for the 1990s

Edited by

William C. Smith, Carlos H. Acuña,
and Eduardo A. Gamarra

Transaction Publishers
New Brunswick (U.S.A.) and London (U.K.)

The mission of the North-South Center is to promote better relations among the United States, Canada, and the nations of Latin America and the Caribbean by providing a disciplined intellectual focus for improved relations, commerce, and understanding in the hemisphere, wherein major political, social, and economic issues are seen in a global context. The Center conducts policy-relevant research and programs of education, training, cooperative study, and public outreach and engages in an active program of publication and dissemination of information on the Americas. The North-South Center fosters linkages among academic and research institutions throughout the Americas and acts as an agent of constructive change in the region.

Library of Congress Cataloging-in-Publication Data

Latin American political economy in the age of neoliberal reform:
   theoretical and comparative perspectives for the 1990s / edited
   by William C. Smith, Carlos H. Acuña, Eduardo A. Gamarra.
        p   cm.
   Includes index.
   ISBN 1-56000-731-1 (paper)
    1. Economic forecasting — Latin America. 2. Latin America —
  Economic policy. 3. Latin America — Economic conditions — 1982 –
  I. Smith, William C., 1946-   II. Acuña, Carlos (Carlos H.)
  III. Gamarra, Eduardo.
  HC125.L3526 1994
  338.98—dc20   93-44981
                                             CIP

ISBN-1-56000-731-1 (paper)
Printed in the United States of America
00 99 98 97 96 95   8 7 6 5 4 3

Contents

Contributors

Carlos H. Acuña teaches comparative politics at the Universidad de Buenos Aires and is an associate researcher at the Centro de Estudios de Estado y Sociedad (CEDES) in Argentina. He is the author of *La burguesía industrial como actor político en la Argentina* (forthcoming), editor of *El nuevo sistema político argentino* (forthcoming), and coeditor with William C. Smith and Eduardo A. Gamarra of *Democracy, Markets, and Structural Reform in Latin America* (1994) and with Catalina Smulovitz of *Los militares como actor político en las nuevas democracias del Cono Sur* (forthcoming).

Luiz Carlos Bresser Pereira teaches economics at the Fundação Getúlio Vargas in São Paulo and is the editor of the *Revista de Economia Política*. His many books include *The Theory of Inertial Inflation* (1987), coauthored with Y. Nakano; *A Crise do Estado: Ensaios sobre a Economia Brasileira* (1992); *Os Tempos Heróicos de Collor e Zélia: Aventuras da Modernidade e Desventuras da Ortodoxia* (1991); and *Economic Reforms in New Democracies* (1993), coauthored with José María Maravall and Adam Przeworski. He is the editor of *Populismo Econômico: Ortodoxia, Desenvolvimento e Populismo na América Latina* (1991). He has served as Brazil's minister of finance.

Marcelo Cavarozzi teaches Latin American and comparative politics at the Facultad Latinoamericana de Ciencias Sociales (FLACSO) in Mexico and is a consultant at the Overseas Development Council in Washington, D.C. He is the author of *Autoritarismo y democracia* (1983) and the coeditor with Manuel Antonio Garretón of *Muerte y resurrección: Los partidos políticos en el autoritarismo y las transiciones en el cono sur* (1989).

José María Fanelli is a senior researcher at the Centro de Estudios de Estado y Sociedad (CEDES) in Argentina and teaches economics at the Universidad de Buenos Aires. He is the author and coauthor of many studies of the Argentine and Latin American economies including, with

Roberto Frenkel, *On Gradualism, Shock Treatment, and Sequencing* (1993); with Roberto Frenkel and Lance Taylor, *The World Development Report 1991: A Critical Assessment* (1992); and with Roberto Frenkel and Guillermo Rozenwurcel, *Transformación estructural, estabilización y reforma del estado en la Argentina* (1992)

Roberto Frenkel is the director of economic studies at the Centro de Estudios de Estado y Sociedad (CEDES) in Argentina and teaches economics at the Universidad de Buenos Aires. He is the author of numerous studies of structural adjustment and economic reform in Latin America and is the coauthor with José María Fanelli of *On Gradualism, Shock Treatment, and Sequencing* (1993); with José María Fanelli and Lance Taylor *The World Development Report 1991: A Critical Assessment* (1992); and with José María Fanelli and Guillermo Rozenwurcel, *Transformación estructural, estabilización y reforma del estado en la Argentina* (1992).

Eduardo A. Gamarra teaches Latin American politics at Florida International University, where he is a member of senior editorial staff of *Hemisphere*. He is the coauthor with James Malloy of *Revolution and Reaction: Bolivia, 1964-1985* (1988); coeditor with William C. Smith and Carlos H. Acuña of *Democracy, Markets, and Structural Reform in Latin America* (1994); and coeditor with A. Douglas Kincaid of *Seguridad ciudadana y seguridad nacional: la policía y relaciones cívico militares en América Latina*.

José María Maravall teaches politics and sociology at the Universidad de Madrid. He is the author of *La política de la transición* (1981) and *Dictatorship and Political Dissent: Workers and Students in Franco's Spain* (1978) and is coauthor with Luiz Carlos Bresser Pereira and Adam Przeworski of *Economic Reforms in New Democracies* (1993). He has served as Spain's minister of education and science.

Guillermo O'Donnell is director of the Helen Kellogg Institute of International Studies at the University of Notre Dame. He is the author of *Bureaucratic-Authoritarianism: Argentina, 1966-1973, in Comparative Perspective* (1988); and the coeditor with Phillipe Schmitter and Laurence Whitehead of *Transitions from Authoritarian Rule* (1986), with Fábio Wanderley Reis of *A Democracia no Brasil: Dilemas e Perspectivas* (1988), and with Scott Mainwaring and J. Samuel Valenzuela of *Issues in Democratic Consolidation: The New South*

Democracies in Comparative Perspective (1992). He is a past president of the International Political Science Association.

Adam Przeworski teaches comparative politics at the University of Chicago. His many books include *Capitalism and Social Democracy* (1985), *The State and the Economy under Capitalism* (1990), and *Democracy and the Market: Political and Economic Reforms in Eastern Europe and Latin America* (1991). He is also the coauthor with John D. Sprague of *Paper Stones: A History of Electoral Socialism* (1986) and with Luiz Carlos Bresser Pereira and José María Maravall of *Economic Reforms in New Democracies* (1993).

Guillermo Rozenwurcel is associate researcher at the Centro de Estudios de Estado y Sociedad (CEDES) in Buenos Aires, Argentina, and teaches economics at the Universidad de Buenos Aires. His is the author of *Fiscal Reform and Macroeconomic Stabilization in Argentina* (forthcoming); coauthor with Roberto Frenkel and José María Fanelli of *Transformación estructural, estabilización y reforma del estado en la Argentina* (1992); and the editor of *Elecciones y política económica en América Latina* (1991).

William C. Smith teaches Latin American and comparative politics at the University of Miami and is the director of the Task Force on Democratization at the North-South Center. He is the author of *Authoritarianism and the Crisis of the Argentine Political Economy* (1989) and coeditor with Carlos H. Acuña and Eduardo A. Gamarra of *Democracy, Markets, and Structural Reform in Latin America* (1994) and with Lars Schoultz and Augusto Varas of *Security, Democracy, and Development in U.S.-Latin American Relations* (1994).

Aldo C. Vacs teaches Latin American and comparative politics at Skidmore College. He is the author of *Discreet Partners: Argentina and the USSR Since 1917* (1984) and has published widely in such journals as *Foro Internacional, Annals of Political Science,* and *Journal of Interamerican Studies and World Affairs.* He has also contributed chapters to numerous volumes, including *Authoritarians and Democrats* (1988), edited by James Malloy and Mitchell Seligson, and *Cuba After the Cold War* (1993), edited by Carmelo Mesa-Lago.

Preface and Acknowledgments

The unraveling and collapse of models of accumulation based upon import-substitution industrialization in Latin America during the 1970s and 1980s were accompanied by profound transformations in relations among the state, civil society, and the economy. The postauthoritarian regimes that emerged in Latin America over the past decade have achieved a degree of democratic consolidation, but they continue to confront severe political and economic challenges. Stable and sustainable growth remains an elusive goal for many countries, despite the modest successes of neoliberal strategies of market-oriented restructuring in achieving external adjustment, taming hyperinflation, and disciplining public sector finance. Sharp declines in per capita income in many countries have exacerbated poverty and worsened already egregious patterns of inequality and concentration of wealth and control over productive resources. Moreover, the often autocratic implementation frequently associated with stabilization and structural adjustment policies has shown a disturbing tendency to undermine representative institutions and the conditions for deepening democratic politics, particularly broadening of citizenship rights beyond the electoral arena.

Understanding these social and economic transformations and their implications for democracy demands a fundamental rethinking of many central issues in Latin American political economy. This is obviously not the first time shifts in prevailing political and economic models in Latin America have provoked theoretical and methodological debates among social scientists or prompted calls for new paradigms better equipped to capture the elusive reality of rapidly changing circumstances; one has only to recall the fervor that informed still simmering debates between structuralists and monetarists or between the defenders of theories of development and modernization and those advocating perspectives privileging questions of external dependency and the region's peripheral or semiperipheral insertion in the world economy. This volume is motivated by a more modest goal. We harbor no illusion of having discovered a new paradigm. Rather, we seek to articulate a perspective that eschews conventional approaches and the

v

theoretico-methodological reductionisms that consider one or the other set of variables, be they political or economic, as "exogenous" or as merely "contextual" to the object of analysis. In this spirit, we hope to offer interpretations of sociopolitical processes in the region that advance beyond the old antimony between "economics" and "politics."

The many themes analyzed in this volume first emerged in the individual research agendas of the editors. Early discussions about the tensions among democracy, markets, and economic reform between Bill Smith and Eduardo Gamarra led to a project supported by the External Grants Office of the North-South Center at the University of Miami. This endeavor was soon enriched by the incorporation of Carlos Acuña into our discussions. Our collective brainstorming, in turn, evolved into a conference held in March 1992 in Buenos Aires. During three, highly stimulating, albeit exhausting days, more than two dozen political scientists and economists from both Latin America and the United States, plus several dozen invited guests from various Buenos Aires research institutions, engaged in collective debate early in the morning and, as is the habit among the *porteños*, recessed only in the early hours of the following morning.

The Buenos Aires symposium was followed by editors' requests to the participants for extensive revisions of their original *ponencias*. The resulting chapters were originally planned for one volume, whose heft caused the editors to refer to it as our *ladrillo*, or "brick." One evening, after a long day's labor on the manuscript, and stimulated by an excellent cabernet sauvignon, it dawned upon us that we really had produced two books, rather than one, with each book capable of standing alone — the present volume provides theoretical and comparative perspectives on democracy, markets, and economic restructuring, while the second consists of matched pairs of contributions from political scientists and economists on the five countries selected for analysis. Readers of this first volume who desire the wealth of empirical materials provided by the studies of Argentina, Bolivia, Brazil, Chile, and Mexico may wish to consult the second volume, *Democracy, Markets, and Structural Reform in Latin America: Argentina, Bolivia, Brazil, Chile, and Mexico.*

The topics and contributors to this volume include Future Politico-Economic Scenarios for Latin America (William C. Smith and Carlos H. Acuña); Politics and Economics in the Argentina of the Nineties (Carlos H. Acuña); Crisis and Transformation of the Argentine State (1978-1992) (Adolfo Canitrot); Crafting Political Support for Stabilization in Bolivia (Eduardo A. Gamarra); Democracy, Liberalism, and Structural Reform in Bolivia (Juan Antonio Morales); The State, Structural Reform, and Democratization in Brazil (Lourdes Sola); Renegade Development: Rise and Demise of State-Led Development in Brazil (Antônio Barros de Castro); The Political Dimension of Processes of Transformation in Chile (Manuel Antonio Garretón); Market Economy, Social Welfare, and Democratic Consolidation in Chile (Pilar Vergara); Making Economic Reform Politically Viable: The Mexican Case (Blanca Heredia); and On the Political Economy of Market and State Reform in Mexico (Jaime Ros).

In this volume, we focus on the multiple interrogations implicit in the problematic relations between economics and politics and their implications for Latin America's present and future. Eduardo Gamarra's introductory chapter opens our discussion with a wide-ranging overview of the challenges confronting Latin American countries as they simultaneously pursue the goals of democratization and profound economic reform. In Chapter 2, Carlos Acuña and Bill Smith examine the relationship between sociopolitical conflict and economic performance in order to understand the logic of support for and opposition to market-oriented restructuring and to identify several alternative politico-economic scenarios for the region. Aldo Vacs, in Chapter 3, probes the international context shaping the twin processes of democratization and economic restructuring and offers some sobering reminders regarding the powerful centrifugal and centripetal forces that make liberal democracy and capitalist market economies such a fragile equilibrium. In Chapter 4, José María Fanelli, Roberto Frenkel, and Guillermo Rozenwurcel critique current neoclassical prescriptions on structural reform crystallized in the so-called "Washington Consensus" advocated by the U.S. government, the International Monetary Fund, and the World Bank, delineate the chief characteristics of the path of "explosive adjustment" followed in many Latin American countries in the wake of the debt crisis, and then advocate a coherent set of alternative policies.

Three essays exemplifying middle-range theories and comparative analyses of contemporary Latin America follow. Marcelo Cavarozzi, in Chapter 5, goes beyond his pioneering formulation of the "state-centric matrix" to highlight the key role that politics and a reformulated state anchored in civil society will play in the transition to new forms of political regulation and economic organization in the region. In Chapter 6, Guillermo O'Donnell builds upon his previous work on "delegative democracy" to examine issues related to citizenship, justice, and the crisis of the "state as law" in Latin America with, as he puts it, a "few glances" at post-communist societies. The volume concludes with a provocative critique in Chapter 7 by Luiz Carlos Bresser Pereira, José María Maravall, and Adam Przeworski of neoclassical approaches to market-oriented economic reform that leads them to propose an alternative "social-democratic" approach for achieving stability with sustainable growth and social justice compatible with the deepening of democratic practices and institutions.

On behalf of all the participants in this symposium, we wish to express our great appreciation to those who made this project possible. For the necessary financial support, as well as for continued advice and friendship, we owe special thanks to the North-South Center and its director, Ambassador Ambler H. Moss, Jr., and to Mary Uebersax, in charge of the External Grants Program, and Robin Rosenberg, who oversees research and studies at the Center. In later stages of the project, the involvement of other Center staff, including Richard Downes, Kathy Hamman, Jayne Weisblatt, Diane Duys, Mary Mapes, and Stephanie Moss were essential to the preparation of the manuscript for publication. We are also grateful to Patricia Rosas, at the University of California at San Diego, who helped bring a sense of clarity and style to the sometimes opaque prose of the editors and contributors.

This project would not have been possible without the collaboration of our respective institutions, colleagues, students, and staff. At Florida International University, the assistance of Francine Bard and René Ramos of the Latin American and Caribbean Center and the Department of Political Science is gratefully acknowledged. In Buenos Aires, the assistance of Mercedes Laplace, then at the Centro de Estudios de Estado y Sociedad, was absolutely *imprescindible* in the organization and smooth operation of the symposium. We also thank Torcuato Di Tella for making available the conference facilities at the Fundación Simón Rodríguez. The countless hours of cheerful and dedicated work in translating and editing manuscripts and managing endless reams of paperwork on the part of Vanessa Gray, Erick Bridoux, Mariela Córdoba, and Pamela Mulder, students at the University of Miami's Graduate School of International Studies, are deeply appreciated. Finally, we happily recognize the patience and inspiration received from María de Lourdes and Gabriela, Elsa and Malena, and Terry and Jackie.

Although the project was originally conceived by Smith and Gamarra, the order of names simply reflects Bill Smith's overall leadership and responsibility for editing the final product. After Smith, names are listed alphabetically. In every way, this book reflects a collective effort on the part of editors and authors.

William C. Smith
Carlos H. Acuña
Eduardo A. Gamarra

Coral Gables, Florida
November 5, 1993

Chapter One

Market-Oriented Reforms and Democratization in Latin America: Challenges of the 1990s

Eduardo A. Gamarra

Introduction

Latin American democracies reached a critical juncture in the early 1990s, nearly a decade after their torturous transitions from authoritarian rule. Owing to a weak tradition in new democratic rules and the relative strength of sociopolitical actors, the outcome of transition still faced a period of great uncertainty. Fragile governments survived and, some would argue, democracy even reached minimal levels of consolidation.[1] Definitions of consolidation (which are mostly minimalist) note that democracy in Latin America is institutionalized through a negative consensus: the armed forces no longer constitute a threat, business supports the system, and labor is too weak to challenge the neoliberal economic project. To claim that consolidation has been achieved, however, overlooks the dynamics of the ongoing democratization process.

To view democratization as a dynamic process enables assessment of how distinct political and social actors appeared and disappeared during the 1980s and early 1990s. This process has no clear-cut outcome and may follow a variety of paths, even a reversion to military rule. Latin American nations most often exhibit a hybrid, which combines authoritarian decision-making processes and democratic legitimation. A careful examination of the dynamics through which sociopolitical actors crafted ways out of the political-economy crisis of the 1980s enhances our understanding of how contenders for political power, who initially subscribed to "populist" or more heterodox economic

1

policies, survived and accommodated themselves to the new economic and political reality of the region.

The first section of this chapter discusses problems of governance faced by democratically elected rulers in Latin America in the context of stabilization and the imposition of market-oriented reforms. The next section analyzes the complex relationship between stabilization measures and the market reforms that followed. The final section examines the challenges posed by neoliberal reforms as governments attempt to bring organized labor, business sectors, political parties, and the armed forces into the policy-making process.

Governance, Democratization, and Market Reforms

The notion that to govern is to manage the economy effectively was one of the most powerful views to emerge in Latin America during the 1980s. Armed with the legitimacy of elections and democratic institutions, governments throughout the region opted to pursue decision-making styles which excluded broad sectors of the population and implemented "correct" economic measures. The tensions emerging from this managerial view of democracy may have implications for the process of democratization now unfolding.

Democratically elected presidents in Latin America faced numerous challenges in the latter half of the 1980s, including declining social indicators and a crisis of confidence in principal political institutions. They focused their attention on the implementation of market-oriented stabilization strategies and profound public sector reforms, such as privatization, deregulation, decentralization, and trade liberalization. Development planners at international financial institutions and bureaucrats in local ministries agreed on the necessity for stabilization and structural reforms; this consensus provided the impetus for neoliberal reforms that swept the region. Stabilization policies, in the context of hyperinflation, generated a core of support. Economists claimed with certainty that stabilization was a necessary, but not sufficient, measure to respond to the profound economic crisis facing Latin America. Stabilization policies were viewed as a prerequisite, while public-sector reform became a long-term element in the battle against the ills facing the entire region.

These strategies had only modest economic success. In the best cases, inflation stabilized at about 20 percent and hyperinflation was brought under control. Economic growth lagged, however, resulting in declines in per capita income and an exacerbation of social inequality. The ambiguous performance of these economies brought out tensions between the logic of democratization and the neoliberal rationale. Social groups — especially labor and the lower middle classes — believed that democratization would allow the redressing of grievances and demands, neglected through years of authoritarian repression.

As numerous studies on Latin American transitions have noted, democratization arrived at one of the bleakest economic periods in history. Facing bankrupt economies, hyperinflation, and declining growth, the newly elected civilian rulers faced a major challenge. Their task was to accomplish two seemingly contradictory objectives simultaneously: to institutionalize competitive politics with expanded political participation and to respond to international financial institutions and foreign governments bent on proving the superiority of marketplace logic. The globalization process in the world economy was a principal force orienting change in Latin America. As Vacs notes in this volume, the dual process of transition in Latin America followed a worldwide pattern of transformation, rooted in developments in the political economies of advanced industrial societies. The Republican and conservative agenda that gripped the United States and Great Britain in the early 1980s radically altered economic policy. Driven by a new economic logic, governments in core nations initiated a decade-long strategy of domestic decentralization, deregulation, privatization, and trade liberalization, although in no case did their reforms go as far as what they have recently required of Latin American nations.

Not surprisingly, these "free market" policies became a crucial ingredient of U.S. foreign policy. During the Reagan and Bush years, promoting free markets and free trade became as fundamental as extolling the virtues of elections and liberal democracy, the other key ingredient of the foreign policy agenda of Republican administrations and Democratic Congresses. Shifts in U.S. foreign policy undoubtedly provided an environment that allowed political and economic transformations in Latin America to occur.

Latin American democratization and economic transformations, however, did not lag behind developments elsewhere. Latin America may have anticipated the monumental transformations in both politics and economics that occurred throughout the world in the 1980s. In fact, the region made its own contributions to these global transformations. Political openings began to occur as early as 1974; moreover, shifts toward market economies occurred in Argentina and Chile under authoritarian regimes before the Reagan-Thatcher experiments. Whereas in the past, U.S. policy supported the relationship between authoritarian regimes and capitalism, in the 1980s Latin America conveniently highlighted a relationship between open, competitive political systems and market economies.

The transition toward democracy and markets in Latin America anticipated the collapse of the Soviet Union and Eastern Europe and the concomitant end of the Cold War. But other transformations occurring worldwide also had an impact on Latin America. The emergence of a transnational and interdependent market economy changed the nature of nation-specific or even region-specific solutions. Global concern for cross-national issues — such as security, health, ecology, narcotics, and technology — eroded traditional definitions of national sovereignty.

Latin Americans displayed a capacity to learn from previous experiences with political instability, inflation, and economic crises. In some measure, each country in the region underwent a learning process. Early heterodox responses to the crisis were simple stabilization measures aimed at controlling short-run disequilibria in the balance of payments and fiscal accounts. As the crisis deepened toward the middle of the decade, Latin Americans provided a great deal of the intellectual and technical expertise that thrust the economies of these nations in the direction of liberalization.[2]

The countries surveyed in this volume were constrained by the limited available choices for economic reform, but additional factors played a significant role as well. First, the context in which neoliberal policies were adopted was important (Whitehead 1992). The experience of Bolivia and Argentina — which were incapable of stabilizing their economies in the early part of the 1980s — suggests that harsh austerity measures work only when an economy has sunk to a historic low point. Second, resolving an economic crisis was not a simple question of "political will." The first generation of political leaders clearly had the will to resolve the dilemmas of their national economies. A series of factors — domestic and international —prevented them from pursuing corrective measures and also dictated the selection of the type of economic policy.

The importance of context concerns a question often neglected in the study of Latin America: the leadership capacity of individuals who took office in the aftermath of authoritarian rule to impose austerity measures and address the economic crisis. For the most part, new civilian leaders were inexperienced and insecure in office; they invariably spent a great portion of their tenure in office dealing with popular and political demands. To satisfy demands, they expanded public employment. As a result, increases in public spending accelerated the fiscal crisis.

The first postauthoritarian leaders could not muster sufficient political support to forge ahead with economic reforms. At the helm of weak coalitions, these leaders often faced hostile legislative assemblies, threatening labor unions, menacing armed forces, and a discontented private sector. In this context, most resorted to rule by decree to overcome impasses. They could not, however, concentrate enough political might in the executive branch to press ahead with reforms. Country-specific variations notwithstanding, the theme was quite similar throughout the region. Presidents modified economic corrective measures, which were primarily standard stabilization programs, and introduced watered-down versions to minimize labor and private sector discontent. This was a fundamental characteristic of the regional crisis of governance. In short, it was not a question of political will, since they all had the desire to end the crisis, but of concrete political capacity.

As a result, in a brief period popular confidence in the principal institutions of democracy declined. Paradoxically, while most Latin Americans continued to support democracy, they were fed up with political parties, legislatures, and judiciaries — the principal institutions of democratic governance.[3] With democracy in its infancy, a crisis of governability and representation hovered over the region's political future. Specifically, political parties and legislatures revealed an incapacity to represent interests or to act as a crucial mediating linkage between society and government during the transition. In some countries, the onset of hyperinflation and the perceivable crisis of representation led to nostalgia for the order of authoritarian regimes. This was the context that gave rise to the neoliberal "medicine" prescribed throughout the region.

With the notable exceptions of Carlos Menem, Víctor Paz Estenssoro, and Carlos Salinas de Gortari, the second generation of leaders came into office with as much inexperience and insecurity as the first. They arrived, however, at a time when each nation faced imminent collapse. This "threshold of crisis" (Whitehead 1992) hit each country at different times.[4] One by one they succumbed — Mexico in 1982, Bolivia in 1985, and Argentina in 1989.[5]

This moment of crisis revealed several underlying tensions. In regard to social representation, the executive preference for an exclusionary policy was rooted not only in the economic crisis and austerity programs proposed. The moment of crisis reinforced a historical pattern of exclusionary decision-making, which transcended conjunctural factors and blurred the differences between authoritarian and democratic regimes. The decision-making style built on a tradition of recruiting "apolitical" technocratic advisors to bolster and lend credibility to the actions of the strong executive. Throughout Latin America in the 1970s, for example, military rulers surrounded themselves with civilian technocrats to help them implement policy. During the economic crisis and beyond, the second generation of Latin American leaders continued to recruit civilian technocrats to deal with the economy and thus continued the tradition of imposing closed policy making.

Thus, the new democratically elected leaders reproduced the style of the authoritarian rulers they replaced. Bypassing congress, utilizing the military to impose states of siege, and neglecting or ignoring the demands of social groups — the style of governance was anything but democratic. Because of its success, however, this authoritarian or "authoritative" decision-making style came to be perceived as the only way to implement neoliberal reforms.

Regardless of regime form, one of the principal issues in Latin America has always been access to the policy-making process. Authoritarian regimes denied access to a variety of groups, including business, which was at the forefront of democratization in the late 1970s and early 1980s. While in the 1990s, the policy-making process is more pluralistic, it is still exclusionary. Business and many other social actors have access. Yet the common factor is that both authoritarian and democratic rulers have determined the degree and the nature of that access. The key to democratic governance in this context rests with how rulers frame access to the policy process.

A couple of additional observations must be made regarding the moment of crisis and the solutions that leadership created. Beyond nation-saving pacts, the record suggests that political agreements between erstwhile enemies were critical to the implementation and the continuation of neoliberal programs. The new leadership underwent a process of political learning. Reflecting on the travails of the first generation, the newly elected leaders crafted both political and economic policies to address the immediacy of the crisis. While the parameters of political action were restricted by the context, the strategies of the new leadership played an important role in overcoming the crisis. Restricted parameters limited political options available to decision makers, but the choices each made were crucial for the implementation of economic reforms. Successful second-generation leaders crafted ways out — *salidas* — rather than long-term solutions to the crisis. These *salidas*, mainly in the form of political pacts, varied from country to country.

This issue brings to mind the current debate about parliamentary versus presidential institutional forms. Bolivian, Argentine, and Mexican experience demonstrates that political *salidas* were not the product of abstract debate among political scientists but the creative response of political leaders to a specific set of circumstances within a nationally defined historical process. In other words, Latin American political leaders have produced hybrids between old-fashioned tools of government and the "modern" thrust of neoliberalism. Again, this reflects a process of historical learning. These hybrids, in my view, are the norm in the region today.

Although domestic policy makers may have played an important role in crafting economic policies, external conditions imposed by international financial institutions (IFIs) caused a severe loss of autonomy. Staff members of IFIs were virtually present at cabinet-level meetings, often holding veto power over government officials. Nevertheless, while international and structural factors were important determinants of the direction of the regional political economy in the mid-1980s, the specific history of each Latin American case was driven by the dynamics of coalition formation and competition.

To govern in this political context involved addressing two key issues. Institutionally, the task of the second generation of leaders was to design and coordinate the institutions of a democratic regime, resolve executive-legislative impasses, exert governmental control over the state apparatus, and design effective electoral systems. Politically, governments faced a crucial need to build coalitions of groups in civil society and bring them into the policy process (Malloy 1992). Coalition building took two forms: electoral coalitions to compete for formal power, and ruling or sustaining coalitions to support governments and specific policy initiatives. An important characteristic of this process was the ability of some leaders to craft coalitions both to get elected and to govern[6] (Malloy 1991, 1992; Malloy and Gamarra 1988). The point is that political coalitions linked the domestic arena with international themes such as neoliberalism, provided support for governments, and enabled the completion of specific policy initiatives.

Mainstream political science has devoted a great deal of study to the importance of the "leadership variable" (Rockman 1984; Neustadt 1981). In sharp contrast, studies of Latin American democratization have long-neglected the study of leaders and their particular behaviors. In my view, the "threshold of crisis" was successfully transcended by leaders who exerted an uncommon capacity to govern.[7] Their feats were accomplished not by altering the rules or changing institutions, as some political scientists would suggest, but by using their command over the institutional features of a given system, concentrating power at the executive level, and deploying enough strength to implement policy. Nevertheless, the constitutionality of their actions was, and still is, extremely questionable.

The crafting of political coalitions to control legislatures and labor involved more than the doling out of symbolic or "patriotic" rewards to politicians and economic incentives to supportive business sectors. As the chapters on Bolivia and Mexico in this volume note, in great measure the crafting of coalitions and implementation of economic reforms relied on the traditional tool of politics — patronage. Many analysts, especially economists, argue that the distribution of patronage undermines the logic of a modern market economy. However, the Latin American record of the late 1980s (and the history of most other regions of the world) suggests that patronage was an important instrument in the implementation of neoliberalism and in securing political stability. It has always been an important tool available to political leaders and the implementation of "modern" economic reforms did not alter this historical reality.[8]

The relationship between patronage, democratization, and the implementation of neoliberal reforms is significant. The attempted coups in Venezuela, the *autogolpe* in Peru, and the recent anti-corruption movements in Bolivia, Brazil, Mexico, and elsewhere reveal that restructuring sources of patronage can have unsettling effects.[9] Economic reforms restrict access to traditional supplies of patronage, but they also create new ones. In many ways, the neoliberal process involves a redistribution of patronage networks; thus, some groups are cut off, a few retain access, and new groups sometimes emerge. From the perspective of governance, this means that a leader must carefully select how to redistribute patronage networks. In short, in Latin America a hybrid form has resulted from the combination of a "rational" logic of neoliberal restructuring and a democracy built on two pillars: the distribution of symbolic rewards (voting, elections, freedom of speech) and the predominance of patronage.

Stabilization and Market-Oriented Reforms

For implementing stabilization and proceeding with public sector reforms, the second generation of post-authoritarian Latin American leaders was credited with inserting their nations into a worldwide consensus, dubbed the "Washington Consensus" on economic policy, inspired mainly by international financial institutions. The Washington Consensus revolves around ten key reforms which economists consider essential to end the downward spiral in Latin America and elsewhere: fiscal discipline, public expenditure priorities, tax reform, financial liberalization, unified exchange rates, trade liberalization, foreign direct investment, privatization, deregulation, and respect for property rights (Williamson 1992). These economic reforms, however, are closely related to the issue of consolidating democratic rule in Latin America.

As John Williamson (1992) puts it:

Democracy should be in no way circumscribed so as to promote good economic policy, but rather that both economic policy and democracy will benefit if all mainstream politicians endorse the Universal Convergence and the scope of political debate on economic issues is de facto circumscribed in consequence. How much consensus on economic policy should be hoped for? As much as is justified by the state of economic knowledge and the convergence in fundamental (ultimately political) values.

The Washington Consensus proposals have led to IFI-imposed agreement on the necessity for state and constitutional reforms throughout Latin America. The predominant IFI aim is to secure neoliberalism in constitutional charters and in major legislation throughout the hemisphere. To carry out this mandate and qualify for loans and other aid, political systems have been tested rigorously. The main method of imposing reforms has been to skirt the niceties of liberal democratic traditions. The coincidence between strong presidential styles, which concentrate power at the executive level, and neoliberal reforms suggests that the only way for Latin American nations to succeed is to do away with some of the formalities of democracy. This can be accomplished by reducing the oversight prerogatives of legislatures, or by packing Supreme Courts.

The notion of "generations" of political leadership follows a distinction made by economic analysts, who examined the period and identified two interrelated stages of economic policy making. During the first generation, stabilization policies aimed to correct short-term problems and did not seek to abolish the state-led development strategy that had been in place since the 1940s. In the mid-1980s, leaders designed stabilization programs with two basic objectives: closures of fiscal and external gaps and controllable levels of inflation. In the current Latin American context, low inflation implies stable, 20 percent annual rates. Thus, the immediate goal of stabilization policies was to attain relatively constant low rates of inflation and stable key relative prices, such as exchange rates and real wages (Fanelli et al. 1991).

Following the lessons of the 1980s, economists widely concurred that stabilization was a precondition for the recovery of growth and the dismantling of state-led economic strategies. Most pointed out that, to restore growth, economies must first address declining production, rising unemployment, sagging investment, and rapidly accelerating inflation. The higher the rate of hyperinflation and recession, the more stabilization became essential.

Stabilization measures raised the level of economic activity and restored the purchasing power of wages. Following Jeffrey Sachs, some argued that the social costs of stabilization were infinitely smaller than the costs associated with hyperinflation. In fact, political support for even draconian measures substantiates this view. These were fragile accomplishments, however, because the persistence of 20 percent inflation rates, the appreciation of exchange rates, and the absence of real growth eroded initial political support.

Nevertheless, conventional wisdom among economists established a neat and causal separation between stabilization and growth. Not only was stabilization to come first; it had to be sustained long enough to satisfy expectations and restore the economy's credibility. Only then would an economy achieve growth. Because stabilization's brief popularity alone was not enough to generate economic reform, economists prescribed that stabilization programs should be conceived as part of a broader structural transformation in which winners outnumber losers. Public sector or state reform and the liberalization of markets became the new panacea. Noting that decades of state-led growth resulted in inefficient state enterprises — which depended mainly on state subsidies, selective credit policies, and tax exemptions — neoliberal proponents called for the dismantling of state enterprises. As Cavarozzi (1992) has pointed out, the dismantling of state enterprises was part of a broader process of eliminating an institutionalized, state-centered matrix.

Concerned mainly with the success of their policies — defined narrowly as the continuous application of neoliberal reforms — Washington Consensus economists paid little attention to the political ramifications of state reform. The implementation was left up to the civilian leaders of the region. Proposals for state reform, including tax reform, reduction of public spending, and privatization, involved decisive, even authoritarian, actions on the part of democratically elected governments. Apart from seeking international approval and support, which came hesitantly despite the rhetoric about a free market, leaders found it necessary to craft alliances to support reforms and make them durable. This was a very difficult task, given the context of regional crisis. The impact of these three proposals has been wide and varied across social classes and groups in Latin America.

As Adolfo Canitrot (1992) points out, because a substantial portion of the revenue generated by tax reform goes to creditor banks, tax reform is the most difficult to enact. Private sector groups and others unaccustomed to paying taxes opposed the measures; thus, governments required a greater measure of political power to make the reforms stick.

The reduction of public spending had a tremendous impact on distinct social groups. By dangerously linking the demands of the military to those of other middle class sectors, such as teachers and retirees, budget cuts produced interesting responses, which did not always seek democratic outcomes. Military spending as a percentage of gross domestic product (GDP) fell to historically low levels. The failure to meet demands for training, equipment, and restitution of social security benefits has already led to severe confrontations between civilians and the military.

Much has been written about the wonders of privatization. In response to the visible deterioration of state enterprises, it was once popular to call for privatization. By linking privatization to debt repayment, advocates claimed that it addressed the demands of creditor banks. Moreover, they argued that resources generated by privatization moderated the severity of tax and public-spending policy.

By generating greater expectations than it will ever be able to meet, privatization has appealed to large business. Governments have achieved a significant trade-off: private sector support for liberalization policies and tax reform in return for privatization. Privatization programs have become an important government tool to reward supporters in the private sector and co-opt opponents. Paradoxically, traditional patronage requirements have been served well by the modern drive toward Latin American privatization.

But privatization has also given rise to discontent and even popular mobilization. Dismantling state enterprises has had an impact on public employment and on the traditional patronage demands of the middle classes. Faced with the disassembling of their enterprises, the armed forces have also been hesitant to get behind privatization programs. The fact remains that beyond purely technical questions, stabilization and public sector reforms are also political matters which are being addressed in the context of Latin America's frail democracies.

Sociopolitical Actors, Neoliberalism, and Democratization

The most significant struggle facing Latin American democracies exists between technocrats, managers, and government officials versus distinct social sectors attempting to find a niche in the unfolding neoliberal policy process. This conflict essentially involves a dispute between two distinct views of democracy. Government officials and their entourage of domestic and international technocrats subscribe to the notion that democracy is simply the effective and efficient management of the economy. This view assumes a strong executive surrounded by a group of "economically correct" specialists who believe that the answers to the problems of the region are to be solved mainly through the proper and continuous application of neoliberal medicine.[10] In short, these managers and advisers will guide the state away from the incorrect "mercantilistic" policies of the past, which led the region into its current debacle, and show the way to a promising future of market capitalism. This view is firmly rooted as Latin America moves toward its third generation of post-authoritarian leaders.

On the other hand, a traditional notion defines representative democracy as access for distinct social groups and organizations to the policy-making process. In the current Latin American scene, pluralist conceptions of democracy are scarce. Political parties are not instruments for aggregating or articulating interests. Legislatures and judiciaries are perceived as obstacles to the institutionalization of rational economic policies. And organized labor is perceived as a threat to the national interest, because it demands higher salaries and other compensation that might undermine fiscal reform.

How have these tensions played out in Latin America? To understand the current climate in the region, one must identify how distinct political actors gain access to the policy process. This determines the nature and the direction of the democratization process in each specific nation. Thus, the challenges facing Latin America's democracies are shaped by how the armed forces, organized labor, political parties, and other groups have been affected by stabilization programs and public-sector reforms. In each case, there is evidence of tension between acquired privileges and the imposition of neoliberalism. How these play out in different countries will define the nature of the democratic system and the depth of neoliberal reforms. Moreover, to address this question requires some attention to the emerging, and perhaps consolidating, second-class citizenship that is the lot of many Latin Americans.

In the 1990s more Latin Americans will vote than ever before, yet the majority of them are largely underrepresented and do not enjoy the rights of full democratic citizenship. One of the most crucial defining characteristics of Dahl's polyarchy is access to the policy-making process, either through interest group or political party representation. Few nations in the region can claim to have institutionalized this practice.

One of the principal reasons for second-class citizenship is the fragility of judicial systems. In many countries, equality before the law is an abstraction. In the Andean region, for example, Indian majorities still face linguistic, racial, and economic discrimination in courts of law. If, as O'Donnell (1993) argues, the judiciary is that part of the state which provides the underlying texture of a democratic social order, then democracy in Latin America faces a very tough task ahead.

In Latin America the liberal democratic notion of "law enforcement" has never existed. Instead, law enforcement has been quite selective. With the advent of democracy the situation for many Latin Americans has not improved. A common saying, "*la movida para mis amigos, y la ley para mis enemigos*" (deals for my friends, the law for my enemies), reflects the perversity of law enforcement. The continuity of these practices alongside the processes of political and economic reform suggests the consolidation of hybrids of old and new patterns of behavior. The weakness of Latin American justice systems has also led to the privatization of security systems and the proliferation of parallel small claims courts. In some countries — Colombia and Panama, for example — private armies and security personnel may already outnumber regular law enforcement personnel. In others — Bolivia and Peru — mechanisms, such as television talk shows, have served in lieu of recourse to small claims courts.

This pattern of privatization has reinforced the hybridization of authoritarian and democratic forms in Latin America. To many members of underrepresented groups, "neopopulist" promises have become attractive; as a result, plebiscitarian decision making is rapidly becoming a preferred governance mechanism. This, of course, runs counter to the liberal democratic character of polyarchic democracy. As Peru's experience demonstrates, demands for greater popular participation and majority-based plebiscitarian decision making erode the prospects for democracy. In most Latin American countries, liberal values of political democracy, are under assault not only by the plebiscitarian fad but also by the imposition of neoliberal reforms.

The question of how social groups access the policy process is related in other ways to the discussion of citizenship. Defined broadly, citizens are all native-born and naturalized individuals in a given country. In Latin America, however, full citizenship is conferred only upon those who function in the formal marketplace, who believe they belong to an interest group or party. In short, they are a "representable" segment of the population. A vast number of Latin Americans, however, are not "representable" because they are part of the informal economy. While individuals in this sector may periodically vote in elections, they have no voice in Congress, they lack fair access to the judicial process, and they do not enjoy the benefits of state spending for such things as better roads, health care, and so on. For these people, citizenship is at best second-rate. The imposition of neoliberal austerity and the process of democratization has not changed the situation of these groups in any visible way. This is the challenge for policy makers and leaders in Latin America and for the neoliberal policies they have pursued.

Notes

1.   In traditional political science literature, consolidation refers to a solidification and routinizing of an institutional framework. Political bargaining becomes more predictable and less disruptive. It also refers to the winnowing out of political actors and the elimination of competing political and economic projects. Full democratic consolidation refers to the emergence of a single, perhaps stable, compromise-consensus project. Consolidation involves the reduction of actors to not fewer than two and the reduction of projects to not more than one. Does the neoliberal consensus fit this single project category?

2.   As John Williamson (1992) points out, books like Hernando de Soto's *El Otro Sendero* were instrumental in shaping market reforms of the 1980s and early 1990s. Moreover, economists in each country (Juan A. Morales and Domingo Cavallo, among others) were important contributors to the "consensus" on neoliberalism. This did not mean that Latin American economists suddenly discovered the wonders of neoliberalism. The learning process occurred within a framework of limited options; thus, under different circumstances they might have opted for a softer approach because, at the threshold of crisis, their options were limited.

3.   See, for example, the polls taken by Bolivar Lamounier in Brazil, ILDIS in Bolivia, and Henry Dietz in Peru.

4.   Following John Polock (1975), James Malloy (1992, 38) describes this threshold of crisis as a "Machiavellian moment... A name for a moment in conceptualized time in which the republic was seen as confronting its own temporal finitude, as attempting to remain morally and politically stable in a stream of irrational events conceived as essentially destructive of all systems of secular stability."

5.   The possibility does exist, however, that for some countries, such as Peru, the abyss may have no bottom and the drop could be permanent. Consult Luis Pásara (1993) for an account which argues that Peru has fallen into a "black hole." This view also suggests that for a country like Peru the term "crisis," normally denoting a temporary situation, has come to mean a permanent condition.

6.   I am indebted to James Malloy for these ideas. This section borrows heavily from ongoing work on a second edition of *Revolution and Reaction* and from an unpublished manuscript by Malloy on business in the Central Andes.

7.   According to James Malloy (1992, 38), the principal task at the Machiavellian moment was to "forge a link between personalized leadership and the secular institutional structures inherent in the concept of republican or rule-bound government. Personality or leadership animates a set of formal institutions through the creative deployment of 'practices' which can be repeated and/or built upon as problems are resolved and new ones confronted over time. Past patterns of leadership

become the accumulated custom or informal rules that underpin a formalized constitutional structure of rules and institutions."

8. As noted elsewhere (Gamarra and Malloy 1993), at least in the Andean region, patronage can also be seen as the only way through which the middle classes have tapped into the surplus of the state. The growth of the bureaucratic apparatus to meet these needs resulted in the consolidation of a "mercantilistic" system. The paradox, however, is that most of the technocrats are a product of the same middle class and, like their predecessors, draw on the state for salaries, jobs, and other remunerations. They have also tapped into the world of international consulting via salary supplements.

9. This view was succinctly expressed to me by a U.S. ambassador to a Latin American country who claimed that with democracy came the institutionalization of impunity. He argued that military governments restricted impunity to the armed forces. Democracy in his view simply means that impunity has been expanded to the civilian sector. The implications of this statement are significant. The left, now devoid of an ideological message, has entered into the game and has been driven by the same logic of political patronage.

10. Guillermo O'Donnell (1992) labels this pattern, "delegative democracy." In his view, the basic premise is that whoever becomes president can govern however he/she pleases. The president is an embodiment of the nation and defines the national interest. I would add that the president defines the national interest on the basis of the advice received from international and national managerial functionaries.

References

Canitrot, Adolfo. 1992. "De la deuda externa a la reforma del estado y la liberalización." Comments delivered at the conference on "Democracy, Markets and Structural Reform in Latin America." March 25-27, 1992. Buenos Aires, Argentina.

Cavarozzi, Marcelo. 1992. "Beyond Democratic Transitions in Latin America." *Journal of Latin American Studies* 24 (3).

Gamarra, Eduardo A. Forthcoming. "Hybrid Presidentialism and Democratization: The Case of Bolivia." In *Presidentialism in Latin America*, eds. Scott Mainwaring and Matthew Shugart. Cambridge: Cambridge University Press.

Gamarra, Eduardo A., and James M. Malloy. 1993. "The Patrimonial Dynamics of Party Politics in Bolivia." In *Building Democratic Institutions: Parties and Party Systems in Latin America*, eds. Scott Mainwaring and Timothy Scully. Stanford: Stanford University Press.

Malloy, James M. 1992. Untitled mimeo. Department of Political Science, University of Pittsburgh.

Malloy, James M. Forthcoming. "Economic Crisis and Democratization: Latin America in the 1980s." In *Latin America and Caribbean Contemporary Record*, Vol. 8, eds. Eduardo Gamarra and James M. Malloy. New York: Holmes and Meier.

Malloy, James M., and Eduardo Gamarra. 1988. *Revolution and Reaction: Bolivia 1964-1985.* New Brunswick, NJ: Transaction Publishers.

O'Donnell, Guillermo. 1992. "Delegative Democracy?" Kellogg Institute Working Paper No. 172.

Neustadt, Richard E. 1980. *Presidential Power: The Politics of Leadership from FDR to Carter.* New York: John Wiley and Sons.

Pásara, Luis. 1993. "Peru in a Black Hole." *Hemisphere* (Winter).

Polock, John Greville Agard. 1975. *The Machiavellian Moment: Florentine Political Thought and the Atlantic Republican Tradition.* Princeton, NJ: Princeton University Press.

Whitehead, Laurence. 1992. "On Reform of the State and Regulation of the Market." Paper presented at the CESDE Conference on Economic Liberalization and Economic Democratization, Forti, Italy, April 2-4.

Williamson, John. 1992. "Democratization and the 'Washington Consensus'." Paper presented at the CESDE Conference on Economic Liberalization and Economic Democratization, Forti, Italy, April 2-4.

Chapter Two

The Political Economy of Structural Adjustment: The Logic of Support and Opposition to Neoliberal Reform

Carlos H. Acuña

William C. Smith

Introduction

Writing a decade ago, Carlos Díaz Alejandro (1984) warned that Latin America "was not in Kansas anymore," echoing Dorothy's surprise when she suddenly found herself in the *Land of Oz*. Since the early 1980s, major watershed transformations have reshaped the Latin American landscape to a degree rivaled only by the events of the 1930s. These events include the emergence, evolution, and partial resolution of the debt crisis, coupled with processes of democratization, profound realignments in global politics, and the growing influence of international financial institutions over the economic strategies adopted in peripheral countries. Consequences wrought by these political and economic transitions and concomitant social changes now permit us to explore the most probable outcomes to be expected from these ongoing transformations.

Most of the civilian regimes that emerged in the 1980s following the transition from military dictatorships have achieved a degree of institutional stability and democratic consolidation,[1] but they still confront severe political and economic challenges. With the significant exception of Brazil, the "free market" policies championed by the so-called "Washington Consensus"[2] have succeeded in taming hyperinflation, bringing greater discipline to bear on

We thank Adolfo Canitrot, Adam Przeworski, Guillermo O'Donnell, Juan Carlos Torre, Thomaz Scheetz, and Scott Mainwaring for their valuable comments on an earlier draft of this paper. The normal caveats apply.

public sector fiscal deficits, and forcing external accounts into equilibrium. For most Latin American countries, however, the goal of sustainable growth has proven elusive. Monetary policies resulting in the overvaluation of local currencies jeopardize trade surpluses and external competitiveness. Concomitantly, since the end of the 1970s, a sharp decline in per capita income in most countries has exacerbated poverty and worsened already egregious patterns of inequality and concentration of income and wealth. The region's modest economic recovery, and events such as the two military coup attempts in Venezuela in 1992, the imposition of a Peruvian civil-military dictatorship in 1992, and continuing megainflation and political uncertainty in Brazil, raise troubling questions concerning the social and political consequences of neoliberal restructuring.[3] Meriting particular attention in analyses of the post-transition period are the sharp erosion of the state's capacity to manage major macroeconomic variables and the problematic tensions between marketplace logic, reinforced by the exigencies of the world economy, and pressures to institutionalize and expand popular participation and citizenship rights beyond the politico-institutional arena of electoral politics.

Some of these issues central to the politics of neoliberal restructuring are addressed in this chapter. We first defend the necessity of rethinking the relationship between politics and economics, and we raise the controversial question of state power in the process of market-oriented economic reform. The second section critiques prevailing notions regarding the relationship between regime type and economic performance. There follows a discussion of the political significance of economic performance for sociopolitical conflict. Dissenting from mainstream analyses, we explain the reasons why an *increase* in sociopolitical tensions should be expected when economic performance *improves*. The fourth section sketches several alternative politico-economic scenarios for Latin American countries: organic crisis, successful neoliberal restructuring along with a fragmented and exclusionary democracy, inclusionary democracy with strong actors and an activist state, and dual democratic regimes with mediocre economic outcomes. In the concluding section we briefly recapitulate our main arguments.

Rethinking Politics and Economics

The external shock of the debt crisis and ensuing structural reforms advocated by Washington and international financial institutions led to the implementation of policies with strong common elements. The process of structural reform was conducive to the emergence of democracies with a high concentration of power in the executive branch and exclusion of the popular sector from participation in the formulation and implementation of social and economic policies. This process also exacerbated tensions between the executive and other branches, resulting in the weakening of parliamentary and judicial institutions. The disarticulation of social actors, particularly those of the subaltern sectors, was also a consequences of this process. Given these important political and economic similarities, can we speak of a single, or common, Latin American political process? Is it legitimate to infer from the narrowing of feasible economic options a necessary tendency toward common political scenarios in which differences among countries will be merely a matter of degree? And finally, what do these similarities tell us about the future of democracy and about the welfare of the people of Latin America?

Inferring politics from economics is bad methodology. This is true especially under Latin America's current highly constrained economic conditions. In contrast to the Great Depression of the 1930s, the external debt crisis of the 1980s and the reinforced dependency of Latin American states with respect to international financial institutions resulted in the imposition of orthodox criteria, the erosion of the relative autonomy of national decision makers vis-à-vis global economic processes, and a narrowing of the range of acceptable strategies of economic stabilization (Stallings 1992; Kahler 1992; and Vacs, Chapter 3 in this volume). Under these circumstances, the organization and behavior of social and political actors frequently are considered, especially by economists, to be a mere epiphenomenal reflection of more "fundamental" economic variables.

But the constitution of social groups and classes and their actions are not determined uniquely by objective conditions. These collective actors' constitution and behavior are the effects of struggles, and these struggles are not determined directly by the relations of production or by market tendencies, regardless of how constraining conditions may be. Even those struggles usually considered as strictly "economic" are historically specific and are defined and shaped by political, institutional, and ideological relations.

Different state institutions, political regimes, and legal arrangements combine in specific ways so that diverse social groups and classes will face widely divergent possibilities of realizing their interests and achieving their objectives. Similarly, non-state institutions, such as political parties, business associations, and unions, that aggregate and struggle for collective interests are the organizational crystallization of each particular actor's resources and capacity for strategic action. These institutional ensembles constitute the social organization of political power (Przeworski 1977; Wright 1978).

An example helps clarify our argument. Imagine a historical conjuncture of crisis so catastrophic that all moderate or gradualist strategies are judged insufficient and the imposition of a recessionary shock program is presented to civil society as the "only" responsible alternative to chaos. This orthodox program, in turn, provokes a sharp fall in wages, an increase in unemployment, a reduction of the fiscal deficit by increasing taxes on consumption and cutting public spending on health, education, and other social services, all leading toward a regressive redistribution of income. Such a crisis and orthodox response are frequently cited as evidence that politics has been driven to it knees, forced to obey the dictates of an implacable economic logic. Majoritarian preferences and elections lose importance in terms of social and economic policy making. Regardless of the leader or party in power, and whatever the government's ideology or ties to different social interests might be, economic policies perforce will, sooner or later, be the same. As the gloomy story goes in many analyses, most actors in Latin American civil societies soon "learn this lesson" and recognize the relative insignificance of politics, elections, and the political system as a whole. *Vaciamiento*, or "hollowing out," of the content of democratic politics and, in extreme cases, abandonment of democratic preferences and commitments as well as the breakdown of democracy are postulated as likely outcomes.

Nevertheless, even in extreme situations in which economic policy making is reduced to only one choice, the political significance of such an event will vary radically as a function of historical contingencies, such as the nature of the political regime, its ideology, or the social or political commitments of governmental incumbents at the time of the crisis or external shock. The tensions exacerbated by the shock of the adjustment might hasten an authoritarian government's decision to liberalize the regime, perhaps eventually leading to a democratic outcome. In the case of democracies, these tensions might lead to a change of government, or even to the regime's crisis and fall. If the crisis occurs within a democratic regime, and neither its governmental nor its institutional stability are undermined, the implementation of adjustment policies by a party that came to power backed by popular sectors and unions may have one outcome. On the other hand, if the adjustment is carried out by a party representing a coalition of the middle class and the bourgeoisie, the consequences may be quite different.

These consequences might range from strengthening long-standing historical patterns of alliance and opposition to a profound historical rupture. In these alternative scenarios, the same economic policies will determine divergent political outcomes in terms of levels of sociopolitical conflict and opposition to economic reform, as well as economic performance and long-term implications for democratic consolidation. The fact that economic crises severely constrain a government's room for maneuver does not mean that the "space for politics" has been foreclosed, nor does it mean that politics have been absorbed by economics. Political choices, strategies, and contingencies remain central determinants of social and economic processes, and their meaning and consequences perhaps gain even greater relevance in a conjuncture of deep economic crises and transformations.

Democratic transitions and consolidations in the context of economic crises with regressive income distributions are not an exclusively Latin

American phenomenon. This pattern characterizes almost all of the transitions and consolidations occurring since the 1970s. As Linz and Stepan (1991) demonstrate, recent European democratic consolidations (that is, those of Spain, Greece, and Portugal) took place, precisely, in contexts of stagnation. Economic growth and employment, as well as salary levels, typically fall during the consummation of democratic consolidations. In these cases, macroeconomic factors related to social welfare did not strengthen the process of democratic stabilization. To the contrary, these consolidations took place *in spite of* the economic reality confronted by these societies.

Similarly, affirmations that state power in Latin America is "weakening" say very little. In fact, such generalizations obscure differences between those countries in which the state is impotent to carry out the neoliberal policies favored by state elites and other countries in which, notwithstanding its "weakening," the state still possesses sufficient power to impose economic reform and to disarticulate troublesome social actors. Underlying the question of state and societal power, there is a striking contradiction. On the one hand, neo-utilitarian prescriptions call for rolling back the state and weakening governmental mechanisms of macroeconomic regulation; on the other hand, the state apparatus must augment its power capabilities to impose a market-driven model of accumulation.

In fact, greater economic orthodoxy may well require not less but *more* autonomy, particularly from the immediate expression of specific entrepreneurial and trade union interests. Similarly, greater orthodoxy may imply not less, but *more* effective coordination and oversight of the private sector (e.g., regulation of the stock and financial markets, broadening the tax base, upgrading skills of workers, promoting technological innovations and competitiveness, and so on) and concentration of expanded administrative power in the hands of state managers and technocratic elites. In short, despite antistatist rhetoric, the state necessarily must play a strong role in this period of rapid transformations.[4]

The current wave of state reform, therefore, does not imply merely the shrinkage and more "efficient" operation of state administrative agencies, but a fundamental redrawing of the existing boundaries between politics and economics and the public and the private. This will be a wrenching experience during which many organized societal interests are, in effect "expelled" from the state and must fend for themselves as individuals in the market.[5] A state more impermeable to societal demands will require a more "authoritative" administrative apparatus capable of neutralizing the reaction of adversely affected groups. The concentration of power in the executive (characterized by *decretazos* of dubious legality with clear authoritarian overtones) characteristic of current market-oriented reforms in Latin America is, therefore, less a result of the psychology of particular leaders — or of alleged traits of Latin American political culture — than a consequence of the political and economic logic inherent in the transition from Keynesian modes of reproduction of consent to more "liberal" models of accumulation and political domination. In short, state strengthening is unavoidable during market strengthening.

But, once the transition has been completed and a new equilibrium is reached, will the state be stronger or weaker than before the neoliberal revolution? In all likelihood, the new, future state will be *both* stronger and weaker. Depending on the specific issue area or public policy arena, for example, neoliberal restructuring may lead to a severe retrenchment of the public sphere's traditional "entrepreneurial" functions related to direct ownership of productive enterprises, thus producing a smaller and much "weaker" state apparatus. Simultaneously, however, in other arenas such as the subordination of the military to constitutional rule and the capacity of civilian elites to exercise civilian control over the armed forces (e.g., formulation of national security policies, severe cuts in military budgets, and so on) or to impose restrictions on organized labor, public authority may be strengthened significantly, surpassing even the power and autonomy achieved by state elites during earlier populist and authoritarian periods. Even with respect to the market, it is not clear that neoliberal strategies necessarily imply a weaker state. For example, in order for markets to function properly, with the efficiency and transparency required by private investors, effective mechanisms of state regulation previously absent must be put into place.

The transformations implied by this "return to the market" are not neutral with regard to prevailing class structures. In fact, neoliberal programs that progressively subordinate public policy making to the logic of marketplace criteria, while concomitantly eroding the significance of political parties and parliamentary arenas of contestation, clearly reinforce the structural power of international capitalist interests and the leading sectors of the domestic entrepreneurial classes. Although fundamental, this observation is still too generic and abstract. The prospects of Latin American democracy cannot be inferred directly and unequivocally as a function of the strengthening of capital, the weakening of parliamentary or judicial power, or the erosion of the "representativeness" of party systems.

In fact, variations in state control and threats to the existing order, the strength of parties and legislative institutions, and the nature of the armed forces' relationship to politics will be manifested in a wide range of situations. For example, in some instances, political control may be imposed on barely half of the national territory (Peru before Fujimori's *autogolpe*) and may confront powerful armed groups with both popular support and military capacity (Peru and Colombia); in other cases, political violence is insignificant, and the territorial scope of the political order is not in jeopardy.

Similarly, cases in which strengthening the legislature requires decision making and negotiation in a fragmented party system with serious difficulties in constituting majorities (as in Brazil and pre-coup Peru) contrast sharply with situations in which strengthening parliamentary institutions implies bargaining between two parties that represent more than 70 percent of the national electorate (as in Argentina, Uruguay, and Venezuela). Challenges to representative institutions may combine with the presence of groups within the armed forces opposed to structural reform, with strong political presence and constitutional right to domestic intervention, repression, and intelligence (as in Brazil and Bolivia). Finally, cases may arise in which some elements of the armed forces support authoritarian attempts to resolve the politico-economic crisis in their societies (as in Peru and Venezuela), or the armed forces may become (or remain) politically neutralized (as in Argentina), and long-term democratic stability may coincide with the military's corporate interests (Acuña and Smulovitz, forthcoming; Acuña and Smith 1994).

By the same token, however, divorcing politics from economics is also bad methodology. Analysis of consolidations under adverse socioeconomic conditions must take into consideration the significance of the specific form of political and economic articulation in each society. Rethinking of the relation between politics and economics should not take place on the terrain of "macro-level" theories.[6] Rather, this rethinking should occur at the level of "middle-range" theories that, while not ignoring or underestimating systemic properties or the structural limitations highlighted by "macro" theories, allow our analysis to incorporate organizational patterns of social and political actors and contingencies inherent in the political struggles of each society. Negative socioeconomic circumstances do not necessarily threaten democratic consolidations. Whether or not stagnation and regressive income distribution will undermine democratic stability is a function of political struggles in the given society. Moreover, although we cannot infer general threats to democratic stability directly from contexts of stagnation and regressive distribution, we certainly can analyze the *type* of democracy that tends to emerge under such circumstances.

To this point, our intention has been to underscore the reasons why similar macroeconomic contexts and similar variations in the "state-centric matrix" (Cavarozzi 1992a and Chapter 5 in this volume) can result in very distinct political processes. Even the same exogenous circumstances, such as those associated with the external shock of the debt crisis, will have very distinct *socioeconomic* consequences in the various Latin American countries.[7] For example, what is the political and economic significance of affirming that "real wages fell in the region," when in some countries wages fell modestly and gradually as a consequence of an annual inflation rate of two or maybe three digits, while in other countries wages plummeted traumatically in the context of five-digit hyperinflationary explosions? How should one analyze statements affirming the "regressive redistribution of income," when in some cases this signified a *decline* in the *relative* income of the popular sectors combined with an *increase* in their *absolute* income levels (as in Brazil), while in others it meant both relative and absolute declines in the income of workers and the popular sectors (as in Argentina)? Why should one imagine that similar trends toward fiscal equilibrium and redefinition of the external debt, similar patterns of state intervention and reconversion of industrial production and export orientation, will lead to similar patterns of price stability or economic growth? Can we assume that there are only differences of degree in terms of the "weakening" of the capacity for state policy making between economies whose domestic savings remain in local currency and those whose savings have been "dollarized"?

The redefinition of Latin America's insertion in the international financial system and world markets during the 1980s has had very different impacts on a variety of fronts across the region. Rethinking Latin American development, questions of democratic governability, the region's insertion in the global political economy, or the transformation of domestic social structures can thus proceed most fruitfully through comparative analyses that place particular emphasis on the specific characteristics of each society. Neither methodologies that study political processes independently from the economy nor those that attempt the "deduction" of political processes from the structural conditions of the region as a whole are likely to be very useful in comprehending the limits and the potentialities of Latin America's present or future.[8]

Democracy, Orthodoxy, Heterodoxy and Structural Adjustment

Theoretical debates and an important body of empirical research have examined the political correlates of economic adjustment policies (Nelson 1989 and 1990; Haggard and Kaufman 1992a; Bresser Pereira, Maravall, and Przeworski 1993). What do we know at this point about the relationship between political regime type and economic performance (i.e., inflation, fiscal deficits, wages, rates of growth, balance of payments), on the one hand, and the relationship between regime and the choice of economic strategy and policies, on the other?[9] Recent literature tends to conclude that conditions of affluence generate relatively similar economic outcomes regardless of regime type. In periods of economic crisis, however, "the political regime variable may be particularly useful in predicting both policy intentions and certain types of economic outcomes" (Stallings and Kaufman 1989, 216).

Two principal generalizations emerge from this literature concerning the choice of economic strategies. First, stable authoritarian regimes as different as Mexico and Chile under General Augusto Pinochet and "established democracies," such as Costa Rica, Colombia, and Venezuela, exhibit a strong preference for "orthodox," market-oriented strategies of stabilization and structural adjustment. The variables shaping these policy choices — and the factors determining the feasibility of their implementation — are to be found in cohesive technocratic elites with strong neoclassical convictions and powerful executives capable of controlling popular protests. Second, in contrast to long-standing civilian and authoritarian regimes, politicians and technocratic elites in "transitional democracies" (e.g., Argentina, Brazil, and Peru in the mid-1980s) have shown an affinity for "heterodox" macroeconomic strategies.

Indeed, the economic teams in many nascent democracies mistakenly diagnosed the crisis as one that could be administered "politically" by negotiating with Washington over the terms of rescheduling payments on interest and principal. Moreover, they minimized the importance of tax reform and control over public enterprises, major obstacles to the resolution of the fiscal crisis and the achievement of medium-term economic equilibrium. This mistaken diagnosis created a false expectation that economic policy could cope with inflation without major structural changes and could induce major economic actors to modify previous inflationary behavior.

By the late 1980s, policy makers in these new or transitional democracies concluded that there was something wrong with "their" entrepreneurs, workers, or middle classes, who were not able or willing to "see" that the numbers were right, inflation was under control, and government policies had created the conditions for abandoning short-term, defensive strategies. Repeatedly, government officials postponed the reform of the state and the tax system, while focusing on the "dysfunctional" economic behavior of political and social actors, which they took as a sign of "domestic irrationality," an exogenous variable undermining chances of economic success. If "correct" economic policies were implemented, this argument held, and governments were indeed operating in a world of "irrational" actors, then it made sense to eschew negotiations and instead to concentrate power in the executive in order to impose needed economic reforms. This perspective is consonant with an analytical logic that separates economics and politics and considers the latter as an exogenous source of inefficiencies.

Consequently, this made more comprehensible the finding that new democracies showed varying degrees of heterodoxy in the economic strategies and policies they implemented and that they shared a common element in the exclusionary character of their decision-making process. In effect, the economic leadership in the new democracies shared a diagnosis that they were confronting an iteration of an "n-irrational actors prisoner's dilemma." State actors, concerned with the continuity of reform policies, potential crises of governability, survival in future elections, possible authoritarian conspiracies, or some combination of these, concluded that for such a game there is a dominant strategy with respect to domestic actors: the unilateral imposition of "Hobbesian solutions" (non-negotiated modifications of the structure of payoffs). All too frequently, democratic leaders have perceived Hobbesian fiats as their most (or, perhaps, their only) feasible choice.[10] This understanding of the relationship between politics and economics, and of the design and implementation of socioeconomic policies, is still present in the shift toward more orthodox strategies that followed the failure of more heterodox economic plans in the new democracies.

Another point to be considered concerns the correlation between political regime and economic performance. Analyses of this question usually compare economic indicators for periods covered by both democratic and authoritarian regimes in order to arrive at conclusions concerning growth, fiscal deficits, balance of payments, inflation, and so on. However, these analyses generally fail to recognize that democratic regimes in Latin America tend to have a higher "survival rate" when facing economic hard times.[11] Therefore, over the long term, democracies will necessarily tend to perform poorly in comparison to authoritarian regimes. But this ignores the greater success achieved by democratic regimes in surviving and managing economic crises. Given that the economic performance of these democracies cannot be measured independently from the crisis that hastened the demise of the dictatorships, and that democracies have a higher survival rate (which determines lower indices of economic performance), a head-to-head comparison of growth, inflation, fiscal deficits, wages, and balance of payments is only marginally useful for understanding the economic capabilities of each of these political regimes.

These indices become meaningful only if the consequences of policy making under the previous authoritarian regime can be isolated from the results of democratic policy making, and if the diminishing impact on economic performance resulting from the greater resiliency of democratic regimes can be controlled for. And none of these econometric operations can be properly completed without a specific, case-by-case assessment of the politico-economic process. Only then we will be able to arrive at meaningful comparative conclusions concerning the differential economic performance of authoritarianism and democracy.[12]

A related question concerns the relationship between new democracies and heterodox economic strategies. The affinity for heterodox strategies on the part of recently installed democratic regimes in the 1980s is transitory and limited primarily to the initial phases of the transition from military to civilian rule. Moreover, the "heterodox shock" strategy embodied in the Austral Plan, the Cruzado Plan, and the Inti Plan — implemented in the mid-1980s in Argentina, Brazil, and Peru, respectively — failed for a variety of reasons only partially related to economics. As we said, many critics frequently blame civilian politicians anxious to curry favor with the electorate. Under the thrall of an apparently "cost-free" adjustment strategy without unpopular measures like recession, unemployment, and high interest rates, the elected leaders of the new democracies procrastinated in enacting urgent policy corrections, not to mention postponomg more "fundamental" reforms. In the view of the critics, this failure of "political will" soon led to an erosion of popular support and opened the way for "macroeconomic populism," which, in turn, led to dangerous hyperinflationary episodes, followed by increasingly harsh stabilization programs in which social costs rose even higher (Dornbusch and Edwards 1991). But this is only one-third of the story.

Adolfo Canitrot (1994) provides another third of the explanation. He notes that such criticism rests almost entirely on retrospective reconstruction; few (or none) of the actors involved — in the government or the opposition — clearly perceived the need for deep reforms until after the initial disasters had already occurred.[13] The final third of the explanation focuses on operation of market forces and the strategic behavior of key collective actors. From this perspective, it is less a question of *political will* than one of insufficient *political capacity* to carry out more far-reaching reforms (see Chapter 1 by Gamarra in this volume). In this context, presidents and their economic teams have little or no capacity to influence 1) crucial economic variables (e.g., international commodity prices or interest rates on the external debt), 2) the uncertainty regarding the behavior of crucial external actors (e.g., the U.S. government, the International Monetary Fund (IMF), or private international banks), or 3) the strategic behavior of powerful domestic actors (e.g., speculative behaviors by capitalist interests leading to runs on the currency).

Also frequently overlooked in retrospective analyses are the fundamental differences among the different heterodox experiments in terms of international posture and domestic political dynamics. For example, both the Hernán Siles Zuazo government in Bolivia and the Alan García government in Peru challenged Washington, the international financial community, and powerful domestic capitalist interests in an effort to mobilize popular support for a "nationalist" development strategy. Less confrontational in their international posture, the architects of Brazil's Cruzado plans during the José Sarney government (1985-1990) sought to prolong a cycle of vigorous economic expansion and even to achieve a modest redistribution of income. To them, heterodox wage and price freezes were a politically attractive alternative to an orthodox stabilization and debt rescheduling program. Raúl Alfonsín (1983-1989) and his economy minister Juan V. Sourrouille pursued a more collaborative strategy, consulting secretly with the Reagan administration and the International Monetary Fund prior to unveiling the Austral plan. In the Argentine case, moreover, heterodox policies were designed to smooth the way for a fairly orthodox, IMF-style stabilization program (acceptance of

Washington's "case-by-case" approach for renegotiating the external debt) and were implemented without significant efforts at "concertation" with labor, capital, or the political opposition. Washington's support not only played an important economic role but was also a key political factor bolstering these heterodox plans. Washington's "OK" helped to neutralize potential reaction from local entrepreneurial groups in both Argentina and Brazil.[14]

Retrospective analyses, focusing exclusively on political will or on technical differences in the degree of heterodoxy, thus may obscure as much as they explain. Of greater significance, from the perspective of political economy, were strategic choices of policy makers, choices embedded in domestic political dynamics that determined the specificities of heterodox failure in each case and the different degrees of confrontation or alignment with Washington. The choices made by policy makers also affected Washington's response (i.e., supporting the Austral Plan or actively opposing the Inti Plan) and who would be charged with responsibility for the politico-economic consequences of each failure, including the choice and the implementation of more orthodox policies.

Comparative analysis shows that, despite the previously mentioned differences between stable authoritarian and democratic regimes and "transitional" democracies, virtually all Latin American countries, regardless of regime, eventually have been obliged to implement similar strategies. These strategies, and their attendant variable economic outcomes, arguably have had little to do with regime type. Following the demise of military dictatorships, the debt crisis and the unfolding of ever more virulent sociopolitical conflicts obliged presidents of social democratic and populist inclinations to enact increasingly orthodox policies attuned to the antistatist discourse and conditionalities emanating from the Reagan and Bush administrations, the multilateral lending agencies, and private international banks. Broadly similar restructuring projects have also been attempted under widely divergent circumstances — and with varying success — in Argentina, Brazil, Chile, Mexico, Bolivia, Ecuador, Peru, and Venezuela.

Throughout the hemisphere, short-term stabilization policies defended during the first years of the debt crisis gave way to increasingly uniform demands for major structural transformations as prerequisites for a market-driven or neoliberal model of accumulation. The growing emphasis on more long-term structural adjustments was part and parcel of a growing sophistication and greater political realism in Northern perspectives. The recognition that the debt crisis was more than a mere liquidity problem was foreshadowed in the 1985 Baker Plan. At the same time, the academic field of development economics, the World Bank, and, more reluctantly, the IMF began selectively to incorporate a different notion of "structural reform," which became thoroughly reconceptualized in accordance with the prevailing neoclassical orthodoxy. By 1987-1989, this change in diagnosis and prescription crystallized in the form of the now-famous "Washington Consensus." As a consequence, Latin American politicians and policy makers saw their autonomy eroded and their alternatives progressively limited.[15] Nevertheless, the relationship between economic performance and sociopolitical tensions during the implementation of restructuring projects is more complex than is frequently assumed.

Economic Performance and Sociopolitical Tensions

What *may* — and probably will — happen if neoliberal strategies are successful? What *might* happen if they fail? What constitutes a "successful" economic strategy? Luiz Carlos Bresser Pereira, José María Maravall, and Adam Przeworski (see Chapter 7 in this volume) note that stabilization policies often are ineffective; moreover, even if (or perhaps especially if) stabilization policies achieve their immediate goal, they may be counterproductive in strictly economic terms, and the consequences may be quite dangerous for nascent democracies.[16] Are continued implementation of the reform packages (e.g., Nelson 1990), or the achievement of stabilization and trade liberalization (Haggard and Kaufman 1990) sufficient indicators of economic success? Bresser Pereira, Maravall, and Przeworski argue convincingly that the economic criterion for judging market-oriented reforms "can only be whether a country resumes growth at stable, moderate levels of inflation [...] Anything short of this is just a restatement of the neoliberal hypothesis, not its test." We agree with this criterion of stable, moderate growth.

In analyzing the relationship between economic performance and sociopolitical conflict, notions of simple linearity were demonstrated to be inadequate by Alexis de Tocqueville more than one hundred and fifty years ago. Surprisingly, however, politicians and economists — key protagonists in the processes we are analyzing — frequently persist in portraying economic performance and sociopolitical conflicts as inversely related: the greater the economic success (measured by continuity of reform policies, achievement of goals such as macroeconomic stability, resumption of growth, and a general increase in income), the lower the level of sociopolitical conflict. This inverse relation informing the generalized "common sense" among policy makers is presented in Figure 1.

Figure 1
Developmentalist Notion of the Relationship
between Economic Performance
and Sociopolitical Conflict

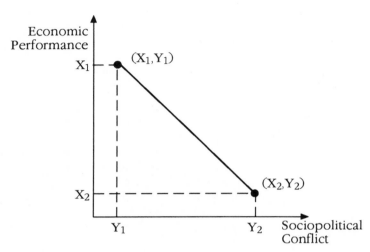

X_1, Y_1 = Buoyant Economy and Minimal Conflict

X_2, Y_2 = Economic Chaos (hyperinflation, fiscal crisis, etc.)
and Sociopolitical Breakdown (riots, coup attempts, etc.)

Empirical observations seem to validate this common sense notion that governments and societies have to prosper economically to reduce sociopolitical tensions and, if they don't, they face increasing political struggles. Societies with vigorous economies, represented in Figure 1 by x_1 (indicating stability, growth, and rising income), have achieved relative political stability and minimal social tensions, represented by y_1. These cases are exemplified by the industrial democracies prior to the mid-1970s and, to a lesser extent, Mexico, Venezuela, and Colombia until the 1980s. Societies on the opposite side of the economic performance axis, at x_2 (indicating hyperinflation, fiscal crisis, high unemployment, deep recession, breakdown of the productive/commercial chain, and so on), experience high levels of social and political conflict (riots and political crises such as those seen in Bolivia in 1984-1985 and Argentina in 1989), as depicted by y_2. In conventional modernization theories, it is assumed that point (x_1, y_1) is linked to point (x_2, y_2) by a toboggan effect: distributional conflicts increase if countries lose their balance and precipitously fall down the slope of the curve. Nevertheless, social relations are seldom as straightforward as Figure 1 suggests, even (or especially) assuming that all actors act rationally.

In contrast to this developmentalist common sense, analysis of microfoundations of social conflict (Acuña 1994) demonstrates that under conditions of economic deterioration and falling income, governments can reduce the virulence of sociopolitical contestation by increasing the costs and reducing the benefits of individual participation in collective action. "Flexibilization" of the labor market and related changes in capital-labor relations are usually at the core of such attempts. Focusing on the speed with which a crisis unfolds, the current literature on the politics of adjustment also recognizes that a gradual *worsening* of economic circumstances does not necessarily result in increased sociopolitical tensions. As Haggard and Kaufman (1992b, 348) observe, long periods of slow growth allow individuals and firms to lower expectations, to implement "nonpolitical" survival strategies (e.g., sending more family members into the work force), and to reduce consumption. Thus riding the toboggan "down" the slope does not necessarily imply a crash landing (x_2, y_2), since a politically more palatable, "softer landing" may be possible. At least two additional dimensions — time and capacity for collective action — must be included for a more accurate specification. Hence, the final outcome in navigating alternative slippery slopes will at the very least depend on 1) a velocity of economic deterioration gradual enough to permit individuals and firms to implement micro-level strategies to adjust to new market conditions and 2) the capacity of the state to disorganize the collective action/contestation capability of those bearing costs of adjustment. A function establishing the relationship between performance and conflict without taking into account these additional variables is simply incorrect.

Beyond what happens when socioeconomic conditions worsen, another fallacious belief also pervades analyses of the "politics of economic improvement." This other side of the coin holds that *improving* economic performance will result in *diminishing* political tensions and social peace. To the contrary, Alexis de Tocqueville's well-known study of the crisis of the *ancien regime* in France observes that "steadily increasing prosperity, far from tranquilizing the population, everywhere promoted a spirit of unrest. [...] Thus, it was precisely in those parts of France where there had been most improvement that popular discontent ran highest. This may seem illogical — but history is full of such paradoxes" (Tocqueville 1955, 176, 177). Following this line of reasoning, we argue that most rational actors (collective or individual) in a recovering economy will, if their capacity for contestation has not been curtailed, increase their demands and the level of conflict *before* either sustainable growth or the possibility of non-inflationary redistribution is assured. This is so for either or both of two basic reasons: 1) because of their knowledge about the *structural* properties of the economy and 2) because of an unavoidable problem of *imperfect information* when assessing the economy and considering probable consequences of alternative actions.

Contestation and Structural Limitations

Let us first focus on the *structural* limitations on collaborative behavior with respect to government policies in the context of a successful adjustment plan. Turning from modernization theories to neoliberal prescriptions, we are instructed that correct market-oriented reforms in response to a stagflationary crisis (t_0) are supposed to initiate a sequence (portrayed in Figure 2): socially painful measures in t_1, macroeconomic stability beginning in t_2, reactivation of the economy (based upon idle capacity) beginning in t_3, and investment, sustainable growth, and noninflationary redistribution beginning in t_4. Moreover, neoliberalism promises that the medium- to long-term future beyond t_4 will be Pareto-superior to the economic performance characteristic of the "good times" under the previous model of import-substition industrialization (ISI). But even if this fable were possible and the "correct" measures, implemented at t_1, actually produced macroeconomic stability in t_2 and some growth in t_3, why would social and economic actors bear the costs of the original economic crisis (as well as of the adjustment policies implemented in t_1) and wait patiently, trusting that their interests finally will be attended to at t_4? Why would a rational actor assume that the large set of contingent variables will remain *ceteris paribus* and that risk in the domestic market will be low enough to elicit substantial investment?[17] Stated differently, even if inflation and fiscal deficits are effectively controlled, given that the debt crisis, the opening of the economy, privatizations, and deregulation of markets have increased the potential domestic effects of external shocks, the probability that the behavior of contingent variables will be functional for the economic plan will be lower than in the previous semi-closed, state-centric model.[18] In a new context of greater uncertainty for investment, a strategy of economic militancy in pursuit of short-term payoffs would *still* be the dominant strategy for rational actors (even though, as in a prisoner's dilemma, this strategy is also the one that leads to the worst possible collective outcome when implemented by all the actors).

Figure 2
Neoliberal Model of Economic Reforms

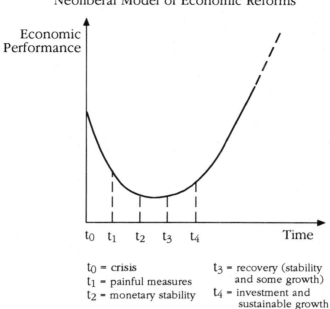

t_0 = crisis

t_1 = painful measures

t_2 = monetary stability

t_3 = recovery (stability and some growth)

t_4 = investment and sustainable growth

A pertinent caveat is that negative outcomes need not *always* occur when neoliberal restructuring takes place in economies such as the Latin American ones. For various reasons related to markets and state capacity, economic openings in some Latin American countries might result in lower risks and higher efficiency of investment and, therefore, less risk for collaborative strategies by those actors who must wait until t_4 to receive the benefits of rising employment and higher wages. Let us first consider the market. If economic liberalization implies integration with the U.S. market (as in the Mexican case), the expectation of a steady medium- to long-term inflow of foreign investment and an increase of manufactured exports might boost domestic investment and (perhaps reinforced by a parallel democratic opening) reproduce the process depicted in Figure 2.

State strength and capacity are also central to increasing the likelihood of collaborative strategies by actors obliged to wait until t_4 to receive payoffs in exchange for their "patience." Despite economic liberalization, political struggles may propel market-oriented reform in a direction in which state capacity to induce efficient investment and allocation of resources is enhanced. This would lower the risk of private sector investment without recreating conditions for the reemergence of the old, bankrupt state-centric model. In this case, instead of directly engaging in productive or extractive activities (steel, petrochemicals, oil) or the provision of services (telecommu-nications, energy), a reduction of the public sector's share of GDP need not be incompatible with more efficient social and industrial policies aimed at increasing welfare and promoting accumulation.

Majoritarian political support, popular confidence in the state's commit-ment and capacity to guarantee redistribution once sustainable growth is assured, combined with state autonomy and bureaucratic capacity to monitor and sanction free-riders, are among the key elements forcing firms to pay taxes and inducing them to invest. Given that these preconditions are the contingent result of political struggles, a society's ability to accomplish these tasks will depend heavily on its main actors' political, institutional, and ideological resources, as well as on what Machiavelli termed the Prince's *buona fortuna*. Argentina could possibly follow this path, although this is not very likely.

Related to state capacity is the question of control over resources. The maintenance of state control over key activities of the economy, particularly one generating an important source of foreign exchange, illustrates how a strong state has a better chance to strengthen the market and induce capitalists to resume investment. Chile is an example of the close relationship between successful market-oriented reform (especially the achievement of fiscal equilibrium with a low level of taxation) imposed by military force and the advantages of state control over the ownership, extraction, and export of copper. Nevertheless, in the following section we will argue, although from a different analytical standpoint, that even when structural conditions for economic growth are favorable, most rational actors will escalate their demands at the first signs of economic stability.

Contestation and Imperfect Information

When one leaves behind the "hard times" of uncontrolled inflation, falling wages, declining production, and increasing unemployment of t_0 and the recessive economic measures of t_1, monetary stability is achieved upon arrival at t_2, the productive/commercial chain is reconstituted, and credit becomes available once again. Consequently, even if low levels of investment persist, idle productive capacity (that resulted from drops in production during t_0 and t_1) means production can expand to accommodate the new, higher level of aggregate demand; sales and profits will rise, and the economy will grow at t_3.

But, if adjustment policies so readily achieve a resumption of growth with rising income, why should the population postpone social and economic demands until a renewal of productive investment at t_4 assures stable, long-term growth? How can actors correctly evaluate when this point has been reached? Workers, the middle classes, and the domestic entrepreneurial class will tend to fall into three distinct groups: those who move resolutely toward an escalation of collective demands, those who support the "need" for social peace and refrain from pressuring the government, and those characterized by a risk-averse attitude and who thus vacillate between militancy and acquiescence. Although influenced by party identity and/or the socioeconomic status of their members, these three groups do not necessarily coincide with either traditional class boundaries or conventional three-way electoral alignments defined in terms of the supporters of opposition parties, the supporters of the governing party, and the "independents."[19] Let's pay closer attention to the foundations of support for and contestation to market-oriented reforms.

In general terms, and particularly with the weakened party identities characteristic of contemporary Latin American democracies, neoliberal reforms are implemented in contexts marked by the presence of two relatively consistent minorities: those who support the reforms "no matter what" and those who oppose the reforms "no matter what." The reasons for one or the other stand might include information that leads actors to believe that prevailing structural limitations undermine (or favor) the probability of successful reform. In either case, actors might choose between collaboration or confrontation as a function of their strong agreement or disagreement with the potential "end state" they believe to be implicit in the reform model. The point is that the actors' knowledge and perceptions, as well as the option to support or to oppose the reform process, are rationally rooted not only in self-interest but also in ideology and/or party identity that helps them to assess the desirability and feasibility of alternative "end states."[20] The minority that opposes reform exemplifies a transition during which actors, who initially lacked the means to act effectively, subsequently gain greater access to resources, which lowers the risk of acting collectively to demand redistribution. Those actors who, for whatever reason, were unwilling from the outset (t_0) to collaborate in the reform effort will move to active opposition once they have accumulated sufficient resources to act collectively. On the other hand, those individuals who collaborate with the government independently of the conjunctural macroeconomic performance are also a minority and, therefore, do not constitute sufficient support to sustain the continuity of the reform process. The size of this minority, as well as its composition — particularly the extent to which it is comprised of those most injured by economic reform — are nevertheless very important. Those sectors of population most hurt by restructuring — and hence, obliged to pay the costs of painful reform — will be willing to endure present sacrifices in exchange for possible future benefits if they have "confidence" in the elites controlling government and macroeconomic policy. And confidence is likely to be a function of whether those in control are "one of us," where "us" means populist, laborite, Peronist, or social democrat. Therefore, neoliberal reforms carried out by parties with a broad base among the popular classes have a higher probability of success than those carried out by parties or coalitions with limited support among the masses.

The third group is also usually a minority, although one of strategic importance in the political struggles over economic reform. Although adversely affected by reform, these actors may see no feasible alternative and thus will support the neoliberal measures "hoping that everything goes well." The strategic character of this group results from the fact that its decision either to collaborate with the reforms or to shift to an active demand for redistribution is the central determinant for the constitution and character of the majority. In other words, it is this third group's decision to join in supporting one or another of the "consistent minorities" that is crucial in assuring majoritarian support for reform or, to the contrary, in crystallizing a majoritarian demand for redistribution.

The social sectors that constitute this strategic third group are willing, up to a certain point, to pay the price entailed by the transition to a new socioeconomic model and carefully weigh the risk of jeopardizing the medium- and long-term stability of current and potential increases in income. For these actors who eschewed militant economism in favor of a collaborative strategy, the empirical references that signal the arrival at the "safe side" of t_4 are greater stability and rising aggregate demand, profits, and growth.[21] The problem is that the *same* observable phenomena characterize the arrival at t_3, although at this moment no significant increase in the level of investment has yet occurred. Therefore, growth will not be sustainable in the long run, and redistributional policies may lead to inflationary consequences.

But actors do not have any reliable and easily available method to assess the (non)existence of investment or readily to distinguish whether economic outcomes (stability, growth, and rising profits) are the enduring consequence of a new development trajectory or, instead, are more ephemeral phenomena associated with a short-term recovery from stagflation. Within the strategic third group, some actors will be convinced that a more buoyant economy is "evidently" a sufficient cause to expect an improvement in their living conditions (without placing reform and growth at risk), causing them to join the first group in voicing demands. The rest will search for "agents" they believe to be better equipped than themselves (because they possess more or better information) to evaluate accurately what is *really* happening in the economy. This situation of asymmetrical information will result in the search by the population for credible "voices" capable of forming opinions over whether to actively demand a larger share of the new pie or, alternatively, to exercise patience.[22]

In brief, there are four important "informed agents" sought by the middle classes, workers, popular sectors, and some capitalists in their attempt to understand what is *really* happening: opposition parties, unions, the government itself, and the independent media. Opposition parties, already paying the political costs of the relative success of the government's economic policies — and awaiting the potential benefits from increased dissatisfaction if those policies fail — will stress the social sacrifices entailed by austerity and, in some cases, will claim that the consolidation of the new economic model will make future redistribution impossible. In a context where the priority is to regain lost electoral support, even those opposition politicians and technocrats who *agree* with governmental economic policies and who accept the need to restrain demands will generally remain silent. If the population chooses to heed signals emitted by the opposition parties, then regardless of the level of investment, an active demand for immediate improvement in their income becomes the rational choice.

Organized labor may express itself in three ways. A few union leaders may be committed to market-oriented reform and voice their support, although this position risks too close an approximation to the government for the pertinent leaders to remain credible and authoritative. The majority of union leaders supporting the government will remain silent. Uncertainty concerning the fate of socioeconomic reform leads them to avoid the potential costs of supporting a plan that might fail. A second group comprising those unions hurt directly by economic reform or particularly threatened by the marketization of capital-labor relations will be militant throughout the reform process and will take a stand coinciding with the opposition parties. A third group remains silent. High costs inflicted by the government in retaliation for unruly behavior (protests, strikes, and so on), as well as the low probability of success if active opposition is adopted, dictate the absence of protest. The actors in this group will refrain from confrontation, alleging that the "right time" for a more activist posture has not yet arrived. For those mindful of these union voices (and strategic silences), the fact that most union leaders willing to express a vocal opinion actively demand increases in real wages means that greater militancy will be seen as the most rational course of action, regardless of whether the level of investment is sufficient to lead to sustained economic expansion.

The government's economic team is the main agent interested in sending a clear signal that conditions for redistribution are still not in place. However, technocrats simultaneously play three "nested games"[23] — one with the middle classes and workers, a second with domestic firms, and the third with international capital — resulting in a contradictory and garbled message. There are two reasons for this confusion. First, those in charge of the economic policies find themselves in a double bind: they must convince domestic and international capitalists that structural problems have *already* been solved and that it makes sense for them to invest. Simultaneously, they must convince the unions and the middle class that ongoing structural reform has *not yet* been completed and demands must be restrained because it is still too early for redistributional policies. Second, government spokespersons and governing party politicians with their finger on the public pulse will be eager to capitalize electorally on declining inflation rates, rising growth, and improving income indicators. Politicians, in particular, will thus stress that, contrary to expectations, adjustment need not imply a long period of recession. In their effort to demonstrate "extraordinary" capacity to achieve stability with growth, these politicians inadvertently heighten the confusion between t_3 and t_4. In this context, rational actors will not be capable of sorting out government messages that reflect the "real" state of the economy from messages that are politically and economically expedient — although false. For most of the population, therefore, the government is not a reliable source of signals either to "move" or to "wait."

The media could conceivably be important allies for state officials in the reform process. The (necessary) ambiguities of the government's discourse in the confrontation with the opposition, however, generally precludes this supportive role. Instead, the media frequently are cast in the role of "neutral" voices in debates over economic policy, thus placing them in a strategic position vis-à-vis the government. Tensions between the media and the government — due to the latter's attempt to influence the former, with consequent accusations of governmental hegemonic aspirations and threats to the "freedom of the press" — are typical of t_2 and t_3 conjunctures.

In view of the problem of asymmetric information regarding the "real" stage of the economic process (t_3 or t_4?), a government bent on economic restructuring is at a serious disadvantage in the competition among the alternative agents in the formation of public opinion. This disadvantage helps explain outcomes, generally counter-intuitive from the perspective of policy makers, in which the exacerbation of sociopolitical tensions frequently goes hand-in-hand with improving economic performance. Many workers, members of the middle classes, and some capitalists who originally were unsure of how to respond to improving economic conditions and, therefore, searched for an "informed agent" begin to voice redistributional demands. They do so because the signals to wait are ambiguous, while the signals to move are both more consistent and probably majoritarian among the sociopolitical leadership. The political timing of the actors' behavior consequently does not follow the timing of the economic model, an eventuality that may jeopardize the success of reform policies. Expectations, demands, and attendant political strategies are not "respectful" of the tempo of the economic sequences by which markets adjust.

Looking at Figure 3 below, let us see in a two-step analysis when and why the assumption of an inverse relationship between economic performance and sociopolitical conflict does not hold. The first step refers to the period when the economy worsens (panel #1) and the second to the period when the economy begins to improve (panel #2). After the outbreak of the economic and sociopolitical crisis at t_0, and once socially painful measures begin to be implemented at t_1, most societies show a paradoxical decline in collective action and mobilization, despite the continued erosion of economic conditions. The novelty is that the population perceives the worsening economic performance as the result of the socially painful measures the government insists are necessary to bring the economy under control. This perception leads risk-averse sectors (who see no realistic alternative to government policies) to close ranks with the "consistent minority" that supports the government "no matter what." In a tradeoff between present sacrifices and future benefits, they demobilize. Demobilization constitutes collaboration with neoliberal reform as the majoritarian strategy. However, the consistent minority that opposes reform "no matter what" has seen its capacity for collective action undercut in the context of stagflation. Therefore, lower economic performance coincides with an easing of sociopolitical tensions, a positive relationship depicted in panel #1 in the movement from t_1 to t_2, when the direction of the curve changes at point A. Panel #2 represents what happens when the economy begins to turn around. After t_2, relative monetary stability begins to improve, showing an inverse relationship between better economic performance and declining sociopolitical tensions. Some growth is achieved following t_3, and the curve continues to reflect a reduction in conflict, although the slope shows a slowdown in the rate of decrease until arriving at point B. Beginning at point B, we again observe a *positive* correlation between conflict and economic performance.

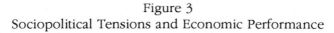

Figure 3
Sociopolitical Tensions and Economic Performance

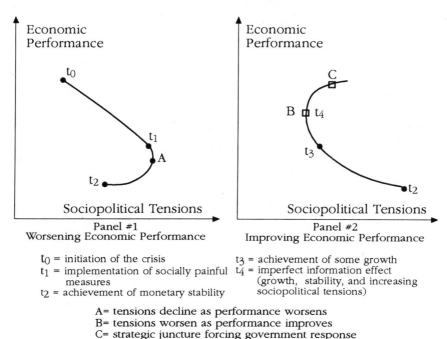

t_0 = initiation of the crisis
t_1 = implementation of socially painful
        measures
t_2 = achievement of monetary stability

t_3 = achievement of some growth
t_4 = imperfect information effect
        (growth, stability, and increasing
        sociopolitical tensions)

A= tensions decline as performance worsens
B= tensions worsen as performance improves
C= strategic juncture forcing government response

   In the previous paragraph, we explained why at certain moments in the reform process (point A) worsening economic conditions tend to go hand-in-hand with declining sociopolitical tensions. Turning to panel #2, which depicts what happens when economic conditions improve, we note that at point B the effects of imperfect information become sociopolitically conflictive. As previously noted, sectors of the risk-averse group, unable to figure out if sustainable growth has been assured or not, begin to shift toward greater militancy, thereby joining the "consistent minority" that had always opposed the government "no matter what." In the context of economic improvement, this opposition minority has more resources for collective action and becomes more militant.[24] The joining of these two groups makes possible the emergence of an opposition majority that threatens the continuation of the reform process. Once this tendency is recognized by governments, at point C, the survival of economic reform policies will, to a great extent, depend on the political capacity and strategies of policy makers and opposition actors. At point C, governments and economic teams face two basic political alternatives: 1) either economic policy making will incorporate political processes as *endogenous* to the model, and the government will undertake negotiations (perhaps leading to social or political pacts) or 2) policy makers will continue to justify their models with a discourse alleging "irrational," "shortsighted," and "selfish" behavior on the part of the social actors they confront.[25] This latter option implies resorting to Hobbesian solutions to the problem of reconciling growth and sociopolitical harmony.

Point C is, therefore, a politico-economic strategic moment because the actions undertaken at this particular location on the curve will determine differential probabilities for subsequent trajectories that, in turn, will have radically different "end states." This logic is reflected in the following analysis of alternative scenarios (S_1, S_2, S_3, or S_4), as portrayed in Figure 4.

Figure 4
Latin American Politico-Economic Scenarios

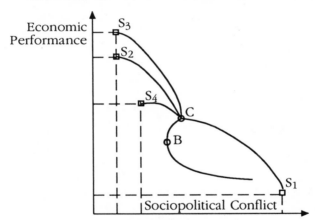

S_1 = Organic Crisis
S_2 = Fragmented, Exclusionary Democracy
S_3 = Inclusionary Democracy
S_4 = Dual Democratic Regime
B = Tensions worsen as performance improves
C = Strategic juncture forcing government response

Alternative Politico-Economic Scenarios

We are interested in two types of politico-economic scenarios. The first scenario (S_1) represents one type and presents a *tendency* toward zero-sum, increasingly conflictive outcomes (where tensions increase and economic performance declines). This scenario does not constitute an equilibrium and is thus inherently unstable and transitory. The other three scenarios

(S_2, S_3, S_4) represent alternative democratic "end states" of self-reproducing relative stability. The particular set of institutions and the structure of conflict in each of these alternatives combine so that none of the main politico-economic actors has sufficient incentive to deviate from the rules of the game if other actors also refrain from deviating. Each of these latter scenarios should, thus, be considered as a distinct mode of democratic consolidation.[26]

If a democratic government enacts an exclusionary style of policy design and implementation, it can succeed or fail in imposing its will on the sociopolitical opposition, alternatives that determine the consideration of our first two scenarios $(S_1$ and $S_2)$. If a democratic government responds to increasing sociopolitical tensions at point C by reducing the degree of Hobbesianism and exclusion in the policy making process, the possible outcomes are described in the last two scenarios $(S_3$ and $S_4)$.

First Scenario: "Organic Crisis" Revisited

If a government fails in its attempt to restructure the economy, performance probably will falter and sociopolitical tensions will increase, thus unleashing a tug-of-war among social and political actors. With the socioeconomic reform effort half completed, S_1 becomes the most probable outcome. In this unstable and stagflationary situation, domestic social actors find themselves in a zero-sum relationship. The differential structural position of capitalists and workers empowers the former to defend their profits more effectively than wage earners can protect their income, a property of capitalism that is at the core of the inflationary spiral. The tendency is toward regressive redistribution in the context of a stagnant or even declining national income base. In this situation, only monopolies or those firms that can effectively play the financial game reap increased profits.

This first scenario usually includes an unresolved, and increasingly critical, external debt crisis (soon reproduced domestically in the form of uncontrollable fiscal deficits) that may force the economic authorities to suspend — with or without an explicit unilateral moratorium — interest payments owed to external creditors. This prospect places international challenges at the center of the government's problems. The typical dilemma is either to reject the demands of multilateral institutions and the foreign private banks (a defiant heterodoxy) or to yield and adjust social and economic policies accordingly to meet external conditionalities.[27] In this first scenario, renewed politico-economic crisis tempts rulers to embark upon even harsher attempts to impose Hobbesian solutions. This might take the form of alternative political outcomes, ranging from a new economic policy (implemented by the same economic team in an attempt to impose new economic "packages"), a new team of economists, the government's replace-ment, or even a crisis of the regime, its downfall, and the threat of an authoritarian regression. Any of these events could lead to a new "starting point," although probably one with higher levels of sociopolitical tension and poorer economic performance than at t_0, when the previous crisis prompted the first efforts at economic adjustment. Political stalemate, escalating distributional conflict, and serious difficulties in capital accumulation combine to produce an "organic crisis" of the society as a whole.

Second Scenario: Fragmented and Exclusionary Democracy with Neoliberal Economics

For a democratic government to implement a full-blown variant of neoliberal restructuring, a series of preconditions must be met. The maintenance of a majoritarian political coalition (both in elections and in congress)[28] in support of governmental policies is necessary but not sufficient. Neutralization of the opposition may be achieved by repression and dismantling the institutional framework that facilitated these actors' capacity for strategic behavior. This entails the progressive disarticulation of social networks and the erosion of collective identities and political solidarities.[29] In a nutshell, the democratic regime's capacity for political domination is based on the "silence of civil society" resulting from the fragmentation of the social actors and the exclusionary design and implementation of social and economic policies.

What we observe in these cases is the accelerated enactment of radical neoliberal reforms abolishing or rolling back laws and regulations related to neocorporatist decision-making institutions, workers' organizations, and collective bargaining. Thus, the deepening of market-oriented reforms may gradually transform traditional societal cleavages and lead to a renovated party system reflecting emergent social and economic realignments. Depoliticization of policy debates, along with competition for electoral advantage within the institutional parameters of the incipient neoliberal order, is also part of this process. Seen from this perspective, the efficient use of the government's majoritarian political support (although this support will probably decline in the interval between points B and C) is necessary to disarticulate the organization and political presence of social actors, in a successful Hobbesian strategy for achieving better economic performance while simultaneously controlling sociopolitical tensions.

The consolidation of this second scenario implies that the government has managed to control the external debt by renegotiating its reduction (historical experience has placed these reductions at approximately 35 percent), that many state enterprises have become private monopolies, that the economy is opened to world trade (with average tariffs hovering at approximately 10 percent), and, above all, that the market has become the main mechanism of resource allocation. These successes reinforce stability, and fiscal reforms may oblige the bourgeoisie to pay more taxes than before the debt crisis, although the lack of state coordination and a state-induced growth strategy may well entail slow and erratic economic expansion, particularly if pragmatism is eschewed and orthodoxy is strictly observed.[30] Also, the weakening of social actors, particularly of labor unions via the marketization of capital-labor relations, will produce a new distributional equilibrium below the pre-1980s historical average. Therefore, successful realization of this scenario implies emergence (and possible crystallization) of a new politico-economic matrix in which neoliberal economic reforms are accompanied by neoliberal political transformations, resulting in the consolidation of a fragmented and exclusionary democracy.

Third Scenario: Inclusionary, Democracy, Strong Actors, and an Activist State

At point C in Figure 1, it is conceivable that the executive could choose to abandon Hobbesian strategies. To do so would imply the reformulation of the decision-making process by strengthening the fundamental social actors and incorporating them more fully into the process of policy design and implementation. This more inclusionary strategy represents an attempt to base democratic stability on sociopolitical pacts that would assure major collective actors their interests would not be seriously hurt by neoliberal reforms. It also implies some sort of redistribution of political and economic resources acceptable to all parties to the pact. If this strategy is successful, the logic underlying democratic consolidation coincides with the "social democratic" proposal made by Luiz Bresser Pereira, José María Maravall, and Adam Przeworski (1993), as well with Przeworski's analysis of democratic class compromise (Przeworski 1985a and 1985b).

The institutional framework and political dynamics associated with this alternative closely resemble neocorporatism (Schmitter 1974; Schmitter and Lehmbruch 1979; Crepaz 1992). This framework implies negotiations of socioeconomic policies at the national level among the state and peak associations of workers and capitalists,[31] as well as parliamentary oversight of neocorporatist pacts to minimize the costs transferred to those actors (consumers, students, feminists, and so on) and public interests (such as the environment) excluded from tripartite negotiations. Three preconditions for the success of this alternative are 1) the organization of the membership of each class with a national leadership capable of obliging its rank-and-file to comply with the terms of negotiated agreements, 2) high institutionalization of capital-labor relations and sufficient state capacity to monitor and sanction breaches of agreements, and 3) low levels of risk and uncertainty for investment required for future higher employment, higher wages, and long-term economic expansion.[32]

Successful pact making with key collective actors would, as in S_2, lead to a politico-economic equilibrium with lower sociopolitical tensions and better economic performance than at point C. Also as in S_2, important economic reforms are completed (privatization, opening of the economy, control over fiscal deficits). Nevertheless, if the arguments advanced in this volume are correct, S_3, which envisions more active state participation in the implementation of social policies and growth inducement than does the "Washingtonian" version of economic adjustment, should produce a similar stable macroeconomic equilibrium, but at a *higher* growth rate (see S_3 in Figure 1). Historical comparisons and the expected consequences of labor union participation in the decision-making process make distributional properties of this third scenario less regressive than in the neoliberal model S_2. Better economic performance with more equitable distribution of income and wealth, plus the abandonment of Hobbesian postures, implies a relative deepening of democracy, when the other scenarios considered.

The problem is that in Latin America this *maximalist* version of democratic class compromise is clearly unfeasible. The fundamental preconditions for democratic class compromise are unlikely to be achieved fully by any Latin American country. Nevertheless, it is politically and theoretically important to underscore the possibility of a *minimalist* version of this scenario under conditions prevailing in Latin America. A more flexible, minimalist version of S_3 would require the *initiation* of closely interrelated, long-term transformations that would point in the direction of maximalist objectives: state reform, negotiation with and strengthening of collective actors, politico-institutional reforms reinforcing parliamentary mechanisms, and the expansion of citizenship rights.

If state reform is to lead toward more just and equitable outcomes under democracy, it is crucial that in the long run the relationship between state capacity and societal actors not be seen a zero-sum game. In this sense, there is a need for an explicit commitment by political and bureaucratic elites to strengthen and incorporate societal actors into the process of formulation and implementation of public policies. In order to generate confidence in the government's sincerity, particularly skillful and courageous "reform-monger-ing" (probably with unmistakable "populist" and "clientelist" overtones) must broaden the scope of negotiations beyond the narrow parameters of social pacts with organized labor and business associations or of political pacts limited to deals with party elites. The incorporation of a broader array of social actors, along with strong measures to reinforce the legal system, would be necessary to combat what Guillermo O'Donnell refers to (see Chapter 6 in this volume) as impoverished "brown spots" and "low-intensity citizenship." Prospects for a minimalist S_3 scenario might be enhanced by changes in constitutional frameworks, such as the introduction of parliamentarism (and certainly enhanced technical expertise and oversight capacity by elected representatives) and extensive reforms of rules governing elections and the party system, as well as a new fiscal pact among the national, state, and local governments.[33]

Although this minimalist project is somewhat more likely than the original maximalist version of S_3, it still confronts important domestic and international obstacles. In addition to the reconstruction of state institutions needed to guarantee the enforcement of pacts, it will not be easy to unify the "voice" of both workers and capitalists. The main obstacles to reducing sociopolitical tensions are rooted in the risks involved for all leaders (state, business, and labor) in carrying out institutional reforms while simultaneously confronting conflicts over substantive issues, such as the exchange rate or wage rates.[34] Finally, the international obstacles to be faced extend well beyond the obvious limitations imposed by the debt crisis and the vagaries of international capital flows to include the more subtle forms of veto power over national policies wielded by multilateral financial institutions, transnational corporations and banks, and the United States government, which still generally view reformist strategies as dangerously "populist" or "leftist" and the cause of economic inefficiency, corruption, and political instability. A governmental leadership able to win the "confidence" of the international community could expand the reform space required for the success of this minimalist scenario.

If progress is made in advancing this agenda of reforms — admittedly ambitious, given conditions currently prevailing in Latin America — it is possible that a trajectory of democratic deepening could be initiated. The key would be a tendency toward a rearticulation of state and societal actors such that elected officials accumulate sufficient political and administrative capacity to sanction transgressors who violate social agreements (on wages, prices, investment levels, and so on). Greater embeddedness of state institutions in civil society would also endow elected officials with the capacity to act gradually to reduce the risks of investment and to provide the incentives required to convince social actors to abandon strategies of confrontation in favor of cooperative strategies tending to institutionalize distributional conflicts within the emergent democratic order. Here a reinvigorated, moderate democratic Left must play an essential role.[35]

A minimalist S_3 could conceivably, over a sufficiently lengthy period, undergo metamorphosis and emerge as a more genuine democratic and more socially just alternative (maximalist S_3). However, a minimalist S_3 scenario could "fall short" and constitute an equilibrium by itself, albeit probably a weak equilibrium. In view of the alternatives, "medium-intensity citizenship," modest redistribution, and reasonable economic growth are not to be disdained.

Fourth Scenario: Dual Democratic Regimes

In the fourth scenario (S_4), state elites seek to establish an alliance with a strategic minority of the opposition for the purpose of excluding the majority of the remaining social actors by disarticulating and neutralizing their capacity for collective action. Political and economic stability in this scenario is facilitated by a dual logic of state power (respect for the organization of the allied minority and disarticulation of the rest) and unequal distribution of resources (benefits are extended only to allied sectors of business and organized labor). The particularly elitist character of this logic of governability defines the dual democratic regimes that emerge in S_4. Of course, all regimes manifest this dual character to some extent because every strategy of inclusion necessarily implies exclusion. The high ratio of exclusion to inclusion, the dependence of the regime's stability on this ratio, and the intention of the main political actors to maintain it are what differentiate dual democratic regimes from others.

As O'Donnell points out (Chapter 6 in this volume), widespread poverty, massive social and economic inequalities, and the weakness of the "state as law" perversely reinforce one another to (re)produce despotic and archaic social relations and what he calls "low-intensity citizenship." O'Donnell's depiction of "delegative democracy," with concentration of power in the executive and inherent hostility to accountability and the institutionalization of mechanisms of representation, also resonates with the syndrome of traits exemplified in S_4.[36]

Economic performance under S_4 will be less dynamic than in S_2 or S_3. Mediocre performance is a likely consequence of inefficiencies and distortions in the allocation of resources stemming from the subsidies and privileges awarded by the government to minority allies in exchange for their political support. But performance will surpass that which is possible under S_1 because the government will have achieved sufficient control over the principal macroeconomic variables to assure at least medium-term stability. On the other hand, sociopolitical tensions in S_4, although higher than in S_2 and S_3, will be lower than in S_1 because the dual logic of power and unequal distribution has been imposed on most of the population. Tensions will be higher than in S_2 because the minority of strategic actors incorporated into the dominant alliance means that a few important actors retain, and will use, their capacity for collective action to pressure the government. Sociopolitical tensions will also be higher than S_3 because the objective of the dominant alliance is not only to disarticulate "the others" but also to restrict the participation of the allied minority as much as possible in the negotiation of "macro" issues, thus setting the stage for constant zig-zags and recurrent confrontations with the opposition.

Relationships Among Scenarios

State elites and societal actors generally do not embark upon the fourth scenario as a consequence of rational calculation. Rather, this scenario usually emerges as the result of the failure of more ambitious elite initiatives (to achieve objectives related to S_2 or S_3) or as the result of the conviction by elites of their own political weakness (S_4 is preferable to the disaster of organic crisis S_1). Each of the paths to the other scenarios thus contains a possible route to S_4. We will examine each path briefly.

Given conditions of organic crisis in scenario S_1, state elites may opt to abandon maximalist objectives with respect to market-oriented reform and economic performance. Instead of a full-fledged Hobbesian strategy to restructure society and the political economy, or a risky option of strengthening and negotiating with societal actors, governing party politicians may select a few representatives from among opposition party elites or among corporate actors (labor unions and entrepreneurial associations) as interlocutors; the precise allies selected will depend on the support required to fashion a minimum winning coalition capable of disarticulating the rest of the society. This divide-and-conquer strategy might succeed, although the cost may be high: the potential members of the privileged minority will only be willing to enter into an alliance with the government in exchange for institutional arrangements that safeguard their own vital interests and capacity for collective action in the future. The obvious risk for the potential allies is that once the government has used their support to neutralize the "others," they themselves could then be "dealt with" by the exclusion of minority allies from the dominant alliance.

From the attempt to achieve S_2, the road is different. At point C in Figure 1, the government may decide to radicalize and deepen its Hobbesian strategy. But the government will be obliged to accept small concessions to strategic minorities, whose support provides the critical margin for success in negotiating specific reform issues (e.g., the privatization of public enterprises where unions could jeopardize the endeavor or the approval of legislation pertaining to the flexibilization of capital-labor relations). However, "partial success" only in some specific aspects of neoliberal restructuring may undermine the long-term consolidation of S_2 and, thus, may favor the emergence of S_4. For example, the contradictions and ambiguities required by concessions to minority allies (e.g., clauses exempting them from the costs entailed in the approval of certain laws) mean that partial reforms may well fall substantially short of the more drastic liberalizing measures typical of the initial period of crisis. As a result, in comparison with S_2, piecemeal economic reforms result in poorer economic performance and higher levels of conflict because of the greater level of organization and capacity for collective action on the part of opposition actors. This determines a different point of equilibrium than the one initially sought by neoliberal reformers.[37] S_4 is, thus, a probable outcome in the event of the failure of an S_2 project.

The transition from attempting S_3 and ending up in S_4 results from a failed effort to strengthen and incorporate societal actors into the decision-making process. At this point, negotiations with minority interests might be initiated with the intention of "waiting out" the crisis in the hope of retaking the original path toward S_3 at some point in the future. Nevertheless, prolongation of the "emergency" and the "circumstantial" exclusion of majoritarian actors might eventually lead to an equilibrium from which none of the organized participants want to depart and the majority would thus be excluded permanently. The government might reason that its attempt to achieve S_3, whether in its maximalist or minimalist version, faces insuperable obstacles and thus conclude that a progressive reform strategy in these circumstances might imply a level of sociopolitical conflict incompatible with its economic objectives. Governing party politicians and government bureaucrats might also realize that the balance of power between state and societal actors required for a radical change in direction toward the full-fledged neoliberal version of S_2 is unattainable. Therefore, in this case, S_4 is preferred as the only feasible alternative.

The failure to achieve S_3 — or the political dynamics to assure the implementation of a series of partial, "micro" reforms needed to attempt S_2 — and the risk of remaining in S_1 or of falling into S_1, are alternative origins for the emergence of S_4 as a stable equilibrium. But some scenarios are simply not present as viable alternatives in many societies. In fact, in a given society certain scenarios may not even form part of the actors' historical consciousness or even their imaginations. Nevertheless, and beyond the fact that no modal pattern can be inferred for the region as a whole, the properties and prerequisites for each scenario, as well as the relationships among the scenarios, suggest that dual democracies (S_4) are the most probable future in most cases.

Conclusions

We began by recalling Carlos Díaz Alejandro's prescient observation that Latin America was "not in Kansas any more." The arguments developed in this essay have advanced some ideas that help us understand the logic of neoliberal policy making and the bases of support and opposition to marketization, as well as locate Latin America more precisely in the maelstrom of political and economic transformations currently reshaping the capitalist world.

Our first step was to redefine in broad terms the relationship between economic and political processes. This is a central issue in the current Latin American context, in which pillars of democracy such as majoritarian choices and preferences are seen by many as having been reduced to empty rituals when governments are perceived as having no feasible alternatives to neoliberal structural adjustments. Are actors indeed learning that democracy is irrelevant? Can it be inferred from the narrowing of the scope of alternative strategies over the last decade and a half that neoliberal reforms will necessarily result in depolitization and the erosion of democratic loyalties and party identities, thus endangering democratic stability and consolidation?

We have argued that inferring politics from economics is bad methodology. Moreover, we have shown that even if the range of choices for socioeconomic policies has been dramatically narrowed, it does not necessarily follow that political consequences must march lock-step in a similar direction. These political consequences might range from strengthening long-standing historical patterns of alliance and opposition to a very different historical rupture. In these alternative scenarios, the same economic policies may set in motion quite divergent political outcomes in respect levels of sociopolitical conflict and opposition to economic reform, as well as produce a variety of economic consequences and long-term implications for democratic consolidation. The fact that economic crises severely constrain a government's room for maneuver does not mean that the "space for politics" has been foreclosed, nor does it mean that politics has been absorbed by economics. Political choices, strategies, and contingencies remain central determinants of social and economic processes, and their meaning and consequences perhaps gain even greater relevance in an era of deep economic crises and transformations. In a nutshell, a common, modal political pattern should not necessarily be expected from the implementation of similar economic strategies. In turn, if a dominant pattern does emerge, it will not be the result of a common economic "cause" but rather a reflection of the contingent aggregation of political and economic processes specific to each society.

By the same token, however, divorcing politics from economics is also bad methodology. Rethinking the relation between politics and economics should occur at the level of "middle-range" theories that allow analysis to incorporate organizational patterns of social and political actors and the contingencies inherent in the political struggles of each society. Although we cannot make general inferences regarding threats to democratic stability directly from contexts of negative socioeconomic circumstances, we certainly can analyze the *types* of democracies most like to emerge.

It is in this sense that we argue that rethinking Latin American development, questions of democratic governability, the region's insertion into the global political economy, or the transformation of domestic social structures can proceed most fruitfully through comparative analyses that place particular emphasis on the *specific* characteristics of each society. Neither methodologies that study political processes independently from the economy nor those that attempt the deduction of political processes from the structural conditions of the region as a whole are likely to be very useful in comprehending the limits and potentialities of Latin America's present or future.

In the same vein, regarding the question of state power and the discussion concerning the recasting of the relationship between the public and the private spheres, affirmations that state power in Latin America is "weakening" may obscure differences between those countries in which the state is impotent to carry out the neoliberal policies and other countries in which, notwithstanding its "weakening," the state still possesses sufficient power to impose economic reform and to neutralize troublesome social actors. State strengthening may be unavoidable during successful reforms leading to market strengthening.

The new, future state emerging from neoliberal reform will, therefore, probably be *both* stronger and weaker. Depending on the specific issue area or public policy arena, for example, market-oriented restructuring may lead to a severe retrenchment of the public sphere's traditional "entrepreneurial" functions and to a much smaller, but not necessarily "weaker," state apparatus. In other arenas, such as the capacity of civilian elites to exercise control over the military or to impose restrictions on organized labor, public authority may be strengthened significantly. Similarly, stronger and more effective mechanisms of state regulation must be put into place in order for markets to function properly, with the efficiency and transparency required by private investors.

Another point considered was the correlation between political regime and economic performance. Analyses of this question usually compare economic indicators for periods covered by both democratic and authoritarian regimes. These analyses generally fail to recognize that democratic regimes in Latin America tend to have a higher "survival rate" when facing economic hard times. Therefore, over the long term, democracies will necessarily tend to perform poorly in comparison to authoritarian regimes. But this ignores the greater success achieved by democratic regimes in surviving and managing economic crises. Unless serious methodological problems are resolved, head-to-head comparisons of economic performance are only marginally useful for understanding the economic capabilities of each of these political regimes.

A key question regarding the relationship between politics and economics in the context of the debt crisis and the subsequent wave of neoliberal reforms deals with the relationship between economic strategy and policy and type of regime. Do democracy and authoritarianism make a difference in terms of the tendency toward more orthodox or heterodox economic strategies? From the comparative literature, we drew two partial conclusions and one overall conclusion. First, the choice of economic strategy or policy does not correlate with the type of regime but with the degree of regime consolidation and stability. While stable authoritarian and democratic regimes tend to implement more orthodox policies, recently installed "transitional" democracies initially show a tendency toward heterodox experiments. Second, despite these differing affinities between stable authoritarian and democratic regimes, on the one hand, and new and only weakly consolidated democracies, on the other, virtually all Latin American countries, regardless of regime type or degree of stability, sooner or later have been obliged to implement broadly similar economic strategies. To be sure, toward the late 1980s the academic field of development economics, the World Bank, and, more reluctantly, the IMF began selectively to incorporate a different notion of "structural reform," which became thoroughly reconceptualized in accordance with the prevailing neoclassical orthodoxy. By 1987-1989, this change in diagnosis and prescription crystallized in the form of the now-famous "Washington Consensus." As a consequence, Latin American politicians and policy makers saw their autonomy eroded and their alternatives progressively limited. The neoliberal strategies linked to the "Washington Consensus" implemented since then by Latin American governments, not to mention their widely divergent economic outcomes, arguably have had little to do with the type of political regime. Our overall conclusion in this respect is, not surprisingly, that the weight of the regime variable in explaining the nature of economic policy is primarily dependent on the scope of maneuvering room and the range of choice, something largely determined in the first instance by the stringency of external constraints. When international circumstances are sufficiently flexible as to allow at least some margin of choice, the determining variable is the regime's degree of political stability and the extent of state capacity and not so much the democratic or authoritarian nature of institutional arrangements.

Another issue at the core of the discussion of the political economy of structural adjustments concerns the relationship between economic performance and sociopolitical conflict. Politicians and economists, key protagonists in the processes we are analyzing, frequently persist in portraying economic performance and sociopolitical conflicts as inversely related — the greater the economic success (measured by continuity of reform policies, achievement of goals such as macroeconomic stability, resumption of growth, and a general increase in income), the lower the level of sociopolitical conflict. To the contrary, in view of an unavoidable problem of asymmetric information regarding the "real" stage of the economic reform process, and using a framework based on strategic analysis and principal-agent models of imperfect information, we conclude that if economic reforms manage to achieve some success leading to an *improvement* in economic performance, sociopolitical tensions will very probably *increase*, rather than subside. The political timing of the actors' behavior consequently does not follow the sequencing of the neoclassical prescription for economic reform, an eventuality that may jeopardize the success of neoliberal strategies. Expectations, demands, and attendant political strategies of rational actors are not "respectful" of the economic timings by which markets adjust.

Once this tendency toward heightening tensions in the context of economic improvement is recognized by governments, the survival of reform policies will, to a great extent, depend on the strategies and political capacity of policy makers and opposition actors. The direction taken by the political process at this stage becomes central not only for the success or failure of the economic reforms but also for the type of long-term politico-economic equilibrium possible for different societies. The composition of the governmental coalition at this particular moment weighs heavily in determining future scenarios. This question underscores an old conclusion in the social sciences that acquires renewed significance in the circumstances we are studying: the likelihood that those most *golpeado* by restructuring will be willing to endure present sacrifices in exchange for possible future benefits will be greater when those controlling the government and macroeconomic policy succeed in eliciting the "confidence" of those paying the costs of painful reform. And, as we noted, confidence is likely to be a function of whether those in control are "one of us," where "us" means populist, laborite, Peronist, or social democrat. Therefore, neoliberal reforms carried out by center-left parties with a broad base among the popular classes have a higher probability of success than those carried out by right-wing parties or conservative coalitions with limited support among the masses.

Finally, in exploring future paths that may spring from present politico-economic tendencies, we have suggested that of the possible alternative future scenarios, full-blown neoliberal restructuring with the consolidation of democratic rule is not a likely future for most Latin American societies. The most probable scenario seems to be dualistic democracies. In this scenario, state elites establish an alliance with a strategic minority of the opposition for the purpose of excluding the majority of the remaining social actors by disarticulating and neutralizing their capacity for collective action. Political and economic stability in this scenario rests on a dual logic of state power (respect for the organization of the allied minority and disarticulation of the rest) and unequal distribution of rewards (favoring allied sectors of business and organized labor and penalizing the rest). The particularly elitist character of this logic of governability defines the dual democratic regimes that emerge. At this stage, rather than firm conclusions, these arguments are interesting hypotheses that we believe merit comparative analysis of specific societies, something we do elsewhere.[38]

As noted previously, the success or failure of structural adjustment is strongly shaped by the fact that the expectations, demands, and political strategies of societal actors are not "respectful" of the macro- and microeconomic timings by which markets adjust. Politics and political timing must be understood as endogenous to the economic process. The problem of "time" for historical analysis and economic policy making is obviously nothing new.

Lord John Maynard Keynes was right when he pointed out the political problems of markets that adjust too far into the future when he observed that "in the long run we are all dead." And policy makers should bear in mind that the meaning of "too far" cannot be ascertained by economic modelling. It was Friedrich Hegel who stressed the importance of "political" time over "chronological" time. In his *The Philosophy of History*, he suggested that historical processes should be understood as ruled by Zeus, the political god, and not by Kronos, the god of time. In Hegel's vision, the struggle between these two gods over the nature of historical evolution ends when Zeus kills and devours Kronos. In other words, "too far" or "close enough" are eminently political questions central to the failure or success of economic objectives. These critical thresholds will be determined by what Hegel identified as those moments when "thinking...flows among citizens and determines their practice, [driving] them to question..." the prevailing order (cited in Marcuse 1968, 239-240).

Díaz Alejandro realized long before most observers that the debt crisis was not a mere passing event, and that Latin America in the early 1980s was entering a sort of *Land of Oz* — a world of uncertainties marked by radical changes of rules, actors, and resources. Not surprisingly, in the years since Latin America "left Kansas," economic strategy and policy making have been dominated by a long series of would-be "wizards" who acted as if they were capable of molding minds and controlling behaviors of societal and political actors virtually at will. The consequences of this autocratic political style are visible for all to judge. The political struggle over structural adjustments still awaits the emergence of new democratic leaders and coalitions who, when confronting the uncertainties of this new phase of capitalism, recognize that in the implementation of market-oriented reform governments necessarily must represent — and confront — rational actors defending legitimate interests. Rather than indulging in political sorcery, and treating them as "selfish" and incapable of understanding what needs to be done, elected leaders and the economic teams of reform-minded governments must consider societal actors as *endogenous* to policy making in a democratic society with a plurality of frequently conflicting interests. Whether included or excluded from policy making, these actors and interests will play a fundamental role in the success or failure of the strategies and reforms undertaken. In the disposition of this inescapable fact hangs the fate of current economic restructuring, as well as the prospects for democracy and sustainable and equitable growth in Latin American and elsewhere.

Notes

1. According to Guillermo O'Donnell (1992, 48-49), one of the key requirements for democratic consolidation is that "...democratic actors no longer have as one of their central concerns the avoidance of a (sudden or slow) authoritarian regression and, consequently, do not subordinate their decisions (and omissions) to such a concern." He also highlights the "habitual nature" of practices compatible with the reproduction of democratic institutions and the requirement that the "procedural consensus" be consistent with the "extension of similarly democratic (or at least non-despotic and non-archaic) relations into other spheres of social life." Adam Przeworski's discussion of consolidation is similar but also underscores that "democracy is consolidated when compliance — acting within the institutional framework — constitutes the equilibrium of the decentralized strategies of all the relevant political forces (1991, 26). Also see Schmitter and Karl (1993) and Valenzuela (1992, 69).

2. Elements of this "consensus" as explained in John Williamson (1990a, 1990b) include extensive reforms of the state (privatization of public-sector enterprises, fiscal reforms, severe retrenchment in public spending, and elimination of subsidies to consumption and "inefficient" producer interests); "getting the prices right" with a priority given to maintenance of macroeconomic equilibrium; sweeping market-oriented reforms (deregulation and demonopolization of the private sector, flexibilization of labor markets); and competitive reinsertion in the world-economy (trade liberalization, promotion of foreign investment). Also see Chapter 3 in this volume by Fanelli, Frenkel, and Rozenwurcel.

3. The term "neoliberalism" refers to the positions defended by contemporary followers of the post-1920s "purists" (Friedrich Hayek, Ludwig von Mises, Wilhelm Röpke) who go beyond the defense of balanced budgets, unregulated markets, and attacks on state intervention to criticize the pernicious effects of state collusion with monopoly and oligopoly private-sector interests and organized labor. For an extensive discussion, see Nylen (1992).

4. This is precisely the reason for the consensus in the literature on the need to enhance the bureaucratic insulation of the "change teams" from societal pressures, particularly in the initial phase of formulation and implementation of neoliberal reforms. Once the reform process is well underway, however, a second type of autonomy becomes crucial in which state elites can elicit the support of key collective actors, particularly among the leading sectors of the entrepreneurial class. In this process of insulation and the construction of support networks in civil society, the two prerequisites for success are autonomy (particularly from capitalists and organized labor) and the administrative capacity to implement policies, even against strong societal opposition. These two elements obviously point toward an important strengthening of the political power of the state, albeit on behalf of market-oriented reforms. See Evans (1992) for a discussion of "reinforced Weberianism" and "embedded autonomy."

5. The social and economic intervention of the "old" Keynesian welfare state resulted in blurring the "liberal" limits between politics and economics and between

the public and private spheres. As Claus Offe (1974, 1975, 1984) and Adam Przeworski (1990) point out, this intervention (fiscal and monetary policy, public investment, labor market regulation, educational and social welfare policies, public production of goods and services, and so on) removed the market as the main mechanism for the resolution of conflicts of interests, placing them under state tutelage in response to priorities determined by political and electoral objectives. Paradoxically, the same process that "strengthened" state power and autonomy since the 1930s also resulted, since the 1960s and 1970s, in its "weakening" and loss of efficiency in achieving objectives. What Offe termed the "politization of the market" prompted the mobilization and organization of societal interests to influence state policies. This accelerated the penetration of the state by multiple, contradictory interests and led to a loss of autonomy, rationality, and efficiency in the extraction of fiscal resources from society. This had two well-known consequences: fiscal crisis and the incorporation within the state apparatus of contradictions and cleavages present in civil society.

6. Addressing the relation between politics and economics in terms of basic properties of the capitalist mode of accumulation, or even examining this relation from the perspective of shifts in the mode of accumulation from import-substitution industrialization and strong state participation to economic opening and strengthening of the market as the allocator of resources is simply not very helpful. For example, the same import-substitution matrix is compatible with a wide range of outcomes in terms of regime stability, strength of sociopolitical actors, composition of class alliances, and so on.

7. Although we are primarily interested in the sociopolitical significance of economic processes, it is also clear that the "same" economic events may have very different economic consequences in different countries. By way of example, we know that since the crisis began, investment rates have fallen far below their historical levels. However, how can the Mexican case, where in the worst years of the debt crisis investment fell to 18 percent of gross domestic product (GDP), be equated with the Argentine case, where investment during "good times" was 22-23 percent and where in the worst of the crisis fell as low as approximately 8 percent of GDP? What new modalities of state intervention in the economy may arise in cases where the state controls the extraction and commercialization of an export good such as cooper (in Chile) or petroleum (as in Venezuela and Mexico)? On the other hand, what sort of state intervention can be expected in situations in which governmental elites confront a politically and economically powerful exporting bourgeoisie (as in Argentina)?

8. Here we are restating the methodological lessons taught by seminal works by such scholars as Fernando Henrique Cardoso and Enzo Faletto and Tulio Halperín Donghi. These authors argued against the search for a single model of development or a modal pattern in Latin American history. Cardoso and Faletto, in particular, persuasively employ a historical-structural and comparative mode of inquiry to delineate the multiple paths and the diversity of historical experiences in Latin America. See Cardoso and Faletto (1979) and Halperín Donghi (1966) among others. Also see Marcelo Cavarozzi's important analysis (1978) of the various historical trajectories eventuating from the crisis of oligarchical capitalism and Ian Roxborough's insightful extension (1984) of the comparative logic implicit in Cardoso and Faletto.

9. The time has long since passed when the notion was uncritically accepted that authoritarian regimes are more efficient than democratic and/or populist ones in coping with economic crises and creating the conditions for higher rates of investment and sustainable growth. For earlier treatments of this problem, see Hartlyn and Morley (1986) and Serra (1979). The last wave of authoritarian regimes in Latin America had a mediocre

record in managing the foreign debt, fiscal deficits, and balance of payments and in promoting investment and growth. Even Chile under Pinochet, frequently seen as relatively "successful" in economic matters, "... did not manage to generate a large amount of investment in productive activities. Most of the Chilean loans, like those of Argentina during the same period, were directed toward speculation and import of consumer goods" (Stallings and Kaufman 1989, 213). The "Brazilian miracle" lost momentum in the mid-1970s and did not survive the foreign debt crisis in the 1980s. Lastly, Mexico's *sui generis* authoritarian regime experienced a stagnant economy in the 1980s, along with high inflation, falling wages, and high fiscal deficits, and its good performance in its balance of payments should be attributed to the oil cycles more than to the authoritarian capacity to design and impose economic policies. In fact, Venezuelan democracy shows similar results in terms of low growth and balance of payments and a better record than Mexico in terms of inflation and fiscal deficits.

10. The prisoner's dilemma (PD) is a game in which the players face the choice to collaborate (C) in a common effort or to defect (D) and free-ride to maximize gains at the others' expense. The particular structure of the payoff matrix in this game makes defection the dominant strategy for both players. The paradox is that while the second best option (to collaborate) is collectively optimal, the payoff matrix makes defection the rational individual course of action, and the resolution of the game implies individual gains that are lower, and hence Pareto suboptimal, than if the players had collaborated. By "n-players" we mean that more than two players are involved in making choices, and by "iterated" we refer to a game that is played in repeated sequences. The "Hobbesian" solution to the PD refers to the presence of a hegemon, operating above and beyond the game to assure the Pareto optimal outcome by acting authoritatively to redefine the payoff structure so as to neutralize the costs of cooperation and reduce the benefits of defection. Of course, as Juan Carlos Torre correctly notes (private communication with the authors), a pure "Hobbesian" solution corresponds to an authoritarian regime under which liberties, rights, and participation by the citizenry are violently negated. An authoritarian regime is one thing and the presence of authoritarian tendencies under a democratic regime quite another. Republican guarantees of rights and democratic forms of participation determine a different political logic shaping the implementation and consequences of Hobbesian strategies. General Pinochet and Carlos Menem, although both are Hobbesians in game-theoretic terms, should not be placed in the *misma bolsa*.

11. Several implications of this discussion of economic performance are pertinent to the analysis of the cases examined in this volume: 1) the indicators commonly used to measure the performance of democracies reflect the profound economic disequilibria bequeathed by the outgoing military dictatorships; 2) the magnitude of the debt burden, the fiscal crisis, and depressed real wages, in a context of deeply rooted inflationary tendencies inherited by the incoming democratic governments, not only severely hampered economic recovery during the transition but also seriously compromised control over inflation and fiscal deficits as well as long-term prospects for economic growth; and 3) given that authoritarian regimes tend to collapse more readily when facing economic hard times, it is not surprising that more frequently it is democracies that confront economic crises. For a discussion of these points, see Przeworski and Limongi (1993). Examining ten South American countries, they found that democracies were not more likely to fall when facing economic crises than when growing, while authoritarian regimes were more likely to fall. In turn, they discovered that the number of other democracies in the region was very important in making democracy in any particular country more likely, while previous democratic break-downs in a country made it less likely. They conclude that political factors seem to have

been more important than economic conditions in explaining the emergence and breakdown of democratic and authoritarian regimes. They also warn that these findings do not necessarily hold true for the world as a whole, where both regimes (particularly poor democracies) seem sensitive to economic conditions. Very different analyses that also highlight the "many ignored advantages of democratic institutions" are offered in Olson (1991) and Remmer (1990 and 1991).

12. Current research by Adam Przeworski and his collaborators examines the empirical basis of this argument.

13. See Adolfo Canitrot's discussion (1994) of the fiscal pact, state reform, and privatization. He notes that pressure for these reforms only gathered in 1988. See Acuña (1989 and 1994), Smith (1990; 1992) and Sola (1991) for analyses reaching similar conclusions about the Argentine and Brazilian heterodox experiences.

14. Similarly, in the case of Israel, Washington's support not only softened entrepreneurial reaction to a similar antiinflationary plan but forestalled expected political opposition from within the cabinet itself.

15. On the evolution of orthodox economic thought among academics and the professional staff of multilateral institutions, see Kahler (1990).

16. Bresser Pereira, Maravall, and Przeworski (see Chapter 7, 182) observe: "Stabilization attempts either fail or induce recessions so profound that they depress investment, undermine the prospects for future growth, and generate social costs that make the continuation of reforms politically unpalatable under democratic conditions. Moreover, the technocratic style in which these policies tend to be formulated and implemented undermines the consolidation of democratic institutions."

17. In Latin America this set of variables includes not only the behavior of n domestic actors that participate in the distributional struggle but also potential changes in the leadership and/or policies of the U.S. Federal Reserve or of the international financial institutions (that have acquired the power to strengthen or veto the monetary policies linked to these countries' economic strategies), or of potential dramatic falls in the international prices of their main export goods with the consequent crises in the country's terms of trade, balance of payments, rate of exchange, rate of inflation, and conditions for growth, all too often determined by trade conflicts among industrialized nations. For example, the international prices of grains, a key export for the Argentine economy, fell an average of 30 percent in the 1985-1986 period due to the "war of subsidies" between the United States and the European Community.

18. The more efficient allocation of resources that is supposed to go hand-in-hand with the opening of the Latin American economies might take place at the level of international markets, something that does not imply that each and every nation will benefit from the inflow of capital and the more efficient allocation of resources that occurs at the level of the international economy. Imputing the properties of a system to its constituent elements is a fallacy. Market distortions, such as trade barriers in countries that have great influence over the global system, only further complicate the possibility for a particular country to benefit from the opening of its economy in terms of improving macroeconomic stability, investment, growth, employment, and redistribution.

19. For example, although most working class supporters of the *Partido dos Trabalhadores* in Brazil probably opposed the Collor Plan, no doubt many PT militants and sympathizers favored the economic measures undertaken by the Collor government and were, therefore, willing to restrain their economic demands.

20. Rationality is neither an attribute of a given behavior nor of a specific objective. Rather, rationality refers to the relationship between an actor's resources and the ends pursued, in a context in which the actor's knowledge defines an expected causal relationship between actions and results and is characterized by certain non-choice features (i.e., perception of interests, identity, values) that influence desires and preferences. In this sense, different courses of action might be rational not only as a function of the differential resources actors possess but also as a function of the different objectives they seek, the knowledge they have, and the non-choice features that characterize them. For a more detailed discussion of this question, see Sen (1986).

21. Note that we have not included falling unemployment among the indicators of improving economic performance because growth at t_3 generally does not imply lower unemployment since firms respond to rising demand without risking the hiring of new personnel (especially in societies where the "flexibilization" of the labor market has not been completed and new personnel would entail medium-term commitments and less flexibility to reduce production costs). Similarly, knowledge about employment would not eliminate the actors' confusion between t_3 and t_4 because for those hurt by the reforms it is not clear that successful neoliberal restructuring will lead, even in the long run, to falling unemployment.

22. Our principal-agent model resembles some of the features of what Eric Rasmusen calls a "moral hazard with hidden information" game (Rasmusen 1992, Chapter 7). Nevertheless, it should be noted that the situation we are analyzing differs somewhat from Rasmusen's description. Our argument concerning t_3 does not assume that when something occurs in the "real world," the *principal* (middle classes and workers in our case) is in the dark, while the informed *agent* takes notice (thus resulting in a situation of imperfect asymmetric information). In our argument, the asymmetric information arises when the *principal* and the *agent* both "know" that something has happened (stability, growth, rising income), but the *principal* does not know its real significance and probable consequences. The "hidden" information for the principal is the behavior of the level of investment — in this case, if investment has risen enough to initiate a period of sustained growth. The difference is not trivial for political analysis. In Rasmusen's case, inaction by the principal (middle classes and workers) should be expected at t_3 because the actor has not noticed any significant changes in the state of the economy; while in our case, the *principal* actively seeks the *agent's* signals to decide upon a course of action.

23. By "nested games" we refer to situations in which an actor plays several games concurrently, each with a different set of actors, different payoff structures, and different rules of resolution. This situation implies the possibility of the simultaneous implementation of different strategies for each game. These games are "nested" not only because the same actor is a player in each but also because the outcome of each game influences the outcomes of the others. For a useful discussion, see Tsebelis (1990).

24. We have deliberately treated "economic performance" as if it were a singular phenomenon constituted by a series of variables (inflation, growth, fiscal deficit, profits, income) that tend to move in the same direction. Nevertheless, we noted that (un)employment was not included in the set of variables used to assess performance. The analysis of the actors' decisions to exercise patience or to increase demands could be disaggregated as a function of specific phenomena such as inflation versus unemployment. This example is not arbitrary; rather we have in mind the observation made by Adam Przeworski and Susan Stokes in their analyses of Poland and Peru. They note that when inflation is very high, actors tend to be willing to accept a tradeoff

between higher unemployment and potential future benefits, but when inflation declines, they are no longer willing do so and, therefore, pursue revindicative strategies. But even if we were to disaggregate our analysis, which is something that lies beyond the scope of this essay, our central argument would still hold: actors are not myopic. Rather, their behavior is a function of rational expectations and imperfect information that characterize them — for example, when suffering unemployment in the context of falling inflation. If less inflation permits some growth, what possible signal could convince these actors that it is *still* necessary to bear the costs of unemployment? What possible agent would be credible enough to contradict the common sense belief that the economy has been "cured"? Is their inability to differentiate whether they are at t_3 or at the "safe side" of t_4 the consequence of myopia or egoism or simply the necessary result of the actors' imperfect information about investment trends (and hence, the prospects for sustainable growth) and the dynamic between "voices" and "silences" described above?

25. Rasmusen (1992, 133) notes that the economist's new generic answer when facing "someone who brought up peculiar behavior that seemed to contradict basic theory" is to say that there "...must be some kind of asymmetric information." It is often the case that most economists in the role of reformers or occupying posts as high-ranking state administrators tend to forget political theory (although it seems that many just never learned this) and resort to fairly shallow politico-economic assumptions when confronting political contestation.

26. Our use of "end state" coincides with the definition of a Nash equilibrium. More technically oriented readers should take into account that of the second, third, and fourth scenarios we discuss, only the maximalist version of the third is a Pareto-efficient Nash equilibrium. In other words, no politico-economic scenario other than *inclusionary democracy with strong actors and an activist state* increases the payoff of one actor without decreasing that of any other actor. Finally, the scenarios we discuss below are not meant to be mere "labels" ranking alternative options faced by the actors from "most" to "least" desirable. Rather, these scenarios — and the genesis of different equilibria — are profoundly rooted in each society's legacies from the past as well as shaped by contemporary structural constraints that inform specific national conjunctures. Situations of equilibrium reflect the shifting contingencies of political struggles among contending actors. In this sense, equilibria are relatively stable resolutions of tensions between memories of the past and perceptions of feasible alternatives on the part of actors set in specific historical struggles.

27. The Austral Plan (Argentina 1985) exemplifies a case in which it was still possible to attempt economic heterodoxy with the agreement of the U.S. government and the international financial institutions. Once the "Washington Consensus" crystallized its stabilization/structural reform agenda (circa 1988-1989), this possibility was foreclosed. See Acuña (1994) and Canitrot (1994).

28. In spite of the diminishing role of congress and the increasing weight of executive decrees in the decision-making process, the legitimacy of the *decretazos*, as well as their effectiveness, tends to rest on signals (public opinion polls, elections, statements by opinion makers and/or influential actors that, in some cases, include the U.S. ambassador) of majoritarian preferences for measures that are presented as urgent and difficult to process through negotiations, a property usually related to congressional debates and decisions. On the other hand, there are issues that in some societies cannot avoid congressional review (either due to political conditions or clear

unconstitutionality), a circumstance which does not allow the executive to "forget" congress when analyzing the political feasibility of certain measures.

29. Although new identities and solidarities might eventually emerge in a process of *embourgeoisement*, it is also possible that the expulsion of blue- and white-collar workers from the formal labor market could lead to deepening anomie and mass withdrawal of citizen participation from the electoral arena as well as from conventional interest-group politics. See Zermeño (1991) for a provocative discussion of anomie and "disidentity" in the context of economic crisis and reform.

30. For elaboration of these arguments, see Fanelli, Frenkel, and Rozenwurcel (Chapter 4 in this volume) and Bresser Pereira, Maravall, and Przeworski (Chapter 7 in this volume). We speak in terms of probabilities because, as we stated before, such contingency variables as international commodity prices or levels of economic activity in the northern industrial economies, which may fluctuate significantly, drastically alter international capital flows, Latin American growth trajectories, and the attendant macroeconomic equilibria.

31. For the particular properties of business peak associations, see Acuña (1992).

32. See CEPAL (1990 and 1992) for important efforts to explore an alternative strategy of development seeking to combine a stress on equity with structural reform and greater external competitiveness.

33. The thrust of these institutional changes would be to increase the probability that electoral coalitions become governing coalitions assuring majoritarian support for reformist initiatives (e.g., industrial policies and, especially, ameliorative social policies) that advance beyond neoliberal recipes. For the parliamentarism versus presidentialism debate, see Mainwaring (1990) and Stepan and Skach (1993). Also see the suggestive discussion of party systems and governability in Haggard and Kaufman (1992).

34. In the case of the state, those members of the executive promoting institutional change are frequently charged by other members of the governing coalition with squandering the government's democratic mandate by "caving in" to pressures from corporate actors. Similarly, business actors and, especially, union leaders face "internal" pressures from rival factions and must calculate the risk of cooperation with state elites to their own positions of power. Maximalist, even unfeasible demands are very often the result of political competition within the union or the business leadership.

35. For recent analyses of transformations of the Latin American Left, see Cavarozzi (1992b), Castañeda (1993), and Carr and Ellner (1983).

36. Some of the features identified by O'Donnell (Chapter 6 in this volume) are also present in S_2.

37. Some of the more radical free-marketeers among the supporters of the attempt at S_2 are likely to perceive this scenario mistakenly as inherently unstable because, from their perspective, it carries the reform process only "halfway" to the desired goal.

38. For an initial effort, see Smith (1993). A more rigorous analysis can be found in Smith and Acuña (1994), accompanied in the same volume by detailed case studies of Argentina, Bolivia, Brazil, Chile, and Mexico.

References

Acuña, Carlos H. 1989. "Intereses empresarios, dictadura y democracia en la Argentina (O, sobre por qué la burguesía abandona estrategias autoritarias y opta por la estabilidad democrática)." Paper presented at the XV Congress of the Latin American Studies Association. Miami, Florida. December 4-6. (An updated version is forthcoming in *Business and Democracy in Latin America*, eds. Ernest Bartell and Leigh Payne. Pittsburgh: University of Pittsburgh Press.)

Acuña, Carlos H. 1992. "Lucha política y organizaciones empresariales de cúpula: Algunos apuntes teóricos con referencias al caso argentino." Paper prepared for the XVII International Congress of the Latin American Studies Association. Los Angeles. September 24-27.

Acuña, Carlos H. 1994. "Politics and Economics in the Argentina of the Nineties (Or Why the Future No Longer Is What It Used to Be)." In *Democracy, Markets, and Structural Reform in Latin America: Argentina, Bolivia, Brazil, Chile, and Mexico*, eds. William C. Smith, Carlos H. Acuña, and Eduardo A. Gamarra. New Brunswick, N.J.: North-South Center/Transaction.

Acuña, Carlos H., and William C. Smith. 1994. "The Politics of 'Military Economics' in the Southern Cone: Comparative Perspectives on Democratization and Arms Production in Argentina, Brazil, and Chile." In *Security, Democracy and Development in United State-Latin American Relations*, eds. Lars Schoultz, William C. Smith, and Augusto Varas. New Brunswick: North-South Center/Transaction.

Acuña, Carlos H., and Catalina Smulovitz. Forthcoming. "Adjusting the Armed Forces to Democracy: Successes, Failures, and Ambiguities of the Southern Cone Experiences." In *Human Rights, Justice, and Society in Latin America*, ed. Elizabeth Jelin.

Bresser Pereira, Luiz, José María Maravall, and Adam Przeworski, eds. 1993. *Economic Reforms in New Democracies: A Social-Democratic Approach*. Cambridge: Cambridge University Press.

Canitrot, Adolfo. 1994. "Crisis and Transformation of the Argentine State (1978-1993)." In *Democracy, Markets, and Structural Reform in Latin America: Argentina, Bolivia, Brazil, Chile, and Mexico*, eds. William C. Smith, Carlos H. Acuña, and Eduardo A. Gamarra. New Brunswick, N.J.: North-South Center/Transaction.

Cardoso, Fernando Henrique, and Enzo Faletto. 1979. *Dependency and Development in Latin America*. Berkeley: University of California Press.

Carr, Barry, and Steve Ellner. 1983. *The Latin American Left: From the Fall of Allende to Perestroika*. Boulder, Colo.: Westview Press.

Castañeda, Jorge. 1993. *Utopia Unarmed: The Latin American Left After the Cold War*. New York: Alfred A. Knopf.

Cavarozzi, Marcelo. 1978. "Elementos para una caracterización del capitalismo oligárquico." *Revista Mexicana de Sociología* XL (4).

Cavarozzi, Marcelo. 1992a. "Beyond Democratic Transitions in Latin America." *Journal of Latin American Studies* 24 (3).

Cavarozzi, Marcelo. 1992b. "The Left in Latin America: The Decline of Socialism and the Rise of Political Democracy." In *The United States and Latin America in the 1990s: Beyond the Cold War*, eds. Jonathan Hartlyn, Lars Schoultz, and Augusto Varas. Chapel Hill: University of North Carolina Press.

CEPAL (Comisión Económica para América Latina y el Caribe). 1990. *Transformación productiva con equidad: La tarea prioritaria de América Latina y el Caribe en los años noventa.* Santiago, Chile: Naciones Unidas.

CEPAL (Comisión Económica para América Latina y el Caribe). 1992. *Equidad y transformación productiva: Un enfoque integrado.* Santiago, Chile: Naciones Unidas.

Crepaz, Markus M.L. 1992. "Corporatism in Decline? The Impact of Corporatism on Macroeconomic Performance and Industrial Output in Eighteen Countries." *Comparative Political Studies* 25 (2).

Díaz Alejandro, Carlos. 1984. "Latin American Debt: I Don't Think We Are in Kansas Anymore." *Brookings Panel on Economic Activities* 2. Washington, D.C.: Brookings Institution.

Dornbusch, Rudiger, and Sebastian Edwards. 1991. "The Macroeconomics of Populism." In *The Macroeconomics of Populism in Latin America*, eds. Rudiger Dornbusch and Sebastian Edwards. Chicago: University of Chicago Press.

Evans, Peter. 1992. "The State as Problem and Solution: Predation, Embedded Autonomy and Structural Change." In *The Politics of Adjustment: International Constraints, Distributive Justice and the State*, eds. Stephan Haggard and Robert Kaufman. Princeton: Princeton University Press.

Haggard, Stephan, and Robert Kaufman. 1990. "Economic Adjustment in New Democracies." In *Fragile Coalitions: The Politics of Economic Adjustment*, ed. Joan Nelson. Washington, D.C.: Overseas Development Council.

Haggard, Stephan, and Robert Kaufman, eds. 1992a. *The Politics of Economic Adjustment: International Constraints, Distributive Conflicts, and the State.* Princeton, N.J.: Princeton University Press.

Haggard, Stephan, and Robert Kaufman. 1992b. "Economic Adjustment and the Prospects for Democracy." In *The Politics of Economic Adjustment: International Constraints, Distributive Conflicts, and the State*, eds. Stephan Haggard and Robert Kaufman. Princeton, N.J.: Princeton University Press.

Halperín Donghi, Tulio. 1966. *Historia contemporánea de América Latina.* Madrid: Alianza Editorial.

Hartlyn, Jonathan, and Samuel A. Morley. 1986. "Political Regimes and Economic Performance in Latin America." In *Latin American Political Economy: Financial Crises and Political Change*, eds. Jonathan Hartlyn and Samuel A. Morley. Boulder, Colo.: Westview Press.

Kahler, Miles. 1990. "Orthodoxy and Its Alternatives: Explaining Approaches to Stabilization and Adjustment." In *Economic Crisis and Policy Choice*, ed. Joan Nelson. Princeton, N.J.: Princeton University Press.

Kahler, Miles. 1992. "External Influence, Conditionality, and the Politics of Adjustment." In *The Politics of Economic Adjustment: International Constraints, Distributive Conflicts, and the State*, eds. Stephan Haggard and Robert R. Kaufman. Princeton, N.J.: Princeton University Press.

Linz, Juan J., and Alfred Stepan. 1991. "Democratic Transition and Consolidation: Eastern Europe, Southern Europe and Latin America." Unpublished manuscript.

Mainwaring, Scott. 1990. "Presidentialism, Multiparty Systems, and Democracy: The Difficult Equation." Kellogg Institute Working Paper, No. 144.

Marcuse, Herbert. 1968. *Reason and Revolution: Hegel and the Rise of Social Theory.* Boston: Beacon Press.

Nelson, Joan, ed. 1989. *Fragile Coalitions: The Politics of Economic Adjustment.* Washington, D.C.: Overseas Development Council.

Joan Nelson, ed. 1990. *Economic Crisis and Policy Choice.* Princeton, N.J.: Princeton University Press.

Nylen, William. 1992. "Neoliberalismo para Todo Mundo Menos Eu: Brazil and the Cartorial Image." In *The Right and Democracy in Latin America*, eds. Douglas A. Chalmers, Maria do Carmo Campello de Souza, and Atilio Borón. New York: Praeger.

O'Donnell, Guillermo. 1992. "Transitions, Continuities, and Paradoxes." In *Issues in Democratic Consolidation: The New South American Democracies in Comparative Perspective*, eds. Scott Mainwaring, Guillermo O'Donnell and J. Samuel Valenzuela. Notre Dame, Ind.: University of Notre Dame Press.

Offe, Claus. 1974. "Structural Problems of the Capitalist State." *German Political Studies* 1.

Offe, Claus. 1975. "The Theory of the State and the Problem of Policy Formation." In *Stress and Contradiction in Modern Capitalism*, ed. Leon Lindberg. Lexington, KY: D.C. Heath.

Offe, Claus. 1984. *Contradictions of the Welfare State.* Cambridge: The MIT Press.

Olson, Mancur. 1991. "Autocracy, Democracy, and Prosperity." In *Strategy and Choice*, ed. Richard J. Zeckhauser. Cambridge: The MIT Press.

Przeworski, Adam. 1977. "The Process of Class Formation from Karl Kautsky's *The Class Struggle* to Recent Controversies." *Politics and Society* 7.

Przeworski, Adam. 1985a. "Compromiso de clases y estado: Europa occidental y América Latina." In *Estado y política en América Latina*, ed. Norbert Lechner. México, D.F.: Siglo XXI.

Przeworski, Adam. 1985b. *Capitalism and Social Democracy.* Cambridge: Cambridge University Press.

Przeworski, Adam. 1990. *The State and the Economy under Capitalism.* New York: Academic Publishers.

Przeworski, Adam. 1991. *Democracy and the Market: Political and Economic Reforms in Eastern Europe and Latin America.* Cambridge: Cambridge University Press.

Przeworski, Adam, and Fernando Limongi. 1993. "Democracy and Development in South America, 1946-1988." Paper presented at the Annual Meeting of the American Political Science Association.

Rasmusen, Eric. 1992. *Games and Information: An Introduction to Game Theory.* Cambridge: Cambridge University Press.

Remmer, Karen. 1990. "Democracy and Economic Crisis: The Latin American Experience." *World Politics* 42 (3).

Remmer, Karen. 1991. "The Political Impact of Economic Crisis in Latin America in the 1980s." *American Political Science Review* 85 (3).

Roxborough, Ian. 1984. "Unity and Diversity in Latin American History." *Journal of Latin American Studies* 16.

Schmitter, Phillipe. 1974. "Still the Century of Corporatism?" *Review of Politics* 36.

Schmitter, Phillipe, and Gerhard Lehmbruch, eds. 1979. *Trends towards Corporatist Intermediation.* Beverly Hills, Calif.: Sage.

Schmitter, Phillipe, and Terry Karl. 1993. "What Democracy Is...and Is Not." In *The Global Resurgence of Democracy*, eds. Larry Diamond and Marc F. Plattner. Baltimore, Md.: The Johns Hopkins University Press.

Sen, Amartya. 1986. "Rationality, Interests and Identity." In *Development, Democracy, and the Art of Trespassing: Essays in Honor of Albert O. Hirschman*, eds., Alejandro Foxley, Micahel S. McPherson, and Guillermo O'Donnell. Notre Dame: Notre Dame University Press.

Serra, José. 1979. "Three Mistaken Theses Regarding the Connection between Industrialization and Authoritarian Regimes." In *The New Authoritarianism in Latin America*, ed. David Collier. Princeton, N.J.: Princeton University Press.

Smith, William C. 1989a. *Authoritarianism and the Crisis of the Argentine Political Economy.* Stanford, Calif.: Stanford University Press.

Smith, William C. 1989b. "Heterodox Shocks and the Political Economy of Democratic Transition in Argentina and Brazil." In *Lost Promises: Debt, Austerity and Development in Latin America*, ed. William Canak. Boulder, Colo.: Westview Press.

Smith, William C. 1990. "Democracy, Distributive Conflict and Macroeconomic Policy Making in Argentina (1983-1989)." *Journal of Interamerican Studies and World Affairs* 32 (2).

Smith, William C. 1991. "State, Market and Neoliberalism in Post-Transition Argentina: The Menem Experiment." *Journal of Interamerican Studies and World Affairs* 33 (4).

Smith, William C. 1992. "Hyperinflation, Macroeconomic Instability, and Neoliberal Restructuring in Democratic Argentina." In *The New Democracy in Argentina*, ed. Edward C. Epstein. New York: Praeger.

Smith, William. C. 1993. "Neoliberal Restructuring and Scenarios of Democratic Consolidation in Latin America." *Studies in Comparative International Development* 28 (2).

Smith, William C., and Carlos H. Acuña. 1994. "Future Politico-Economic Scenarios for Latin America." In *Democracy, Markets, and Structural Reform in Latin America: Argentina, Bolivia, Brazil, Chile, and Mexico*, eds. William C. Smith, Carlos H. Acuña, and Eduardo A. Gamarra. New Brunswick, N.J.: North-South Center/Transaction.

Sola, Lourdes. 1991. "Heterodox Shock in Brazil: Técnicos, Politicians, Democracy." *Journal of Latin American Studies* 23 (February).

Stallings, Barbara. 1992. "International Influence on Economic Policy: Debt, Stabilization, and Structural Reform." In *The Politics of Economic Adjustment: International Constraints, Distributive Conflicts, and the State*, eds. Stephan Haggard and Robert R. Kaufman. Princeton, N.J.: Princeton University Press.

Stallings, Barbara, and Robert Kaufman. 1989. "Debt and Democracy in the 1980s: The Latin American Experience." In *Debt and Democracy in Latin America*, eds. Barbara Stallings and Robert Kaufman. Boulder: Westview Press.

Stepan, Alfred, and Cindy Skach. 1993. "Constitutional Frameworks and Democratic Consolidation: Parliamentarism versus Presidentialism." *World Politics* 46 (1).

Tocqueville, Alexis de. 1955. *The Old Regime and the French Revolution*, trans. Stuart Gilbert. New York: Doubleday.

Tsebelis, George. 1990. *Nested Games: Rational Choice in Comparative Politics*. Berkeley and Los Angeles: University of California Press.

Valenzuela, J. Samuel. 1992. "Democratic Consolidation in Post-Transitional Settings: Notion, Process, and Facilitating Conditions." In *Issues in Democratic Consolidation: The New South American Democracies in Comparative Perspective*, eds. Scott Mainwaring, Guillermo O'Donnell, and J. Samuel Valenzuela. Notre Dame, Ind.: University of Notre Dame Press.

Wlliamson, John. 1990a. *The Progress of Policy Reform in Latin America*. Washington, D.C.: Institute of International Economics.

Williamson, John, ed. 1990b. *Latin American Adjustment: How Much Has Happened?* Washington, D.C.: Institute for International Economics.

Wright, Eric Olin. 1978. *Class, Crisis and the State*. London: New Left Books.

Zermeño, Sergio. 1991. "Desidentidad y desorden: México en la economía global y en el libre comercio." *Revista Mexicana de Sociología* LIII (2).

Chapter Three

Convergence and Dissension: Democracy, Markets, and Structural Reform in World Perspective

Aldo C. Vacs

Introduction

The current shift toward liberal democracy and self-regulating markets in Latin America, the former Soviet Union, Eastern Europe, Africa, and Asia has created a need to address questions concerning the scope, timing, and nature of this unprecedented trend. Why are similar liberal democratic regimes and self-regulating markets emerging in countries with such disparate political regimes, economic systems, and social structures? Are there any international systemic situations that create auspicious conditions for these developments? What are the most significant international conditions and actors that encourage this change? What kinds of linkages are established between the international and domestic forces supporting these processes?

This chapter examines these political-economic developments starting with the hypothesis that the current worldwide trend toward liberal democracy is partially the result of changing global situations. These situations include the emergence of a transnational and more interdependent global market economy, the transformation of the world strategic scenario, the crisis of the bureaucratic-socialist and national-populist experience, the processes of political and economic disintegration of existing countries and blocs and the ascendance of new ones, the growing conviction among influential economic and political actors that liberal democratic regimes create more adequate conditions for capitalist growth than do authoritarian ones, and the multiplication of security, ecological, technological, and health issues whose resolution requires global management. In this setting, the emergence of democracy, markets, and structural reform policies appears as an adaptive process which contributes to the development of more efficient market economies better able to insert themselves into the world economic system, to the promotion of interdependent economic links, and to the reduction of the uncertainty and waste of resources characteristic of confrontational international situations.

The fact that the rise and consolidation of these liberal democracies is closely related to their continuous association with free-market economic policies creates conditions that may affect the stability of these regimes. Current political-economic trends have heightened the importance of the socioeconomic components of the equation — market structures — over the political ones — democratic procedures. This raises the possibility of conflictive situations where the preservation of market structures is secured at the expense of democratic procedures. At the domestic level, support for liberal democracy might ebb if the expectations of economic and social progress held by important sectors of the population are frustrated, or if there are attempts to promote, through democratic means, structural changes or redistribution policies that might affect the interests of powerful socioeconomic groups. These latent or open contradictions are reinforced by the advent of two forces that threaten the ascendancy and stability of liberal democracy as a global phenomenon: the rise of regionalism, especially in the form of integrated economic blocs, and the emergence of subnational separatisms taking ethnic, linguistic, and religious forms.

The Revival of Liberal Democracy

The democratic transitions of the 1980s shared several characteristics in their content and outcome. One basic feature of this democratic trend has been the procedural nature — as opposed to the substantive content — of the phenomenon. Previous democratic waves, such as the turn toward democracy in Western Europe, Latin America, and Asia in the periods immediately following the two world wars, the tide of political change associated with decolonization in the late 1950s, or the participatory political movements of the 1960s, emphasized in differing degrees the importance of social equality, economic justice, and grass roots political participation as essential components of democratic regimes.[1] The push toward democracy on these occasions included explicit or implicit calls to introduce substantive structural reforms able to eliminate — or at least reduce — the legacy of social inequities, economic disparities, and limited political participation bequeathed by the old regimes, leading to the emergence of welfare states in the developed world and of national populist regimes in the less-developed countries.

Unlike these historical precedents, the democracies that arose in the 1980s underscored the importance of the procedural elements that characterize liberal democratic regimes. The features of these emerging democracies can be related to Joseph Schumpeter's interpretation of the modern democratic method as an "institutional arrangement for arriving at political decisions in which individuals acquire the power to decide by means of a competitive struggle for the people's vote" (Schumpeter 1976, 279).[2] However, unlike some appraisals of Schumpeter's approach, it is important to emphasize that the functioning of this democratic institutional arrangement requires the presence of features, such as free elections and real competition, to legitimize the liberal democratic regime including its actors (candidates and political parties), agents (elected officials), products (laws, decrees, regulations), and enforcement mechanisms. Thus, although in practice citizens make choices between politicians and not between issues and policies, to be democratic these choices should take place in a context characterized by the existence of some basic conditions that legitimize through a noncoercive popular mandate the right of those elected to decide between policy alternatives.[3] In most cases, these transitions to democracy have been directed toward the creation or reestablishment of a political system that meets the basic criteria for a liberal democracy: a government whose legitimacy rests on a claim to represent the citizenry, individual consent, equality before the law, separation between the private and public domains, majority rule with constitutional limitations, competitive periodic elections, possibility of citizens' participation as voters and candidates, and guarantees for the freedoms of expression, assembly, and organization.[4]

At the same time, the liberal democratic discourse of the 1980s disregarded or rejected as inadequate, unrealistic, or dangerous the demands for structural socioeconomic change and broadened participation raised by some sectors of the political spectrum. The former were identified with the forms of state intervention that led to the economic, social, and political crises of the 1970s and 1980s; the latter were denounced as advocating approaches that, in practice, would lead to situations of ungovernability and thus would threaten democratic stability. The notion of liberal democracy that guided these transitions and that appeared to be shared by different sectors of the population — including upper, middle, and low income groups — linked politics and economics with the underlying notion of an efficient allocation of resources, power, and wealth, respectively. From this perspective, elections are considered to be the mechanism through which citizens convey their political choices by electing representatives, while the market is regarded as the mechanism through which consumers express economic preferences by exchanging goods and services. Both are considered efficient and mutually reinforcing activities that create adequate conditions to preserve and foster individual freedom and prosperity.[5]

It is obvious that these ideas and their underlying assumptions are open to criticism from different perspectives. These ideas and assumptions include an incomplete conception of human nature which prizes individualism while dismissing social traits, an emphasis on choice over participation, an assumption of overall consensus and lack of polarization, and a narrow concept of efficiency (understood in terms of following formal procedures and not of securing substantive outcomes).[6] However, pointing out these shortcomings does not alter the fact that substantial numbers of people in Latin America, Eastern Europe, the former Soviet Union, Asia, and Africa have espoused this liberal democratic model, which, despite its limitations, appears as a welcome alternative to the different political and economic regimes that prevailed until the 1980s. Elections and markets have become the hallmarks of change in the 1980s, and the main actors and intended beneficiaries of these processes are the individual voters and consumers.[7]

Similarities among the emerging liberal democratic regimes are as remarkable as the fact that these transitions have taken place simultaneously or in a short period of time in areas of the world that exhibited very different political, economic, and social systems. In the past there were cycles of democratization that happened simultaneously in different countries, but most of these experiences were brief and confined to one particular region. After the end of World War I, Wilsonian democratic ideals prevailed for a short period in Europe but were rapidly displaced by the eruption of authoritarian ideologies and regimes. The defeat of fascism in World War II was followed by the advent of democracy in Western Europe and Japan but led only to the incomplete and temporary democratization of some Latin American and Asian countries. The process of decolonization encouraged an ephemeral democratization in Africa and parts of Asia, but in most cases, these regimes were superseded by the ascent of single-party systems and military governments. In contrast, the democratic wave of the 1980s has been geographically widespread, diverse in terms of the polities, economies, and societies affected, and more enduring than the previous tides.

It is the combination of these elements — similar features and simultaneous occurrence in such different situations — which suggests the convenience of exploring the role of global factors in influencing the transitions to liberal democracy and the prospects for stability.[8] It is clear that in each case domestic economic, social, and political factors have fostered the democratization process. Economic mismanagement and crises, the rise of new social movements, military defeats, the political weakness of authoritarian coalitions, and the growing strength of opposition forces are among the most significant domestic circumstances that facilitated these political transformations. However, analysis of these factors is not sufficient to explain similar contents and timing of liberal democratic developments. There are few observable similarities between the domestic situations of the different Latin American countries — and practically none when we compare them with the former Soviet Union, the Eastern European, Asian or African countries — that can be used to explain the contents and timing of the democratic phenomenon. And even if it is possible to point out that most —but not all — of these countries were affected by economic setbacks and social crises, this generalization would not help to explain why the socioeconomic crisis did not lead, as on previous occasions, to a reinforcement of the authoritarian tendencies instead of facilitating the demise of nondemocratic regimes. These considerations indicate the importance of exploring the global dimension of liberal democratization with the hope of finding some clues that might shed light on the genesis of these processes, their current characteristics, and their future prospects.

The New World Order: Transnationalization, Interdependence, and Liberal Democracy

The 1970s and 1980s were years of crucial transformations for the international political economy that emerged after 1945. Although it is beyond the scope of this chapter to analyze all the momentous changes that happened during this period, it is important to mention some of the trends and situations that created favorable conditions for the emergence of liberal democracies in Southern Europe, the Third World, and the Socialist bloc. The 1970s marked the end of the political-economic order established after the Second World War under the hegemonic leadership of the United States. The network of trade, monetary and financial regimes created in the postwar years helped to consolidate a liberal international economic order. International institutions, such as the General Agreement on Trade and Tariffs (GATT), the International Monetary Fund (IMF), and the World Bank, as well as a number of regional organizations, were created to liberalize trade and secure the necessary financial flows among capitalist economies. However, as John G.Ruggie has observed, this liberal order was not an orthodox one designed along classical free trade and market principles but a compromise based upon "embedded liberalism" that comprised primarily the Western industrial nations and was never fully extended to the developing countries (Ruggie 1983). In Ruggie's words:

> unlike the economic nationalism of the thirties, [this embedded liberalism] would be multilateral in character; unlike the liberalism of the gold standard and free trade, its multilateralism would be predicated upon domestic interventionism...that [this] multilateral order gained acceptance reflected the extraordinary power and perseverance of the United States. But that multilateralism and the quest for domestic legitimacy were coupled or even conditioned by one another reflected the shared legitimacy of a set of social objectives to which the industrial world had moved, unevenly but "as a single entity"...Ironically, then, the foremost force for discontinuity at

present is not "the new protectionism" in money and trade, but the resurgent ethos of liberal capitalism (Ruggie 1983, 209, 213-214, 229).

This political economic order generated the conditions in which the United States, Western Europe, and Japan were able to attain and sustain adequate rates of economic growth, social consensus, and political stability and successfully confront the challenge posed by the socialist countries while maintaining the subordination of the Third World nations. However, as the hegemonic leadership of the United States eroded, the international economic order shaped under its influence experienced a parallel decline.[9] The multiple manifestations of this phenomenon included the Vietnam debacle, the new challenges to the United States in the Third World, the emergence of strategic parity with the USSR, the disagreements among the members of the Western alliance, the decline of the dollar and the deterioration of the Bretton Woods system, the world inflationary surge associated in part with growing U.S. deficits, the rise of stagflation in the industrial countries, the oil shocks of 1973 and 1979, the spread of neoprotectionist policies in the 1970s, and the economic rise of the European Economic Community (EEC), Japan, and the newly industrializing countries (NICs) vis-à-vis the United States accompanied by growing commercial competition and internationalization of production.

In the early 1970s, these developments led to a reluctant retrenchment of the United States from many of its global strategic and economic commitments, manifested through a declining capacity to project its military power and reductions in the disbursement of resources necessary to maintain control over the international financial, trade, and monetary regimes. This erosion of U.S. hegemony was accompanied by a gradual transition in the Western political-economic system from "embedded liberalism" toward more liberal orthodox economic arrangements. Powerful private actors — such as the international banks and multinational corporations — took advantage of the more unregulated environment and proceeded to reorganize capital flows and production in their favor. The privatization of financial flows related to the surge of the Euromarket and petrodollars, together with the integrative internationalization of production and commercialization brought about by the global transnational corporations, appeared to mark the end of an era in which advanced capitalist states had been able to control or influence the behavior of these economic variables.

In the late 1970s, the apparent irreversibility of this trend forced the United States to adapt itself to the changing political economy by gradually discarding any attempt to restore the embedded liberal order while embracing a more orthodox, market-centered approach. Starting in 1979, the application of stringent monetary policies by the Federal Reserve increased real interest rates, reversed the capital flows, created a non-inflationary — even deflationary — environment, and strengthened the dollar while helping to generate the debt crisis in less-developed countries and forcing the rest of the world to finance the U.S. fiscal deficit. Under the Reagan administration, the trend toward economic orthodoxy was reinforced by implementing liberal economic measures such as trade and financial liberalization, deregulation, and reductions in social expenditures. All these economic moves were combined with increasing military expenditures and a more aggressive foreign policy aimed to restore U.S. hegemony.[10] This objective was not fully attained — the United States was unable to meet the essential condition of again becoming the most efficient economy in the system — but there was a partial revival of U.S. hegemony under different conditions in the financial and monetary spheres and, more importantly, an acceleration in the pace of transition in the global political economy toward a liberal capitalist order dominated by self-regulated markets.

A crucial factor that facilitated the spread of liberal capitalist orthodoxy was the expansion and deepening of the twin phenomena of transnationalization and interdependence.[11] These phenomena have multiple facets including international mobility of capital in its productive and financial forms; development of complex networks of production, distribution, and consumption into the context of a single world capitalist market; global revolution in information technology, telecommunications, and transportation; expanding influence of multinational economic groups and noneconomic international organizations; and the rise of new forms of voluntary or imposed cooperation between nations to confront a context of increasing economic, ecological, and strategic interdependence problems and challenges that can only be solved at the global level.

In this context, international mobility of productive capital results in the gradual replacement of vertically and horizontally integrated multinational corporations (corporations with headquarters in one country and subsidiaries in others that typically produce final products and act to increase the real income of their home country's citizens) by transnational corporations (corporations that allocate different stages of production among units located in different countries and act to increase global corporate profits).[12] In its financial form, transnationalization resulted in the creation of Eurobanks, offshore facilities, and globally spread financial institutions that promote and facilitate the free cross-border circulation of capital. These developments led to the emergence of complex private economic networks that allocate investment, production, and distribution according to differential profit opportunities assessed at the level of a single world capitalist market and not in the domestic or regional arenas. Breakthroughs in information technology, telecommunications, and transportation create adequate means for this global expansion while removing the obstacles for its acceptance on the part of individual nations. Interdependence, understood as "situations characterized by reciprocal effects among countries or actors in different countries,"[13] is one of the main factors that facilitates this process of global integration into a single political economy as the number of issues which are not open to any isolated or individual solution multiply. Currently, issues such as the utilization of shared natural resources, atmospheric or oceanic pollution, nuclear proliferation, and epidemics are examples of problems that cannot be solved by individual countries and that require voluntary or imposed international cooperation to be addressed successfully.

Taken to its logical conclusion, transnationalization and interdependence would culminate in the creation of an integrated global political economy in which the role of states is severely limited by their growing incapacity to control crucial variables that affect economic, social, and political developments within and across national boundaries. Well before this process is completed, state sovereignty is clearly "at bay" and the classical laissez-faire model of a minimalist state unwilling — or unable — to intervene effectively in the economy to modify the nature or the outcomes of free market interactions is accomplished in practice. This happens even if the liberal ideal of a minimalist state is still rejected by significant groups in each society whose collective identity and interests are affected by the decline of the role and influence of the nation-state.

Nevertheless, the factual development of this liberal capitalist order is not enough to ensure its permanence. As one of the champions of modern capitalism, Peter Berger, has emphasized:

> capitalism has a built-in incapacity to generate legitimations of itself, and it is particularly deprived of mythic potency; consequently, it depends upon the legitimating effects of its sheer facticity or upon association with other, noneconomic legitimating symbols (Berger 1986, 208).

In terms of "sheer facticity," the appeal of capitalism, in comparison with other earlier or contemporary economic systems, results from the superior capacity of market systems to heighten material production. The demonstration effect of this superiority intensified as transnationalization made it possible to exhibit this material prosperity in the most remote corners of the globe and to contrast capitalism's accomplishments with the poor economic performances of other economic systems, while interdependence reduced the chances of formulating new strategies for development that attempted to escape a liberal capitalist framework. However, in the long term neither this material appeal nor the international constraints are always sufficient to legitimize liberal capitalism and to defend it against challenges posed by reformist or revolutionary alternatives. If the legitimacy of a capitalist order is based solely on the expectation of material benefits (that is, if it relies exclusively on interest situations), its stability might be jeopardized by every downturn in the business cycle that affects a significant portion of the population. This is especially problematic in those cases in which the role of the state has been greatly reduced and a self-regulating market economy allocates the cost of economic decline unequally among different socioeconomic groups. What has been pointed out in the case of post-communist societies is also valid in many other transitions to liberal democracy taking place in nonsocialist settings:

> However, as has been repeatedly remarked, the destruction of a social and political system is far easier than the construction of a new one. In particular, the post-communist reformers face a major dilemma. In introducing the institutions of Western democracy they are bringing in forms that do not match social and political realities. Their aim is to transform those realities until the mismatch diminishes. This raises the problem of how far these societies are to be guided by elites — enlightened or otherwise — and how far they are to respond to what the citizens demand now. Indeed,...there are currents in the post-communist world that are not in every respect friendly to representative democracy but look to the immediate implementation of their desires as the definition of democratic order. Above all, throughout the area there are social strata which believe that democracy means that they should enjoy a Western standard of living at once. Those who voted for the self-made millionaire emigré Tyminski in the presidential elections in Poland exemplify this (Schopflin 1991, 236).

To guarantee a longer lasting stability of the capitalist order, it is necessary to introduce a value rational element of belief in its validity (legitimacy) that is normally obtained from its association with liberal democracy (Weber 1978, 31-36). This political economic construction becomes legitimate by upholding values such as freedom, individual progress, popular representation, and equality before the law that appeal to significant portions of the population. At the same time, liberal democracy prescribes protection of private property, separation between the public and private spheres, and the existence of a minimal state that is confined to the maintenance and reproduction of a liberal capitalist order characterized by the preservation of civil liberties and economic freedom.

From this perspective, it is clear that laissez-faire capitalism and liberal democracy reinforce each other. However, historically, it is clear that there rarely have been favorable conditions in which this amalgamation could take place around the globe. Until the 1980s, market economies with minimal state intervention and liberal democracies were the exception and not the rule. In the 1980s, the process of transnationalization and increasing interdependence, along with the revival of liberal orthodox capitalism, created both the opportunity and the necessity to establish liberal democratic regimes not only in the advanced industrial nations but also in those countries where democratization had previously been unnecessary to facilitate global economic growth and stability.

The Collapse of the USSR and the Impact of Global Strategic Transformations

The decline of the traditional hegemonic role of the United States that began in the 1960s was mirrored in the 1970s by the decay of the Soviet hegemonic power in its own sphere of influence. Long before Gorbachev's inauguration, the launching of *perestroika*, the collapse of Soviet-sponsored regimes in Eastern Europe, and the disintegration of the USSR, the Soviet Union had begun to undergo a process of economic and social decline that was translated into a growing inability to maintain control or to influence the pro-Soviet regimes abroad.[14] Among the socioeconomic problems that led to the crisis of the Soviet system, the most frequently mentioned are the slowdown of economic growth; the lack of incentives for technological innovation; the excessive bureaucratization, centralization, and corruption plaguing the planning systems; the waste, inefficiency, and irresponsibility associated with an imbalanced economic structure that disregarded consumer needs, thus leading to shortages and growing unrest; decaying health, educational, and social services; a general decline in the quality of life of the majority of the population; increasing apathy; and a progressive atrophy of the party and state organs.

These domestic problems affected Soviet ability to project power, especially when confronted with the more aggressive U.S. stand in the 1980s, as well as to promote the Soviet system as a socioeconomic model for Third World countries. By the early 1980s, the Afghan quagmire, the growing waste of resources associated with the arms race, the rise of Solidarity in Poland, the stalemate between pro-Soviet and pro-U.S. forces in different parts of the Third World, and the proliferation of "deviant" socialist experiences all indicated that the USSR was losing its capacity to maintain its hegemonic position. The point had been reached at which it was impossible for the USSR to increase further its resource expenditures to maintain its hegemonic influence without suffering dramatic domestic consequences. Like the United States before it, a Soviet Union assailed by domestic and international problems opted for reducing its commitments abroad and attempted to insert itself into the global political economy by accepting the existing international division of labor and the need for peaceful coexistence.

Initially, the hegemonic decline of both superpowers created a relative vacuum in which third countries attained a higher degree of autonomy and an enlarged capacity to engage in political economic experimentation. But, as time went by, it became clear that this relative autonomy was only a temporary, if not illusory, phenomenon. The revival of the liberal economic ethos at the international level and the transnationalization and interdependent character of the new global order made it apparent that, as the superpower confrontation ebbed, a new international order was rising and that this new arrangement imposed severe constraints on the capacity of individual countries to make autarchic decisions and to pursue deviant models of political and economic development.

As Gorbachev himself pointed out, the new international order that was emerging in the 1980s was "a contradictory but interconnected, interdependent and, essentially, integral world" in which security and economic growth became global phenomena that could not be secured by isolated countries (Gorbachev 1987, 139-142). The successful insertion of the USSR into this new world order required not only market reforms and political liberalization at home but also relaxation of international tensions to facilitate the access to foreign capital, goods, and technology; redirection of wasteful military expenditures to investment in the modernization of productive activities; and reduction of Soviet involvement in conflictive areas of the world to attain these previous objectives.

From this perspective, the new Soviet approach helped to reduce the international tensions that nourished the Cold War climate of confrontation and had facilitated the emergence and consolidation of pro-Soviet and pro-U.S. authoritarian regimes. The abatement of superpower rivalry lessened the perception of threat that had been used by leftist and rightist groups alike to justify the establishment of repressive regimes and obtain military and economic support from the superpowers. In these new conditions, it was difficult or impossible for most authoritarian governments to legitimize their rule and obtain material support against their democratic opponents by agitating the specter of Soviet subversion or of U.S.-sponsored destabilization.

Moreover, the changing Soviet views of the global political economy, with their acceptance of the inevitability of transnationalization and interdependence, converged with and reinforced the global trend toward economic and political liberalization. When combined with similar positions upheld by the United States and shared by the other Western developed countries, this convergence not only eliminated many of the misgivings that powerful groups in different countries had concerning the dangers of democracy but bolstered the impression that, under existing conditions, the only viable type of regime acceptable to the great powers was one that embraced the tenets of political and economic liberalism.

The Demise of Alternative Political Economic Models

Another important factor that influenced the emergence of liberal democracies in the 1980s was the lack of alternative political-economic models that could promise — with an adequate degree of credibility — an attractive political, social, and economic environment.[15] Thus, the aforementioned international economic and strategic shifts were accompanied by an ideological shift in support of democracy that resulted from a growing awareness of the inability of authoritarian political regimes to deliver, in the long run, economic growth, social peace, and political stability.

The gradual elimination of political-economic alternatives took place by stages during the last fifty years. The end of World War II resulted in the collapse of fascism as an attractive or viable alternative to liberal, populist, and socialist models. The catastrophic defeat of the Axis powers was seen as a clear demonstration of their incapacity to compete successfully with the liberal democratic and socialist authoritarian nations and, since 1945, no explicitly fascist regime has emerged.

The 1960s and 1970s represented the turning point for the Third World authoritarian and semi-authoritarian populist import-substitution industrializing experiences and for the remnants of semi-autarchic authoritarian regimes in Southern Europe. The former collapsed together with the decline of the economic models of import-substitution industrialization that had provided their social and economic basis of support. The latter disintegrated as the rise of a European Economic Community that excluded the participation of authoritarian regimes condemned them to isolation and decline. However, in this period there were still some political alternatives to liberal democracy. These alternatives enticed some elites who wanted economic growth but distrusted the disrupting effects of democracy and counterelites who demanded rapid socioeconomic transformation but doubted the effectiveness of democracy in promoting it. In parts of Latin America and Asia, bureaucratic-authoritarian models offered elites the option of fostering economic growth through the export promotion of manufactures without altering the patterns of economic, social, and political domination. And, as the examples of some of the newly industrializing countries demonstrated, these regimes were able to attain some of these goals, albeit only temporarily. In the Caribbean Basin, Africa, the Middle East, and Southeast Asia, the rise of revolutionary socialist-oriented regimes gave counterelites the opportunity to test the viability of alternative political-economic paths aimed at introducing radical economic and social transformations.

However, by the early 1980s, most of these experiments had been wrecked by a mix of economic, social, and military reversals, including the debt crisis, domestic upheavals, foreign-sponsored insurgencies, and costly external wars. Meanwhile, the decline of welfare states in the West and growing economic and political distress in the Soviet bloc and China had considerably pared down the menu of political options. While the economic crises and the breakdown of the different variants of authoritarianism pushed elites and masses away from this option, the example of the stability and prosperity enjoyed by liberal democracies in the United States, Japan, and Western Europe pulled people into accepting this model as a plausible option to escape economic stagnation and political decay.

Moreover, free markets and liberal democracy together appeared as the most viable political alternative because it offered some degree of freedom of choice and adaptability to different circumstances within the narrow confines of the model. Prospective liberal democracies could opt for different constitutional arrangements as typified by U.S. presidentialism and the diverse forms of Western European and Japanese parliamentarianism. The prospect of instituting a constitutional framework that could limit popular participation and reduce the state's capacity to interfere with private property and individual liberties helped to lessen the elites' distrust of liberal democracy as a mere preamble to the rise of anti-establishment populist — or demagogic — governments interested in promoting state-led and redistributionist developmental strategies. For the opposite reasons, the model's relative flexibility served to attract support for liberal democracy from those groups disenchanted with the authoritarian socialist or populist experiences, but which had not relinquished their hopes of promoting progressive socioeconomic reforms through peaceful means in a democratic context.[16]

In the late 1980s and early 1990s, the collapse of the Eastern European and Soviet regimes and the emergence of the unsuccessful mass democratic movement in the People's Republic of China confirmed that liberal democracy, as a reality or as a goal, was on the rise as practically the only political choice acceptable for a substantial portion of the world population. With authoritarian socialism and command economies destroyed or in disarray, and with the alternative forms of capitalist regimes extinct or in decline, liberal democracy and free markets appeared to be the only legitimate political and economic option still open to those societies trying to escape from authoritarianism and stagnation.

International Actors and the Liberal Democratic Impulse

The pro-democratic impact of the systemic economic, strategic, and ideological developments discussed in the preceding pages has been enhanced in the last decade by the emergence of an array of actors committed, for different reasons, to the promotion of liberal democracy and free markets. Some of these actors had always explicitly promoted democratization; others espoused this goal more recently after having justified or even encouraged authoritarian forms of domination. Some of them appeared in the international political arena only in last few years; others had been a factor in international politics for centuries. But in all cases, their new or revitalized commitment to liberal democracy and free markets became a distinctive feature of the effective international campaigns waged in the 1970s and 1980s.

The relevant actors included diverse governments, international organizations, and nongovernmental groups with sometimes conflicting political, economic, humanitarian, religious, and ecological interests and goals. However, in recent years all of them have coincided in advocating the establishment and consolidation of liberal democratic regimes that were seen as effective means to pursue their otherwise disparate goals. While it would be impossible to analyze here in detail the motivations underlying the pro-democratic activities of each of these actors, their particular features, and their ultimate goals, it is important to examine briefly some of their activities to appreciate the global significance of this phenomenon.

The occasional promotion of democracy by the governments of some Western developed nations is not a completely novel situation as the two postwar experiences, decolonization, and other waves of support for democratization tend to indicate. The uniqueness of the governmental promotion of democracy in the 1980s stems from the widespread, less rhetorical, and more enduring nature of the commitment to liberal democracy demonstrated in the last few years by the governments of some of the developed and less-developed countries.

In the United States, several new developments accounted for the elimination of some of the apprehensions associated with democratization in the past. These developments include the waning of the Cold War, the fact that in many nations liberal democracy had become the only acceptable alternative to disintegrating authoritarianism, and the unpredictable and unstable behavior of right-wing authoritarian regimes — witness the Greek junta, Leopoldo Galtieri, Manuel Noriega, Ferdinand Marcos, and others. The promotion of democracy was seen as one of the most effective ideological weapons in the global competition with noncapitalist systems and as one of the best practical alternatives to the proliferation of radical left-wing regimes and untrustworthy right-wing dictatorships. This approach, combining pressure for free markets and democratization, became even more attractive when the collapse of the Soviet bloc removed the last remaining misgivings concerning the possibility of Kerenski-like situations — that is, the emergence of weak democratic regimes that could be overthrown by foreign-supported revolutionary groups and replaced by regimes promoting noncapitalist strategies for development. Political pressure or outright intervention were used to remove authoritarian regimes considered inimical or detrimental to U.S. interests and to replace them with restrictive liberal democracies that, due to their institutional characteristics, guaranteed that there was no danger of populist or socialist aftermaths.[17]

Western European governments, which had begun to promote democratization in Southern Europe in the 1970s, continued to press for democratization in the 1980s.[18] The Western European motivations for endorsing liberal democracy did not significantly differ from those held by the U.S. government in terms of the expected economic and political outcomes of these transitions, but the Western European commitment to liberal democracy appeared to be stronger, more formal and binding — probably as a result of fresh memories of the devastation brought about by right-wing authoritarian regimes and close contact with the Eastern European experience. Hence, democracy was ascribed, in treaties and protocols, as a condition for certain types of relations, and the Western European governments offered economic incentives to entice prospective democracies, such as the Southern European nations, which wanted to share the economic benefits resulting from membership in the EEC. This European commitment to democracy was strengthened by multilateral agreements in which formal provisions supported the maintenance of democratic regimes and opposed attempts to overthrow them. These stipulations, initially established as preconditions for the incorporation of Western European countries to the EEC, emerged in the 1980s as an important element in the relations established between Western European nations and developing countries when the bilateral and multilateral accords began to include clauses that made economic cooperation conditional on the establishment and maintenance of democratic regimes.[19]

Governments of those countries that had successfully completed democratic transitions also exerted significant influence in favor of liberal democratization. In Latin America, Eastern Europe and Africa, newly democratic governments not only had a demonstration effect on neighboring countries that remained under authoritarian rule but also engaged, individually or collectively, in a number of actions to promote or accelerate the transition to democracy in their respective regions. In the Southern Cone of Latin America, democratization became, in practice, a prerequisite for the incorporation of new members into emerging common market and integrative structures. Elsewhere — in Central and South America and in Eastern Europe —the nascent democratic governments offered their solidarity and support to the democratic forces in neighboring countries, convinced that one of the best guarantees for domestic democratic stability was the development of liberal democratic regimes in the surrounding areas.

At least until the late 1980s, the most important intergovernmental economic organizations — such as the IMF, the World Bank, and the GATT — had not usually stated their preference for any particular political regime, but they strongly advocated market-oriented reforms, especially in LDCs and former Socialist countries. By the early 1990s, the so-called "Washington Consensus" emphasized the importance of implementing specific neoliberal measures as the means to create conditions for sustained economic growth in most countries (Williamson 1990, 7-38). The recommendations resulting from this "consensus" included the promotion of fiscal discipline, elimination of subsidies, broad and moderate taxation, market-determined interest and exchange rates, trade and foreign investment liberalization, privatization of state enterprises, deregulation, and respect for private property rights. The advocates of these measures try to preserve the "technical" or "apolitical" nature of their recommendations by carefully avoiding any reference to the political frameworks that can facilitate or hinder the operationalization of these policy instruments.

However, it is clear that some political regimes are better equipped than others to ensure the successful application of these policies and their long-run stability. Although authoritarian regimes may implement with relative success some of these measures — as was illustrated by the Augusto Pinochet regime in Chile — the maintenance in the long run of this neoliberal strategy seems to require the institution of liberal democratic procedures to legitimize the continuity of this strategy from the political perspective. Moreover, liberal democratic environments create more favorable conditions for the accomplishment of certain market-oriented goals. For instance, liberal democratic regimes are more inclined or better prepared than their authoritarian counterparts to reduce certain types of governmental expenditures — such as military budgets — to impose broader systems of taxation, to promote trade liberalization favoring consumers over specific groups of producers, to obtain support for privatization and deregulation decisions, and to reduce the uncertainty concerning the respect for property rights by underscoring the rule of law and reducing the chances of arbitrary decisions.

Most of the time, international organizations promoting these structural reforms prefer to emphasize the technical nature of their recommendations, although the governments of the developed countries that participate in these organizations have explicitly pointed out in official statements the connection between market reforms and liberal democracy. Nevertheless, in the last few years, some of the multilateral institutions have also started to recommend political democratization openly, in conjunction with market reforms and a minimalist state, as the only means to reduce corruption and inefficiency and generate conditions for sustained economic growth. Thus, a 1989 World Bank report on Sub-Saharan Africa contains the usual economic recommendations — less government, privatization, market discipline, and administrative reform — but it goes a step further in the political direction (World Bank 1989).[20] The report strongly supports democratization, decentralization, community participation, and respect for civil liberties as the only way "to empower ordinary people to take charge of their lives, to make communities more responsible for their development, and to make governments listen to their people" in order to make these governments more accountable, less corrupt, more efficient, and less interventionist in a market-oriented process of economic growth.

Among the nongovernmental organizations that promoted liberal democracy during the 1980s, human rights groups, political parties, and religious organizations played a significant role. Human rights groups — including Amnesty International and a host of other organizations, such as the International Commission of Jurists, International League for Human Rights, Survival International, and the Helsinki Watch Committees — documented, publicized, and denounced human rights violations and, thus, weakened the repressive regimes, thereby enhancing conditions for democratization (Nanda, Scarrit, and Shepherd 1981). Political parties, especially European members of the Social Democratic, Christian Democratic, and Liberal internationals, also played a significant role by exerting pressure for the departure of authoritarian regimes and by supporting the democratic forces fighting against them.[21]

Among the religious groups that played substantive roles in the transitions to democracy, sections of the Catholic Church and the World Council of Churches gradually departed from their traditional apoliticism in the defense of human rights and began to espouse liberal democracy as the political regime most likely to guarantee the preservation of civil and religious liberties and human dignity.[22]

Lately, other interest groups with particular agendas, such as the preservation of the environment, protection of minorities, and promotion of women's rights, have also reached the conclusion that the existence of a liberal democratic milieu creates more advantageous conditions to attain their objectives and to empower groups in different nations which are the recipients of their support.

A crucial aspect of the evolution of these nongovernmental groups is their diminishing proclivity to dismiss liberal democracies as politically formalistic and socioeconomically unfair contraptions. In the last few years, most human rights groups have made a strong commitment to the defense of political rights while paying less attention to the elimination of economic and social injustices that continue to plague many societies after democratization. The European socialist parties have supplanted their early propensity to back democratic-socialist transformations with a commitment to support liberal democratic regimes that have regularly implemented neoconservative economic policies. The progressive, grass roots-oriented, and sometimes anticapitalist sectors of the Catholic Church that played an important role in the initial phases of the struggle for democratization have been forced to retreat to secondary positions while the more traditional, hierarchical, and procapitalist groups supported by the Vatican have assumed influential roles in support of liberal democracy. Similar tendencies toward compromise and acceptance of liberal democratic regimes as the only viable alternative to authoritarianism seem to be emerging among the other internationally active interest groups.

As expected, this shift toward liberalism among international actors has influenced their links with domestic actors in the post-authoritarian societies and reinforced the trend toward homogenization of political outcomes. In each of the nascent democracies, conservative and moderate political groups and organizations have profited from this shift by establishing close relations of cooperation with these international actors in order to strengthen their positions in both the international and domestic arenas. Groups seeking socioeconomic transformation and the deepening of political participation are dismissed as utopian dreamers who threaten the only viable type of democracy and who, consciously or unconsciously, pave the way for the return of authoritarianism. In most cases, these arguments are accepted as valid by international actors and help to isolate dissenting groups from external sources of support while enhancing the international prestige of proponents of liberal democracy who project the impression of being attacked by antidemocratic forces. Thus, the interests of the foreign govern-mental and nongovernmental actors in promoting liberal democracy con-verge with the interests of those local groups that — for material or ideological reasons — support the consolidation of this type of regime. This serves to create solid transnational linkages facilitating similar political-economic outcomes in many geographically, economically, and socially diverse pro-cesses of transformation.

A Delicate Balance:
Markets, Democracy, and Domestic Consensus

The analysis of the international factors that promoted the global trend toward markets and democracy in the 1980s suggests that these powerful influences will continue to encourage liberal democratic expansion. Most of these developments are the consequences of structural transformations in the distribution of power and wealth in the international arena and represent the culmination of long-term shifts in ideological and political beliefs. Transfor-mation of the international political economy, changes in the strategic scenario, lack of alternative models, and activities of international actors are forces intersecting at a single point — the promotion of liberal democracy — and which, by all indications, will continue to exert considerable influence in the coming years.

However, change of these international conditions cannot be completely dismissed. Thus, it is important to examine some of the problems that particular characteristics of these transitions to liberal democracy create in securing their consolidation and further expansion. The current international trend toward democratization seems to be inextricably linked to the establishment of liberal regimes that protect the free market and formulate relatively orthodox structural reforms. If there were a situation in which the political and economic sides of this equation no longer complemented each other — if, for instance, parties opposed to neoconservative policies came to power or were able to hinder the application of these policies — the commitment by powerful international and domestic forces to liberal capitalism might take precedence over the allegiance to political democracy. In this case, conflict might lead to antidemocratic initiatives and, depending on the correlation of forces, to the breakdown of democracy or a serious deterioration of the regime's capacity to maintain control over economic and political circumstances.

Concern over the stability of new democracies that rely in part on an international support that is conditioned on the maintenance of specific economic conditions and policies is compounded when one considers the strength and durability of the commitment to democracy of different domestic groups in these societies. Domestic support for democracy depends on variables such as the degree of devastation attributed to the previous authoritarian regimes and the intensity of the population's revulsion against these regimes, the depth of the popular belief in the legitimacy of democracy, the ability of democratic governments to establish effective institutional arrangements and to preserve peace and order, the existence of representative political parties, and other political conditions. Even more crucial to the stability of liberal democracies is the commitment not only to the political elements of the regime but also to the continuous support for the socioeconomic features of the system — namely private property, free markets, consumer sovereignty, and minimal state intervention in the economy.

A critical problem is that this support is largely based on the expectation of material benefits — the belief that a market economy will generate prosperity and that most of the population will eventually partake in the benefits of economic growth. Thus, if as seems to be the case in many new democracies, the market system is unable to generate adequate rates of economic growth and satisfactory income distribution, there will be generalized frustration among the marginalized sectors and growing pressures to abandon some of the basic tenets of liberalism and to implement more interventionist state policies aimed at redistributing income, promoting employment, and improving social services. On the other hand, if structural changes appear imminent, powerful domestic socioeconomic groups and foreign actors might experience a resurgence of old fears of democracy — any kind of democracy — as the prologue to state intervention and arbitrary restrictions on private property rights. In either case, domestic support for liberal democracy may recede rapidly, leading to situations of increasing political-economic instability characterized by the rise of more authoritarian regimes. What has been accurately said in reference to East Central Europe applies to other liberal democratic transitions:

The transition to free market economies involves, at least in the short run, drastic measures resulting in the aggravation of economic dislocations and hardship for large segments of the population. The rhetoric of social justice, however, has been deeply engraved in people's minds in all state-socialist societies and therefore unemployment, decreasing living standards and new market-induced inequalities represent a potential source of conflict and division which may decisively modify the strength and capabilities of political actors and affect the extension of citizenship and the creation of truly democratic institutions (Ekiert 1991, 312-313).

In the absence of a strong domestic commitment to democracy, the permanence of these regimes becomes more dependent on the maintenance of favorable international conditions. However, support given by international forces to a particular type of democratic regime — the liberal one — raises the question of what their reaction will be to situations in which some domestic groups want to maintain democracy but discard the liberal economic component, while others want to maintain economic liberalism even at the cost of eliminating political democracy. Such a situation can lead to a wide range of responses, from open support of different forms of democracy to a complete endorsement of authoritarianism. But in practice, if we consider the experience of the liberal democratic regimes established in the 1980s and early 1990s in Latin America, Eastern Europe and Asia, the response seems to be univocal. When confronted with the emergence of such tensions, support goes to those solutions which, without eliminating entirely the liberal democratic elements, lead to a consistent effort to reduce political participation and to a concomitant increase in the use of legal methods of repression.

Some basic elements of liberal democracy, such as periodic elections, party competition, and majority rule with constitutional limitations, are normally preserved. But, at the same time, there have been a number of initiatives aimed at further limiting popular participation or influence on policy decisions. In many cases, power has been concentrated in the executive branch, especially to facilitate the application of economic policies aimed to strengthen the free market. These policies include privatization; liberalization of the financial, monetary, exchange, and foreign trade sectors; and rationalization of the public sector. Legislatures and even the judiciaries have been excluded from any meaningful participation in these decisions. There have been successful attempts to curtail certain rights and freedoms (including the right to strike, collective bargaining, unionization, access to mass media, and publicity of state actions) while opposing expansion of the remaining ones. The use of repressive measures to deal with challenges from opposition forces has intensified, while the role of military and security forces in domestic affairs — which at the beginning of the democratic periods had been reduced to a minimum — has been enhanced. The members of these institutions have begun to occupy more central positions in the new regimes. In sum, participatory elements of democracy and the possibility of a socioeconomic restructuring adverse to free markets have been severely curtailed while democratic procedures remain in force. The emphasis on the definition of democracy as a liberal regime excludes any other alternatives. If there is a continuous deepening of this trend, it may open to discussion the usefulness of the term "democracy" to describe these regimes. But it seems clear that, as the emphasis on liberalism increases, the notion of democracy becomes more ambiguous and the commitment to its preservation more uncertain.

Centrifugal Forces: The Challenge of Separatism

In liberal democracies, the delicate balance established between market structures and democratic rules is many times threatened by the inability of the self-regulating markets to satisfy the expectations of material improvement held by substantial sectors of the population as well as by the possibility of empowerment of groups opposed to market reforms. As mentioned before, this conflict between the economic and political components of the liberal democratic formula may result in the breakdown of the democratic regime or, more frequently, in the implementation of measures aimed to limit participation and to narrow the scope of political rights and freedoms in order to preserve the free markets. However, in a more radical and fundamental way, this precarious balance may be disrupted by the emergence, at the domestic level, of centrifugal forces unleashed as a reaction against the disruptive effects of markets on the sociopolitical structure. Unrestrained market interactions may cause the disarticulation or destruction of fragile social networks, eroding collective identities and solidarities and creating conditions for important groups to separate themselves from the existing national polity or to withdraw from the prevailing political-economic order.

The development of self-regulated markets and the establishment of minimalist states in a context of growing transnationalization and global interdependence reduces the capacity of these states to influence the evolution of crucial economic, political, and social variables. This decline in the state's sovereign power profoundly affects its ability to generate loyalty and support among the population and to foster the creation and maintenance of all-embracing national identities and solidarities. Market forces, whose universalistic features and dynamics ignore national boundaries and ascriptions, generate conditions that are simultaneously necessary and detrimental for the continuous functioning and expansion of free markets at the global level. On the one hand, markets thrive when state involvement is minimal and barriers hindering economic exchanges are removed. On the other hand, the unleashing of market forces and the establishment of "laissez faire" states disrupt or destroy the delicate and complex networks that link citizens to their respective nation-states. As the citizenry realize the growing ineffectiveness of the state to address and resolve their problems, the capacity of the state to generate or recreate a national identity is diminished, and it becomes more difficult to foster allegiance to it. In this context of growing anomie on the part of important sectors of the population, the notion of national citizenship and the basic consensus on the "national interest" necessary for the functioning of liberal democracies is eroded and challenged by the rise of competing subnational ethnic, linguistic, regional, religious, socioeconomic, and other loyalties. These forces, that had been until then checked by the overarching existence of a conviction of belonging to a legitimate nation-state, are now unleashed and threaten to cause its collapse.

The potential of this situation to cause the actual destruction of existing nation-states is obviously greater in those cases in which the political and social heterogeneity is expressed under the form of subnational and ethnic differences, especially if these differences are associated with and reinforced by linguistic, religious and socioeconomic disparities. Multinational states and plural ethno-cultural societies are the most vulnerable to the rise of this type of tension. The former situation is well illustrated by the violent explosion of centrifugal forces that has affected the former USSR and Yugoslavia or by the less dramatic partition of Czechoslovakia, and rise of secessionist demands in Canada. The rise of separatist nationalism in the Baltic states, Central Asia, Azerbaijan, and Armenia, the civil war in Yugoslavia, the growing tensions between English Canadians and Quebecois are some of the manifestations of these forces that aim to create new national identities in a context of the growing importance of market and liberal democratic trends. The case of plural societies moving in a similar direction is well illustrated by the demands raised by Tartars, Cossacks, and Kazahks in the Commonwealth of Independent States; the Tamils in Sri Lanka; the Ibos in Nigeria; the Kurds in Iran, Iraq and Turkey; the Kashmiris and Sikhs in India; and other ethnic-based rebellions in different parts of the world.

In some cases, the reassertion of ethnic identities has not yet reached the level of demanding a separate statehood — as is the case with the Gypsies in Romania, the Moldavians in the former Soviet Union, or the Quechua and Mayan groups in the Andean countries and Central America — but the intensification of liberal economic policies that worsen the situation of these weaker groups may lead in the future to growing demands for autonomy if not to de facto separation from the existing national polities. What has been noted in the African case can also be applied to similar situations in other regions of the world:

A return to communal self-reliance will...not resolve the acute problems of material underdevelopment and political authoritarianism. In fact, it may well intensify the salience of ethnicity and consequently promote conflict, nepotism, and traditionalism. The urban and rural masses' powerful attachment to ethnic sentiments would heighten the competition for scarce resources between kinship communities; it would also lend itself to selfish manipulative appeals of the elites...As Kwame Ninsin has argued, withdrawal is a 'mechanism by which the state gradually abandons its legal and moral obligations toward the weaker sections of society as a result of its growing incapacity to discharge them effectively'. Indeed, withdrawal implies the breakdown of the rules of normalcy and the dissolution of traditional legal structures; it breeds the cruel conditions of severe insecurity that nurture the ghastly emergence of African *macoutes* (bandits) and the potential war of all against all (Fatton 1990, 470-471, 472).

The emergence of these centrifugal forces creates unfavorable conditions for the establishment and maintenance of liberal democracies and market policies. The attempt to build new nation-states might be accompanied by the implementation of exclusionary domestic and foreign policies and by large degrees of state intervention that directly clash with some of the basic tenets and features of liberal democracies. As the current situation tends to indicate, the new Azerbaijani, Slovak, Quebecois, Tamil, or Kurdish states would most probably try to consolidate their national identities by practicing discriminatory policies against minority groups found inside their boundaries and by using state intervention to promote economic gains for the majority ethnias in detriment to other groups. These situations collide with the economic and political foundations of liberal democracy and could finally lead to the rise of ethnic-based authoritarian regimes which would impose restrictions on free market interactions. Moreover, this nationalistic trend may generate protectionist and isolationist attitudes that, though very difficult to sustain in the long term, may disrupt and hinder the process of global liberal democratization and the formation of a global free market. Finally, these separatist, exclusionary, and nationalistic developments can and have created the conditions for acute conflict and open wars — witness the crises in Yugoslavia, Nagorno-Karabakh, Somalia, Peru, and Sri Lanka, among others — that hinder the process of global liberal democratization by disrupting the stability and peace necessary for free market economic exchanges and the application of democratic rules. In a world split by national, ethnic, religious, and linguistic conflicts, markets cannot operate nor can democracy be established and maintained in the long term.

Centripetal Forces: The Challenge of Regionalism

The possibility for disintegration of existing nation-states into ever-smaller units that practice isolationist and exclusionary policies is not the only danger faced by the global liberal democratic ethos. The delicate balance necessary to maintain liberal democratic regimes also is threatened by forces that promote the integration of countries into regional communities. These communities embrace the notion of economic and political liberalization within their confines but, at the same time, raise barriers that impede free economic exchanges with the rest of the world while further reducing the citizens' capacity to influence policy decisions through their elected representatives.

For authors like Walt Rostow, the current technological revolution, the rise of new powers, the global environmental threats, and the end of the Cold War create the conditions for the "coming age of regionalism" in which "the political structure of the global community would require greatly strengthened regional institutions if we are to deal successfully with the agenda history has set for, say, the next half-century" (Rostow 1990). The proposition that the convergence of these four forces may encourage regional-based outcomes is valid. But, it appears that, contrary to Rostow's optimism and in lieu of the peaceful emergence of a "federal pattern of regional and global cooperation," the rise in regionalism may increase international tensions and conflict that could threaten the stability of global markets, while simultaneously increasing a bureaucratization that may impair the functioning of liberal democracies.

In the contemporary international political economy, the appearance of regional communities, such as the EC, or the potential consolidation of diverse regional arrangements, such as Mercosur, the North American Free Trade Agreement, the Organization of South Asian Regional Cooperation, and the Economic Cooperation Organization, raise the possibility not of global harmony but of renewed conflict that may affect the efficiency of the global markets. Growing regionalization is likely to lead to new restrictions on international trade, financial flows, and investment involving competing regional blocs instead of individual countries. However, the impact of this new situation on the existence of global free markets will be as negative as the nationalistic policies that in the past hindered international economic exchanges. The restrictions currently imposed by the most advanced of these regional organizations — such as the EC — on agricultural and service trade suggest that the emergence of other regional communities might lead to the widespread application of similar protectionist policies and the decline of global free markets as each bloc imposes its own restrictions and other blocs retaliate with yet more exclusionary policies. In fact, the creation of regional communities may create a situation that gradually resembles the logic of the "tragedy of the commons" in which most nations have the incentives to create regional blocs to obtain more benefits by practicing regional protectionism and taking advantage of the existence of a global free market. But, as the number of blocs that act in this way multiplies, the free market environment disappears and all the regional participants lose their opportunity to profit from free market transactions.

At the domestic political level, the emergence of regionalism creates another problem and may result in the further erosion of the already limited participation characteristic of the existing liberal democratic regimes. The creation of economic and political regional communities has the effect of further removing the decision-making power from the domestic population and its elected representatives and transferring it to international bureaucrats. The decisions concerning the increasingly complex monetary, investment, productive, and financial issues affecting countries that belong to a regional bloc are no longer under the jurisdiction of local politicians or even bureaucracies but tend to be concentrated gradually in the hands of the regional organization bureaucrats. Thus, new layers of decision makers are added to the already existing ones, and the gap between national electorates and the agents that make the decisions that affect their lives widens to such an extent that the notion of democratic participation becomes meaningless. As it has been pointed out:

> As a consequence, not only does the influence of the ordinary voter disappear almost to vanishing point but that of the national politician is severely weakened as well. Within the new global politics, decisions get made through multibureaucratic rule by a mandarinate of officials working within various international agencies...whose accountability to anything outside the norms and hierarchy of their respective organizations is very hard to achieve. (One needs to think of the tirades of successive British governments against the EC, including their own appointees amongst the commissioners, for a vivid illustration of this fact) (Bellamy 1991, 513).

In sum, the rise of regionalism may threaten both the continuity of a global free market environment as well as the ability to maintain democratic conditions at the domestic level. However, the emergence of these threats is one of the potential but not inevitable consequences of the regional impulse. It is always possible that the conscious attempts by the regional organizations to prevent commercial wars and isolationism, and the growing demands of the national populations to regain some influence on the decisions, might help to reverse these trends.

A Tentative Conclusion

At the end of this journey through newly emerging liberal democratic and free market systems, it seems appropriate to make a few observations about the prospects for their consolidation and stability. The forces that converged to create this global trend are still powerful enough to sustain the new political-economic order in the near future. Transnationalization and interdependence, the end of the Cold War, the lack of viable political-economic alternatives, and the promarket and pro-democratic influence exerted by international actors are powerful factors that will not suddenly vanish. On the contrary, the potential of these factors to shape international and domestic political-economic configurations increases as they reinforce each other and narrow to a minimum the range of options. Given the current circumstances, it is impossible to discern any feasible alternative to the deepening of the trends toward democracy, markets, and neoliberal structural reforms.

However, favorable global circumstances today do not mean a continuous unfolding of the liberal democratic trend. In fact, the fragile balance between democracy and markets and the disruptive forces of separatism and regionalism strongly suggest that we have not arrived at the "end of history" in which the triumph of liberal democracy and free markets marks the beginning of a long-lasting period of supremacy of economic and political liberalism. The stable and peaceful new world order announced by those who see the victory of liberal capitalist democracy as irreversible is threatened by those forces that — from below or increasingly above the surface of calm and homogeneity — promote political and economic changes, which under the guise of demands for economic redistribution and social equality, ethnic and national identity, or regional integration, clash with liberal principles.

It is difficult to predict what will be the most likely outcome of this conflict between the global liberal democratic trend and the dissenting forces that challenge its ascendancy. It seems, however, that from a longer-term perspective, the chances for institutionalization of the current forms of liberal democracy and market systems are limited. If past experiences with the global rise of political-economic models contain any lesson, it is that pressures for reform, change, and even radical transformation will inevitably arise. Thus, the future may bring renewed calls for the transformation of the current political-economic configurations, especially in terms of promoting broader and more effective citizens' participation in the decision-making processes and restraining and controlling the impact of free market forces on different sectors of civil society. These calls for restructuring may assume the form of demands for transitions from liberal democracy to democratic liberalism, the creation or resurgence of forms of consociational democracy, and even the possibility of new longings for workable forms of democratic socialism. As was argued by Karl Polanyi almost fifty years ago when pondering the demise of another seemingly permanent global order organized around the liberal creed and market systems:

> Nineteenth-century civilization was not destroyed by the external or internal attack of barbarians; its vitality was not sapped by the devastation of World War I nor by the revolt of a socialist proletariat

or a fascist lower middle class. Its failure was not the outcome of some alleged laws of economics such as that of the falling rate of profit or of underconsumption or overproduction. It disintegrated as the result of an entirely different set of causes: the measures which society adopted in order not to be, in its turn, annihilated by the action of the self-regulating market. Apart from exceptional circumstances such as existed in North America in the age of the open frontier, the conflict between the market and the elementary requirements of an organized social life provided the century with its dynamics and produced the typical strains and stresses which ultimately destroyed that society. External wars merely hastened its destruction (Polanyi 1957, 249).

The internal tensions generated by the self-regulating markets in the new world order might produce once again the conditions for change in what today appears to be the irresistible ascendancy of liberal democracy, thus opening a new historical chapter whose political-economic features cannot yet be anticipated with any degree of certainty.

Notes

1. On the ideals of democratic reconstruction and their association with the resolution of social, economic, labor, and minority problems after World War I, see, for instance, Cleveland and Schafer (1919). On a similar attempt to combine political democratization with socioeconomic transformations after 1945, see Mannheim (1950). For studies of the democratization processes in West Germany, Italy, Austria, France, and Japan after the end of World War II, see Herz (1982). On decolonization and the association of democracy with the search for socioeconomic transformation, see Clapham (1985). On the demands for participatory democracy in the late 1960s, see, for instance, Benello and Roussopoulos (1971).

2. For a brief but excellent discussion of Schumpeter's ideas on capitalism, liberalism, and democracy, see Bellamy (1991).

3. As José Nun has pointed out, it is possible that in some cases the use of "narrow and formal definitions of democratic liberalism" associated with the Schumpeterian vision of democracy might be only a device used by analysts to manage the aggregation of disparate cases (Nun 1991, 5). However, the features of the current trend toward democracy give substantial reason to consider that a procedural definition of democracy adequately captures the essence of the type of democratization that appeared in the 1980s.

4. Among the most influential studies of liberal democracy that define its formal operative aspects and analyze its empirical manifestations are Dahl (1971) and Powell Jr. (1982). On the procedural aspects of democracy, see Dahl (1979, 97-133). The current wave of democratization appears to have generated what Dahl calls "procedural democracy in a narrow sense" rather than the more inclusive "full procedural democracy."

5. For a widely read exposition on the connection between liberal economics and political democracy, see Friedman (1982). For a more philosophical presentation of similar ideas, see Hayek (1960). Hall (1987) presents a critically informed analysis of these links from a historical perspective.

6. There are numerous criticisms of these notions. Among the most cogent arguments are those presented in Bowles and Gintis (1986), Hirschman (1970), and Macpherson (1977).

7. Good illustrations of the rise in Latin America of these liberal - in the classical sense - political and economic expectations can be found, for instance, in de Soto (1989) and Ribas (1988). For the emergence of similar notions in the Soviet Union, see, for instance, the articles collected in Gwerztman and Kaufman (1990), and in Part I of Lane (1990). On the USSR and Eastern Europe see Bermeo (1992), Kittrie and Volgyes (1988), Ekiert (1991), Bunce (1990), and Schopflin (1991). On Africa, see Fatton Jr. (1990), Ronen (1986), and Cheru (1989). On East Asia, see Bello and Rosenfeld (1990).

8. For an excellent theoretical discussion of the impact of the international system on domestic political developments, see Gourevitch (1978).

9. Among other excellent studies of the decline of U.S. hegemony, see Calleo (1987), Gilpin (1987), and Keohane (1984).

10. On the partial revival of the U.S. hegemonic power in the early 1980s, see Tavares (1985).

11. On these trends and their political-economic repercussions, see Dicken (1992), Wachtel (1990), Varela (1982), and Lichtensztejn (1982). Relevant analyses of the transnational processes from the interdependence perspective can be found in Keohane and Nye (1977) and Keohane (1984).

12. This distinction is related to the one made by Robert Reich (1983) between "national multinationals" and "pure multinationals."

13. On the notion of interdependence and its manifestations, see Keohane and Nye (1977, 3-37).

14. For studies of the growing socioeconomic problems that affected the USSR since the early 1970s and the alternative proposals for their resolution, see, for instance, the articles compiled in the multivolume collection by Shtromas and Kaplan, eds. (1988), Aslund (1989), and Clemens, Jr. (1990). For Soviet diagnosis of the crisis, see Aganbegyan (1988) and Gorbachev (1987).

15. On the current lack of appealing alternatives to political democracy, see the cogent analysis by Markoff (1990, esp. 34-48).

16. For an interesting analysis of how the Southern European elites were reassured by the example of institutional diversity offered by the EEC countries and cast off their rejection of democracy, see the article by Whitehead in O'Donnell, Schmitter, and Whitehead (1986). On the expectations concerning liberal democracy held by the Latin American reformist groups, see, for instance, Tironi (1986) and Delich (1986). For critical analyses of similar expectations in post-communist Eastern Europe, see Dahrendorf (1990) and Dahl (1990).

17. On the U.S. role in promoting democracy in Latin America during the 1980s, see, for instance, the chapter by Thomas Carothers in Lowenthal (1991). On the U.S. support for democratic transitions in Eastern Europe, see Gordon et al. (1987) and Starr (1989). On the U.S. role in East Asia, see Schlossstein (1989). On the late developing U.S. support for democratization in different Third World countries, see Staniland (1991), and on the particular case of the Philippines, see Bonner (1987).

18. The Western European attempts to promote democracy abroad, especially in Southern Europe, Latin America, and Eastern Europe are analyzed in Whitehead (1986), van Klaveren (1986), and Gordon et al. (1987).

19. For instance, the inclusion of prodemocratic clauses in the economic cooperation agreements signed by Argentina with Italy and Spain in 1988 and with the EC in 1990 as well as the pressures exerted on Kenya by the Western European countries (and the United States) in 1991 to promote structural economic and political changes.

20. For a critical discussion of this new World Bank approach, see Sandbrook (1990).

21. On the role of political parties, and particularly of the European Social Democrats, in promoting democratization, see Feld (1978) and Whitehead (1986). An interesting case study that highlights the importance of foreign political party support for the democratic forces in Chile can be found in Angell (1989). On the role of political foundations, see Pinto-Duchinsky (1991).

22. On the role of the Catholic Church in Latin America's processes of democratization, see, for instance, Lehman (1990) and Mainwaring and Wilde (1989).

References

Aganbegyan, Abel G. 1988. *The Economic Challenge of Perestroika.* Bloomington, Ind.: Indiana University Press.

Angell, Alan. 1989. "La cooperación internacional en apoyo de la democracia política en América Latina: El caso de Chile." *Foro Internacional* 30:2.

Aslund, Anders. 1989. *Gorbachev's Struggle for Economic Reform.* Ithaca, N.Y.: Cornell University Press.

Bellamy, Richard. 1991. "Schumpeter and the Transformation of Capitalism, Liberalism and Democracy." *Government and Opposition* 26 (4).

Bello, Walden, and Stephanie Rosenfeld. 1990. "Dragons in Distress: The Crisis of the NICs." *World Policy Journal* 7 (3).

Benello, C. George, and Dimitrios Roussopoulos, eds. 1971. *The Case for Participatory Democracy.* New York: Grossman.

Berger, Peter L. 1986. *The Capitalist Revolution: Fifty Propositions about Prosperity, Equality, and Liberty.* New York: Basic Books.

Bermeo, Nancy, ed. 1992. *Liberalization and Democratization: Change in the Soviet Union and Eastern Europe.* Baltimore: The Johns Hopkins University Press.

Bonner, Raymond. 1987. *Waltzing with a Dictator: The Marcoses and the Making of American Policy.* New York: Times Books.

Bowles, Samuel, and Herbert Gintis. 1986. *Democracy and Capitalism. Property, Community, and the Contradictions of Modern Social Thought.* New York: Basic Books.

Bunce, Valerie. 1990. "The Struggle for Liberal Democracy in Eastern Europe." *World Policy Journal* 3 (3).

Calleo, David P. 1987. *Beyond American Hegemony.* New York: Basic Books.

Carothers, Thomas. 1991. "The Reagan Years: The 1980s." In *Exporting Democracy: The United States and Latin America. Themes and Issues,* ed. Abraham Lowenthal. Baltimore: The Johns Hopkins University Press.

Cheru, Fantu. 1989. *The Silent Revolution in Africa. Debt, Development and Democracy.* London: Zed Books.

Clapham, Christopher. 1985. *Third World Politics. An Introduction.* Madison: University of Wisconsin Press.

Clemens, Jr., Walter C. 1990. *Can Russia Change? The USSR Confronts Global Interdependence.* Boston: Unwin Hyman.

Cleveland, Frederick, and Joseph Schafer, eds. 1919. *Democracy in Reconstruction.* Cambridge, Mass.: The Riverside Press.

Dahl, Robert A. 1971. *Polyarchy. Participation and Opposition.* New Haven, Conn.: Yale University Press.

Dahl, Robert A. 1979. "Procedural Democracy." *Philosophy, Politics and Society.* Fifth Series, Peter Laslett and James Fishkin, eds.. New Haven: Yale University Press.

Dahl, Robert A. 1990. "Social Reality and 'Free Markets': A Letter to Friends in Eastern Europe." *Dissent* (Spring).

Dahrendorf, Ralph. 1990. *Reflections on the Revolution in Europe: In a Letter Intended to Have Been Sent to a Gentleman in Warsaw.* New York: Times Books-Random House.

Delich, Francisco. 1986. *Metáforas de la sociedad argentina.* Buenos Aires: Sudamericana.

Dicken, Peter. 1992. *Global Shift: the Internationalization of Economic Activity.* 2nd ed. New York: The Guilford Press.

Ekiert, Grzegorz. 1991. "Democratization Processes in East Central Europe: A Theoretical Reconsideration." *British Journal of Political Science* 21 (3).

Fatton, Jr., Robert. 1990. "Liberal Democracy in Africa." *Political Science Quarterly* 105 (3).

Feld, Werner J. 1978. *The Foreign Policies of West European Socialist Parties.* New York: Praeger.

Friedman, Milton. 1982. *Capitalism and Freedom.* Chicago: University of Chicago Press.

Gilpin, Robert. 1987. *The Political Economy of International Relations.* Princeton, N.J.: Princeton University Press.

Gorbachev, Mikhail S. 1987. *Perestroika: New Thinking for Our Country and the World.* New York: Richardson-Harper & Row.

Gordon, Lincoln, et al. 1987. *Eroding Empire: Western Relations with Eastern Europe.* Washington, D.C.: Brookings Institution.

Gourevitch, Peter. 1978. "The Second Image Reversed: The International Sources of Domestic Politics." *International Organization* 32 (4).

Gwerztman, Bernard, and Michael T. Kaufman, eds. 1990. *The Collapse of Communism.* New York: New York Times-Random House.

Hall, John A. 1987. *Liberalism: Politics, Ideology and the Market.* Chapel Hill: University of North Carolina Press.

Hayek, F. A. 1960. *The Constitution of Liberty.* Chicago: University of Chicago Press.

Herz, John H., ed. 1982. *From Dictatorship to Democracy: Coping with the Legacies of Authoritarianism and Totalitarianism.* Westport, Conn.: Greenwood Press.

Hirschman, Albert. 1970. *Exit, Voice, and Loyalty.* Cambridge, Mass.: Harvard University Press.

Keohane, Robert O. 1984. *After Hegemony: Cooperation and Discord in the World Political Economy.* Princeton, N.J.: Princeton University Press.

Keohane, Robert, and Joseph Nye. 1977. *Power and Interdependence: World Politics in Transition.* Boston: Little, Brown and Co.

Kittrie, Nicholas N., and Ivan Volgyes, eds. 1988. *The Uncertain Future: Gorbachev's Eastern Bloc.* New York: Paragon House.

Krasner, Stephen D., ed. 1983. *International Regimes.* Ithaca, N.Y.: Cornell University Press.

Lane, David, ed. 1990. *Soviet Society under Perestroika.* Boston: Unwin Hyman.

Laslett, Peter, and James Fishkin, eds. 1979. *Philosophy, Politics and Society.* Fifth Series. New Haven, Conn.: Yale University Press.

Lehman, David. 1990. *Democracy and Development in Latin America: Economics, Politics and Religion in the Post-War Period.* Philadelphia: Temple University Press.

Lichtensztejn, Samuel. 1982. "Internacionalización y políticas económicas en América Latina." *Comercio Exterior* 32 (7).

Lowenthal, Abraham F., ed. 1991. *Exporting Democracy: The United States and Latin America. Themes and Issues.* Baltimore: The Johns Hopkins University Press.

Macpherson, C. B. 1977. *The Life and Times of Liberal Democracy.* Oxford: Oxford University Press.

Mainwaring, Scott, and Alexander Wilde, eds. 1989. *The Progressive Church in Latin America.* Notre Dame, Ind.: University of Notre Dame Press.

Mannheim, Karl. 1950. *Freedom, Power and Democratic Planning.* New York: Oxford University Press.

Markoff, John. 1990. "The Great Wave of Democracy in Historical Perspective." Paper delivered at the Conference on Global Trends of Democratization, November 3-4, Skidmore College, Saratoga Springs, New York.

Nanda, Ved P., James R. Scarrit, and George W. Shepherd, eds. 1981. *Global Human Rights: Public Policies, Comparative Measures, and NGO Strategies.* Boulder, Colo.: Westview.

Nun, José. 1991. "Democracy and Modernization, Thirty Years After." Paper presented at 15th World Congress of IPSA, July 21-26, Buenos Aires, Argentina.

O'Donnell, Guillermo, Philippe Schmitter, and Laurence Whitehead, eds. 1986. *Transitions from Authoritarian Rule: Comparative Perspectives.* Baltimore: The Johns Hopkins University Press.

Pinto-Duchinsky, Michael. 1991. "Foreign Political Aid: The German Political Foundations and their U.S. Counterparts." *International Affairs* 67 (1).

Polanyi, Karl. 1957. *The Great Transformation: The Political and Economic Origins of Our Time.* Boston: Beacon Press.

Powell, Jr,; G. Bingham. 1982. *Contemporary Democracies: Participation, Stability, and Violence.* Cambridge, Mass.: Harvard University Press.

Reich, Robert. 1983. *The Next American Frontier.* New York: Times Books.

Ribas, Armando. 1988. *El retorno de Luz del Día: Liberalismo y desarrollo.* Buenos Aires: Sudamericana.

Ronen, Dov, ed. 1986. *Democracy and Pluralism in Africa.* Boulder, Colo.: Lynne Rienner.

Rostow, Walt W. 1990. "The Coming Age of Regionalism: A Metaphor for Our Time?" *Encounter* 74 (5).

Ruggie, John Gerard. 1983. "International Regimes, Transactions and Change: Embedded Liberalism in the Postwar Economic Order." In *International Regimes,* Stephen Krasner, ed.. Ithaca, N.Y.: Cornell University Press.

Sandbrook, Richard. 1990. "Taming the African Leviathan." *World Policy Journal* 7:4 (Fall).

Schlossstein, Steven. 1989. *The End of the American Century.* New York: Congdon & Weed.

Schopflin, George. 1991. "Post-Communism: Constructing New Democracies in Central Europe." *International Affairs* 67:2.

Schumpeter, Joseph A. 1976. *Capitalism, Socialism and Democracy.* New York: Harper & Row.

Shtromas, Alexander, and Morton A. Kaplan, eds. 1988. *The Soviet Union and the Challenge of the Future.* New York: Paragon House.

Soto, Hernando de. 1989. *The Other Path.* New York: Harper & Row.

Staniland, Martin, ed. 1991. *Falling Friends.* Boulder, Colo.: Westview Press.

Starr, Richard F., ed. 1989. *United States-East European Relations in the 1990s.* New York: Crane Russak.

Tavares, Maria da Conceição. 1985. "The Revival of American Hegemony." *CEPAL Review* 26 (August).

Tironi, Eugenio. 1986. *El liberalismo real.* Santiago, Chile: Sur.

Van Klaveren, Alberto. 1986. "Europa y la democratización de América Latina." *Nueva Sociedad* 85 (September-October).

Varela, Gonzalo. 1982. "Transnacionalización y política." *Comercio Exterior* 32 (7).

Wachtel, Howard M. 1990. *The Money Mandarins: The Making of a Supranational Economic Order.* London: Pluto Press.

Weber, Max. 1978. *Economy and Society.* Berkeley: University of California Press.

Whitehead, Laurence. 1986. "International Aspects of Democratization." In *Transitions from Authoritarian Rule: Comparative Perspectives,* Guillermo O'Donnell, Phillipe Schmitter, and Laurence Whitehead, eds. Baltimore: The Johns Hopkins University Press.

Williamson, John, ed. 1990. *Latin American Adjustment: How Much Has Happened?* Washington, D.C.: Institute for International Economics.

World Bank. 1989. *Sub-Saharan Africa: From Crisis to Sustainable Growth.* Washington, D.C.: World Bank.

Chapter Four

Growth and Structural Reform in Latin America: Where We Stand

José María Fanelli

Roberto Frenkel

Guillermo Rozenwurcel

Introduction

This chapter examines issues related to the problem of restoring growth in Latin America in order to extract some conclusions from the adjustment-with-stagnation phenomenon experienced by most Latin American countries throughout the 1980s. To achieve this objective, it is necessary to analyze the structural disequilibria that arose during the adjustment period of the 1980s. But it is also important to examine the policy reform proposals put forth by the World Bank and the International Monetary Fund (IMF) and the literature produced by the Washington think tanks, which gave rise to the so-called "Washington Consensus" (Williamson 1990). These proposals have determined, in great measure, the direction of market-oriented reforms implemented by the largest countries in the region. Part of this chapter assesses the suitability of the theoretical framework supporting the Washington Consensus and its concrete policy reform proposals. Apart from analyzing the economic disequilibria in some economies of the region and evaluating the Washington Consensus, an additional objective is to advance and evaluate some alternative policy proposals aimed at restoring growth.

We have opted to discuss the economic liberalization paradigm in some detail not only because it is the most influential development paradigm, but also because — independent of our judgment about the theoretical underpinnings of the liberalization approach — it is correct in some of its criticism of the postwar development process in terms of resource misallocation. We deal more specifically with two contemporary constraints to growth: first, the magnitude of the adjustment needed to achieve a savings rate compatible with a reasonable growth rate, which we label the "Smithian" constraint to growth; and second, a "Keynesian" constraint, in which the mechanisms operating in the present disequilibrium situation preclude the use of available savings to finance investment in real assets. Capital flight and lack of financial intermediation are analyzed in connection with this second point.

The last section discusses policy reforms for achieving adjustment with growth that our analysis suggests are suitable, given the constraints to growth that Latin American countries currently face. Policy reforms concerning the fiscal budget, the trade structure, and the external sector are emphasized.

Stabilization with Growth and the Washington Consensus

The imbalances in most Latin American economies are not short term in character. Disequilibria in the current account, the government budget, and the propagation mechanisms (in the form of high inflation or increased financial fragility) have led to a situation that cannot be quickly reversed because it calls for a complete change in the prevailing economic regime. The present context of disequilibrium is not the traditional, short-run maladjustment between absorption and domestic income that could be reversed by implementing a traditional IMF-inspired policy package. This fact is broadly perceived by both economic policy makers and scholars. There is a wide consensus that not only short-run stabilization measures but also others oriented to introducing structural changes are needed to ensure the closing of the aforementioned gaps.[1]

One of the most important and influential responses to the need for stabilization is the policy package based on what John Williamson (1990) termed the Washington Consensus[2] (WC) approach to stabilization with growth. The WC diagnosis is based on both empirical and theoretical arguments. In this approach, the roots of Latin American instability and lack of growth lie in the import-substitution strategy of industrialization (ISI) adopted in the postwar period in Latin American countries. According to the WC, this strategy entailed an inward-oriented model of growth and a serious misallocation of resources, especially because of the central role played by the public sector as an "engine of growth."

From a purely theoretical point of view, the WC takes as a benchmark to judge the ISI strategy the neoclassical model of development put forth by McKinnon, Shaw, Krueger and the staff of the World Bank.[3] The intellectual influence of this view is so pervasive that Fischer (1990) argued that there are no longer two major competing economic development paradigms. The only paradigm is the market-oriented one. Consequently, all participants in the development debate now speak the same language.

Given that this development paradigm has little to say about how to stabilize an economy in the short run, its basic notions are, in fact, coupled with the traditional IMF approach (Kahn et al. 1986). This marriage between the neoclassical approach to stabilization and development provides the basis for WC structural reform proposals designed to restore both growth and macroeconomic stability in Latin America. The set of objectives pursued by the policy proposals based on this paradigm has been summarized by Fischer (1990) as the search for 1) a sound macroeconomic framework, 2) an efficient and smaller government, 3) an efficient and expanding private sector, and 4) policies for poverty reduction (such as targeted food subsidies, medical and educational programs).

We believe that this approach has been successful in highlighting some important weaknesses in the development strategy adopted by Latin America in the postwar period. We also believe, however, that certain flaws render it an inappropriate tool for overcoming the disequilibria outlined below. The empirical interpretation of the ISI model and of the role of the state, as well as the theoretical foundations of the liberalization approach, are too general and abstract to represent a firm base on which to diagnose, design, and implement sound policies oriented to achieve stabilization with growth. It also shows weak theoretical foundations regarding the relationship between short-term and long-term policies designed to stabilize the economy and restore growth. In our view, the neoclassical approach is a static comparative exercise which lacks the dynamic elements that bear on the relationship between stabilization and growth.

Given the strong influence the WC has on policy making in present-day Latin America, it is worthwhile to discuss its basic components, focusing on its theoretical underpinnings and the policy proposals presented by Williamson (1990). The principal assumption behind WC policy recommendations is that, because most of the output growth during the first stage of the reform period should come from a better reallocation of existing resources and a better utilization of existing capacity, a fundamental complement between adjustment and economic growth exists (Guitian 1988). Long-run, self-sustained growth can be achieved only when individuals prefer to invest domestically instead of abroad. Such a thing can occur only after structural reforms and macroeconomic stability are firmly established (Selowsky 1990).

Based on this view of the relationship between stabilization and growth, the liberalization literature specifies that an economy moving from stabilization to growth should go through at least two stages. During Stage I, economic policy should focus primarily on establishing a sound macroeconomic setting. Given that instability is the result of excessive and volatile borrowing from domestic sources to finance the public sector deficit, achieving a fiscal surplus is the priority. Thus, major fiscal reform to fulfill this policy objective should follow WC guidelines regarding the public sector.

The specified policy package lacks essential elements to structure a true stabilization package aimed at attacking the most important short-run disequilibria, such as a high inflation rate or the existence of a misleading structure of relative prices (typically, overvalued exchange rates and lagging public prices). As a result, the policy package of the WC is normally appended to the standard IMF stabilization procedures. Explaining the relationship between the IMF and the World Bank policies, Guitian (1987) argued that a key function of economic management at this stage is to keep the level and rate of growth of aggregate demand in a sound relationship with the level and growth prospects of an economy's production capacity. The IMF understands this to mean a tight control over the aggregate demand, which, in turn, entails not only eliminating fiscal imbalances but also keeping domestic credit expansion in an appropriate balance with the prospective path of desired money holdings in the economy (see Guitian 1987). More often than not, this produces a deep recession.

Stage II encompasses the implementation of a set of policies aimed at bringing private incentives more in line with "true" economic scarcities. During this stage, the core of the liberalization package should be applied, including the policy reforms recommended by the WC for the financial sector, trade structure, deregulation of the labor market, and so forth.

Only after successfully passing through Stages I and II could a country expect to recover solid growth and, perhaps, creditworthiness. More optimistically, a country that has shown a firm political commitment to implementing structural reforms could expect some support from the official multilateral creditors. Yet according to Fischer and Husain (1990), it is necessary to achieve some success in reforming the economy prior to being eligible for support from international financial institutions (IFIs). Countries like Argentina under Raúl Alfonsín, for example, which showed a willingness to reform but suffered from a certain lack of conviction during the process, found themselves in an uncomfortable situation. Fischer and Husain are pessimistic about countries that have yet to put in practice a "realistic and sustainable program of economic reform." In their view:

> ... as things now stand they will be left out of the strengthened debt strategy and continue to carry a heavy burden of external debt until they achieve the political will to adopt the necessary adjustment measures. For such countries, the main thrust should be to persuade them to undertake credible and lasting economic policy changes that can make them eligible for debt and debt-service reduction (Fischer and Husain 1990, 27).

WC views carry the conviction that liberalization is the appropriate framework to restore growth and that the IMF model is the correct one to address stabilization. This, in turn, implies that the sequence of policy reforms should follow broadly the stages mentioned above. Nonetheless, one could ask whether there are sound bases for this consensus regarding the necessity and timing of the adjustment-with-growth process. One might also question Fischer's notion of the uniqueness of the development paradigm. In principle, there is an ambiguous answer. Even the authors who adopt the analytical framework provided by the liberalization approach claim that, with regard to several key points, "more research is needed." This is particularly true with issues that bear on the dynamics of the economy during the transition from "repression" to liberalization. Moreover, empirical evidence from countries that have achieved stabilization with growth appears to contradict the idea that the economy should fulfill the policy sequence entailed by stages I and II.

We specify several of these weaknesses because they have a determinant influence on the correct design and implementation of the policy reforms. First, the "division of labor" between the IMF and World Bank, with the former addressing stabilization and the latter designing the policy package for growth, has no firm theoretical basis. Kahn et al. (1986) provide a unique attempt to mix both the Bank's and the Fund's approaches (Fischer 1987). However, while the liberalization approach rests on the mechanism of relative prices for achieving a better resource allocation, relative prices are scarcely mentioned by Kahn and his associates.

Second, as Michalopoulos (1987) recognizes, because of the poorly understood dynamics of reform, uncertainties are prominent in the implementation stage. Michalopoulos concludes that although the framework provides a good basis for the design of adjustment in most countries, one can be more confident about the long-term outcome of the policy reform than about the precise consequences of the program's implementation. Two conflicting issues are raised by Michalopoulos: 1) the sequencing of policy measures aimed at stabilization and those that focus on structural adjustment, and 2) the optimal sequence of reforms to remove distortions when many markets are initially regulated. Again, in another form, the problem of the relationship between short-term stabilization and structural reform appears unresolved. If, as Michalopoulos recognizes, economic theory (read "the liberalization approach") offers little guidance concerning the optimal sequence for overcoming market distortions, why should one assume *a priori* that the dynamics of the process would never be explosive? And, how can one evaluate the costs and benefits of policy reform? In fact, substantial empirical evidence from many Latin American countries counsels against disregarding the possibility of explosive paths in which the adjustment process in the domains of the public accounts, inflation, the domestic financial system and the evolution of external public-sector debt may evolve in disastrous fashion with unforeseen consequences.

The issue of the costs and benefits of the policy reform is no less relevant. A "mistake" in the sequencing of the implementation of the financial, trade, and capital account liberalization in the Southern Cone programs of the late 1970s had a cost of billions of dollars in terms of increased external indebtedness. Was it wiser to pay the cost of these failed liberalization attempts than to pay the cost of preserving the economy's repressed structure? Colombia, which did not experience a major crisis and is an example of successful market-oriented reforms, implemented piecemeal changes rather than pursuing the immediate eradication of the ISI development strategy. This case may suggest that a calculated aversion to risk may be advisable with regard to policy design and implementation.

Third, the WC takes for granted the contention that a strong complement exists between domestic policies and external financing. Sound policies will be rewarded with the almost automatic return of debtor countries to normal and voluntary access to the international capital markets. Or, if this were not the case, sound policies would at least make the country eligible for handling commercial debts in the framework of Brady-like initiatives.

The Latin American experience presents an empirical challenge to this contention. Countries that undertook deep reforms, such as Uruguay, Bolivia, or even Mexico, did not receive any immediate or significant amount of additional external financing. When external financing did arrive, it did so after a long delay, and the amount was insufficient to restore growth. It should be taken into account that the total amount that the IMF and the World Bank are expected to provide within the Brady initiative will be no more than $20 to $25 billion, whereas Latin American debt amounts to $500 billion. Moreover, the most successful adjustment-with-growth experience in Latin America is Chile. This country received preferential treatment with regard to external financing. The amount of external credit received was significant and was available from the beginning of the adjustment process.

A fourth point, which provides mixed evidence on both empirical and theoretical grounds, concerns the sources of growth. The core of the liberalization approach's contribution to development theory lies in the potential for fostering growth due to improved resource allocation. Referring to the World Bank's experience, Jagdish Bhagwati (1987) made this point clearly:

Aid conditionality reflected in the 1950s the dominance of the Harrod-Domar type of thinking. Since that model basically related growth to investment with the productivity of investment (in the shape of the capital-output ratio) taken as technologically given by the composition of output, the performance of the aid recipient was measured by how much was done to raise the contribution of domestic savings to domestic investment. Hence, savings performance, and therefore tax effort, became the key elements of conditionality. By now, it is well known that investment is a necessary, but not a sufficient, condition for developmental success. Conditionality has thus moved on to include questions of efficiency in the use of resources, which brings into the picture the question of outward orientation, in turn (Bhagwati 1987, 257-8).

For at least three reasons this bold contention raises some doubts on empirical grounds.[4] First, research on the determinants of growth usually finds that resource allocation does not explain much, while most of the improvement in growth rate results from gains stemming from advances in knowledge and education. Second, successful liberalization in countries like Korea, Turkey, and Chile exhibits both improvements in resource allocation and a high level of disposable savings either from domestic sources or from abroad.[5] Third, countries like Uruguay and Bolivia, which have undertaken structural reforms to liberalize the market, show very low levels of investment and have achieved only moderate growth.

Structural Reform and Stabilization with Growth

In Latin America, different adjustments to the debt crisis depended on the structural features of each country, the initial preadjustment conditions, and the availability of foreign finance for each economy. For the region as a whole, general policy prescriptions have had limited validity. Consider the countries that performed well. For several reasons — good luck and prudent precrisis economic policies being among the most important — Colombia was less affected by the debt crisis. Thus, it successfully adjusted to the new international environment without major changes in its growth strategy. From a long-term perspective, the main challenge for Colombia was how to deal with the "neoclassical problem" of improving resource allocation.

Chile, unlike Colombia, was severely affected by the crisis and its adjustment implied a profound change of regime, involving both trade liberalization and a fundamentally different role for the state. Chilean success in restoring growth, however, is still very fragile. Its balance of payments and fiscal accounts remain highly dependent on the behavior of foreign finance and the terms of trade. Owing to its high debt/GDP ratio, the Chilean economy faces an uncomfortable tradeoff between domestic consumption and investment if it fulfills all of its external commitments.

In most other countries of the region, the external shock of the early 1980s was equally severe. The initial impact was exacerbated by different propagating mechanisms. The result was a highly uncertain economic environment with destabilizing tendencies reflected in the extreme volatility of the principal macroeconomic indicators — level of activity, rate of inflation, key relative prices, public internal debt, degree of monetization, and so forth.

Given these characteristics, the sharp declines experienced by investment and growth rates in these countries are not surprising.

In addition to resuming growth, Brazil has yet to overcome the consequences of hyperinflation and has been unable to stabilize its economy. Argentina has made substantial progress in pursuit of stabilization, but long-term growth remains uncertain. Mexico achieved stabilization, but the restoration of growth was delayed for many years (the so-called "bottom-of-the-well equilibrium"), which widened the external gap. These experiences suggest that stabilization is still precarious.

Our analysis will focus on the experiences of several Latin American nations which attempted some sort of growth recovery through four strategies: 1) stabilization, 2) fiscal reform, 3) external sector and trade, and 4) money and finance.

Stabilization

Supported by the experience of several Latin American countries, economists reached a consensus on the priority of stabilization as a precondition to growth. In most economies, sagging production levels, high unemployment, and falling investment were coupled with acceleration of inflation. The stabilization processes which followed led to rising levels of economic activity. Beyond this basic notion, consensus is hard to find. The dominant view establishes a neat separation between stabilization and growth. Stabilization must come first and must be sustained long enough to consolidate expectations and credibility. Only then is the economy ready to grow.

The conventional view of stabilization relies heavily on pre-1980s' diagnoses and prescriptions that arose when stabilization policies were conceived to resolve short-run disequilibria in the balance of payments, fiscal accounts, or monetary aggregates. This type of disequilibria might result from shocks or policy mistakes disturbing the normal functioning of the economy. Stabilization policy was a set of measures intended to push the economy to stable equilibrium through a quick correction of deviations.

In each concrete episode, stabilization programs combined short- and long-term measures. Moreover, in many cases, stabilization was presented as a precondition of reforms aimed at improving the allocation of resources and increasing the long-term rate of growth even though structural reforms had little to do with the success of the short-run stabilization effort. These notions of stabilization are no longer relevant for Latin American economies. Disequilibria cannot be managed with the instruments traditionally used in stabilization policies: closing external and fiscal gaps requires structural reforms that condition the possibility of stabilization.

There is a new character of stabilization, which is derived from its new target. According to our diagnosis, many Latin American economies follow paths characterized by the steady deterioration in their functioning and productive capacities. Under these circumstances, stabilization must be conceived of as a set of measures and policies capable of stopping this deterioration.

A stabilization policy has to obtain sustainable closure of the fiscal and external gaps and a quick reduction of the rate of inflation to a (relatively) low level. The objective should be to achieve a lower, stable inflation rate and the stability of key relative prices, such as the rate of exchange and real wages. Achieving these two goals is necessary for stopping the flight of physical and financial assets overseas. Even when fiscal and financial gaps are narrowed and inflation reined in, complete reversal of previous tendencies should not be expected to take place immediately. In the short run, capital flight will probably stop, and some remonetization may take place. Nevertheless, domestic financial assets will show very short-term maturity, and the interest rate will continue to be high for a long period.

The stickiness of pre-stabilization financial behavior can be attributed to coordination failures or credibility problems. In any case, the post-stabilization financial situation will be fragile and very sensitive to signals from fiscal or external fronts. The sustainability of the fiscal-gap closure has two aspects. First, because it requires deep changes in the amount and structure of fiscal expenses and receipts, a permanent closure involves state reform rather than merely marginal adjustments. This will take time. In the meantime, the fiscal gap has to be externally financed, as was the case in Chile and other successful adjustments. Second, given the budgetary importance of the external debt, a sustainable closure of the fiscal gap requires a firm agreement on debt payments, which means that the fiscal and external gaps have to be closed simultaneously. In all cases, state reform involves tough actions. Governments must craft a consensus in favor of reform. Reaching these targets without external agreement and support will be nearly impossible.

To reduce uncertainty and to signal stability, the closure of the external gap should take the form of an extended agreement with foreign governments, multilateral lenders, and commercial banks. The time, structure, and amounts of the agreed-upon flow of funds should be compatible with the fiscal program and the financing of some investment recovery. Agreements should also contain contingent clauses to cushion unfavorable shocks, given that voluntary lending will be nonexistent in the foreseeable future.

The durability of a low rate of inflation will require persistent anti-inflationary activity instrumented by a broadly accepted incomes policy. Stability of key relative prices is both a target and a necessary condition of this policy. Thus, a tradeoff exists between the anti-inflationary role of the nominal rate of exchange and the required stability of the real exchange rate. The success of anti-inflationary policy requires the utilization of all possible tools to perform a very difficult task. These measures include the use of the nominal exchange rate as an anchor for price and wage decisions and expectations. Because residual inflation is always higher than the nominal rate of devaluation, there is a post-stabilization tendency for the domestic currency to appreciate. The lower the residual inflation, the weaker the tendency, but this problem has no neat solution. In each case, stabilization policy has to combine the two conflicting targets in a specific mix.

If all the necessary conditions for stabilization are fulfilled, it will be possible to reach financial and monetary equilibrium with a low rate of inflation. The economy then will stabilize with explosive tendencies brought under effective control. Is it possible to consolidate this stability without also returning to a positive growth rate? The main difficulty lies in the fragility of the equilibria and rates of inflation achieved by the stabilization effort. It will be very difficult, if not impossible, to sustain the post-stabilization equilibrium without some positive signals from the real side of the economy. In a situation of economic stagnation, the probability of falling back to destabilization because of exogenous shocks or distributive conflicts increases with time.

Beyond quantitative considerations, stabilization-cum-growth recovery implies a reconstruction of the state's ability to perform coordinating and promoting functions. This requires a far-reaching political effort to formulate and implement social rules and discipline. Together with the aforementioned external agreement, a politically sustainable fiscal pact and a social agreement appear essential. In many Latin American cases, the heroic character of stabilization policy also comes from the need to reverse pessimistic expectations after nearly a decade of destabilized economies and repeated policy failures.

We have argued that stabilization without growth is not impossible but will be difficult to sustain. Until very recently, Bolivia and Mexico still belonged to the stabilized-but-stagnant category. Aside from fragility, their economies suffer from high real rates of interest, a tendency for their domestic currencies to appreciate without a reversal of monetization or an increase in domestic financial intermediation. In both cases, but more emphatically in Bolivia, a "wait-and-see" strategy dominated growth policy.

Public Sector Reform

From our analysis of the fiscal gap, it follows that not only the external shock of the early 1980s but the subsequent adjustment period induced serious and long-lasting effects on the structure and functioning of the public sector. The public sector appears to have endured the shocks relatively well in Colombia and Chile. In contrast, there was a deep disarticulation of the state's normal functioning in Argentina, Brazil, and Mexico. Countries like Venezuela, Bolivia, Uruguay, and Peru also experienced major crises of their public sectors. In fact, Chile and Colombia are the exceptions rather than the rule in Latin America today. The deterioration of the state is observed throughout the region. Consequently, the need for restructuring both the public sector and its role in the economy is also widely accepted.

Our hypothesis is that the role of the state will become crucial in the transition to a more stable situation. The state has an irreplaceable role to play in a society's effort to overcome Keynesian, neoclassical, and Smithian constraints to growth. Obviously, making the state more efficient would help in attaining growth and stability. To weaken the state hinders the prospect of overcoming those constraints.

Some of the adjustment policies implemented during the 1980s, and the emphasis on the notion that the inefficiencies observed stem primarily from government-induced misallocation of resources, led to a progressive weakening of the public sector's institutional and administrative capabilities. In the future, the reversal of this process will have significant economic costs. An institutionally strong and economically efficient public sector, whatever its size, is necessary for restoring growth.

Owing to the fact that Latin American countries have always faced significant obstacles in confronting the Keynesian problem of ensuring the effective investment of domestic savings in real assets within the country, the state has played a fundamental role in Latin America in both generating savings and maintaining the investment rate. This problem is closely related to the issue of efficiency in the intermediation of funds between savers and investors (because of the existence of market failures that have impeded financial deepening of the economy).

During the ISI growth process, state intervention partially solved this problem via subsidies, selective credit policies, tax exemptions, direct public investment through state enterprises, and huge infrastructure projects. Such policies received the bulk of neoclassical criticism. They produced, however, better growth performance than that attained by the Southern Cone economies during the liberalization attempts of the late 1970s and the adjustment period of the 1980s. During these two periods, capital flight absorbed a good portion of domestic savings, thereby depressing both public and private investment. The observed growth rate during the ISI years was higher, although the mechanisms for intermediation between savings and investment, ensuring a high investment rate, resulted in an overaccumulation of capital and a serious distributional bias. The postwar strategy cannot be repeated because a high capital/output ratio resembling that of the postwar period could not be financed. The fact that these policies are not feasible today should not lead to the conclusion that any role assigned to the state in the investment-saving process would be unfeasible.

Currently, two main threats to Latin American economies are percep-tible. First is the failure to attain some minimal degree of stability, with the economy jumping from one unstable path to the other, as in Brazil and, until recently, Argentina. The second threat is to attain stability at the cost of falling into a "bottom-of-the-well" equilibrium, as in the cases of Uruguay and Bolivia. Unlike Fischer (1990), in our view the best strategy to avoid either of these situations will necessarily have a significant component of the "pick-the-winners" strategy in which the state should assume greater responsibility for speeding up growth and promoting economic development.

Again, this is not an abstract contention. Empirical evidence reveals that countries like Colombia and Chile, where the state did not renounce its role as a major investor and where state institutions suffered a much lower degree of erosion during the adjustment process, were the most successful. State reform should seek to improve the effectiveness and the efficiency with which governments aim to stabilize the economy and promote growth. What are the principal constraints facing state reform?

The restrictions that policy makers will have to face stem from three problems. First, in many Latin American countries, the task entails much more than just restructuring public sector economic institutions. In some countries, the distorting effects of the crisis and its duration have been so strong that the public sector has lost a good part of its administrative and management capacity. The most important factor explaining this situation is that the external adjustment was intended to maximize both the amount of the external transfer and the speed of the process. The cost of such a strategy was the increase in what Vito Tanzi (1991) termed "fiscal tension." A trade surplus was attained in a very short period of time by — among other measures — a reduction of the current public deficit without taking long-run implications into account. We agree that this fiscal tension resulted from policies intended to remedy the fiscal imbalance by 1) compressing real public sector wages to levels that are well beyond what is politically sustainable or advisable in terms of efficiency; 2) applying temporary and highly inefficient taxes; 3) postpon-ing essential operation and maintenance expenditures, thus reducing the productivity of the public infrastructure and often sharply reducing the usable life of valuable assets (roads, buildings, cars); 4) building up arrears owed domestic suppliers and foreign lenders; and 5) depleting inventories of public enterprises.

The maintenance of a high degree of fiscal tension for a long period resulted ultimately in permanent changes to the structure of the economy in general and the public sector in particular. The maintenance of very low wages in the public sector over a long period was especially negative because it resulted in a kind of "brain drain" that severely undermined government planning and administrative capacity. Even the notion that a "public service career" is needed for improving public sector efficiency appears to have almost disappeared today from conventional policy reform proposals (which only seem to seek the reduction of public expenditures at any cost). The maintenance of negative net investment rates in many areas of the public sector is as bad as the loss of skilled workers. As a consequence, a severe deterioration of the public infrastructure followed, particularly in health, education, and transport. Over time, this resulted in a significant deterioration in the provision of public services and also in an incredible waste of resources, since the cuts in investment and dismissals of employees or wage reductions were not carried out according to a coherent, overall program. Achieving quick improvements in the treasury's cash flow, while minimizing political conflicts, was the "golden rule" of adjustment.

The major restriction that this process puts on reform policies is that today there is almost no room for "macro" policies of the kind applied during the 1980s under IMF-inspired stabilization packages. During the 1980s, IMF policy packages were designed to achieve a given reduction in overall expenditures (targeted as a function of an exogenously set amount for public sector borrowing needs). This process usually failed to take into account the kinds of expenditures which were being reduced in terms of their impact on short- and long-term efficiency consequences. If the use of resources by the public sector is to be improved, future restructuring policies must be much better planned at a "micro" level.

The second problem is closely related to the relationship between stabilization and growth. While governments have to apply aggressive policies to restore growth, they cannot generate significant deficits as they did in the past. In fact, in many Latin American countries, such as Argentina, Brazil, and Peru, the government cannot run fiscal deficits higher than the available flow of external financing to the public sector. The reason is that real demand for new issues of domestic assets in the form of either "bonds" or "money" is zero. Moreover, to preserve financial stability, the rate at which authorities increase the supply of nominal domestic assets cannot be greater than the sum of the rate of growth and the rate of inflation. (And, it is assumed that to achieve stability, the latter must be very low.) It is true that the maintenance of a stable environment might result in an increase in the real demand for domestic assets, but this will surely not occur in the short or even the medium term.

The third problem that governments face in implementing a "pick-the-winner" strategy is that many of the policy tools used in the past for growth promotion are now obsolete, either because the economic situation has changed (at the domestic as well as the international level) or because it had distorting consequences both on the micro incentives (work, investment and efficient portfolio selection) and on the macro equilibrium.[6] One of the main challenges is to implement selective promotion policies. But, at the same time, the rules for their implementation should not leave much room for discretionary case-by-case decision making, nor should they absorb the same quantity of fiscal resources as in the past. Investment resources are extremely scarce, so the public sector must use them more efficiently.

We now turn to some guidelines for public sector structural reforms consistent with the goal of increasing public investment and public savings, without generating further distortions at either the micro or macro level. On the expenditure side, not much room is available for further dramatic reductions in government outlays. In fact, in some items, such as public investment or the improvement of public sector administrative capabilities, there should be significant increases. Thus, policy reform should aim at significantly improving the allocation of existing expenditures. There are many institutional obstacles, however, that will emerge while performing this task. The most important are 1) the existence of a variety of interest groups (industrial and commercial chambers, trade unions, political lobbies) acting in their own interests (this is one of the most important reasons for the strengthening of the state autonomy resting on a democratically generated consensus); 2) the operation of an international demonstration effect, which has led Latin American governments to emulate the distribution of expenditures observed in developed countries by implementing expensive social security programs (that either could not be financed or ultimately favored socially privileged sectors) and by initiating wasteful investment projects promoting sophisticated industries just for the sake of national pride; and 3) pressure of external creditors through the conditionality of multilateral agencies for speeding up the reforms and further reducing expenditure at any cost.

The restructuring of expenditures should aim to increase the amount of resources allocated to public investment and antipoverty programs. In addition, the structure and design of subsidy policies should be greatly modified. Recovery in public investment should start by supporting well-designed strategies to increase maintenance and operation expenses. The second step to be taken should aim at financing public infrastructure projects. Particularly important are projects to improve the infrastructure closely related to export expansion (roads, harbors, storage capacity, and so forth) and targeted programs dealing with public health, education, and poverty reduction. In other words, the main purpose of public investment policies should be to halt and, if possible, reverse the ten-year process of deterioration affecting the public sector. This deterioration has been so grave that a "pump-priming" strategy, based on public investment to prevent the economy from falling into a bottom-of-the well equilibrium, could well last for a long period without the danger of crowding out the private sector.

The bulk of the costs of external adjustment has been born by the poorest sectors of society. Thus, it is necessary to implement well-designed and targeted antipoverty programs. There have been some recent attempts to implement such programs, but with the exception of Chile, most have failed. Apart from the problem of funding, these failures stem from lack of experience with similar large-scale programs and lack of a well-trained staff in the public sector. It should be taken into account, however, that the increase in poverty has been closely related to deep recession in certain sectors of the economy. In Argentina, for example, an increase in construction activity would improve the situation of the urban poor.

One of the WC's strongest criticisms of growth-promoting policies of the postwar period concerns the difficulty in calculating the impact of subsidies that were carefully hidden in public-sector budgets. We believe that such criticism is fairly accurate. The restructuring of public sector expenditures should induce a radical modification in the allocation and recording of subsidies in the budget.

As a general rule, all subsidies should be explicit and consistently targeted as a part of a specific program. Much misallocation of resources generated by the granting of subsidies stemmed from policies aimed at improving income distribution and promoting growth. Restructuring policies should focus first on improving efficiency in these areas. In particular, governments should avoid distributional measures implemented through the pricing policies of public enterprises, which lead to a massive subsidization of overall consumption. Growth-promoting policies that entail subsidies channeled through the Central Bank, public enterprises, pricing policies, or tax exemptions should also be avoided. These policy tools have significant fiscal costs in terms of loss of government revenues, while their benefits are difficult to assess.

While it is true that explicitly targeted subsidies recorded in the budget are much more efficient, it is also true that they call for a much more efficient budgeting process. Many past mistakes were not made because of the perversity of public officials, but because it was administratively easier to grant massive subsidies through public enterprises or the banking system. Once again, improving resource allocation calls for strengthening the management capacity of the public sector. The alternative to poor subsidy policies is not a "no-subsidy policy" but rather a more efficient one.

The WC emphasizes policies aimed at the reduction of expenditures rather than targeting the revenue side of the government balance sheet as a means of reducing fiscal deficits. An increase in the ratio of tax revenue to GDP is posited as having serious deterrent effects. When the overall macroeconomic setting is taken into account, it is obvious that the positive effects of an increase in public savings might largely compensate for any worsening in the incentive structure. In short, they will contribute to an easing of the "Smithian restriction." Likewise, a disincentive effect on private savings does not mean that the available funds for financing investment domestically would decline, because part of the resources saved by the private sector are now allocated in foreign assets. In fact, a policy aimed at increasing public sector savings constitutes one of the few available measures to stop capital flight. If, in turn, the government invested the additional portion of savings stemming from the accrued revenues, it would also help to weaken the Keynesian constraint.

It follows from the previous argument that the principal aim of fiscal reform regarding the revenue side should be to increase the tax revenue/GDP ratio. Any tax policy oriented to generating higher revenues, however, must attain a significant degree of success in stabilizing the economy. As we argued in our analysis of the evolution of the fiscal gap, the erosion of the tax base was closely related to the acceleration of inflation. Fiscal reform also must rationalize and simplify the existing tax structure. In most Latin American countries, the tax system shows severe maladjustments. Tax systems have been systematically and even abusively used to attain objectives relating to the allocation of resources (under the ISI and the liberalization attempts of the late 1970s) and to obtain loosely defined distributional aims.

Also, the present system has suffered many *ad hoc* modifications over the adjustment period that were closely related to short-run stabilization objectives, with little or no concern about the long-term effects on both the efficiency of the tax system or the amount of taxes collected. In this manner, short-term buoyancy in the tax system resulted in a decline in the income elasticity of taxes. In addition, the recurrent reliance on tax increases to fill temporal gaps in fiscal accounts (which usually induced negative effects on income and wealth distribution) severely affected the community's sense of fairness and, in some countries, gave rise to a kind of "fiscal rebellion" that contributed to widening the size of the underground economy.

The principal elements of a tax reform should be the following:

1. The ability of the government to collect should be strengthened. This calls for greater resources allocated to improving financial manage-ment and allocated for the monitoring and oversight systems of the central tax bureau. This should lead to a decrease in tax evasion and a widening of the tax base.

2. Temporary or *ad hoc* taxes should be reduced or eliminated to make both the amount of taxes that the private sector expects to pay and the amount of government revenues less uncertain.

3. The administrative control and efficiency of the tax bureau could be greatly improved by eliminating those taxes that are unproductive and minimizing the use of multiple rates.

4. In accordance with the policy for restructuring the allocation of subsidies, tax expenditures to pay for subsidies should be eliminated, while the use of the tax system to grant incentives to the private sector should be carefully planned and implemented. Tax policies imple-

mented under the ISI providing incentives for real investment, as well as the tax exemptions on interest payments carried out by the liberalization policies, more often than not resulted in tax evasion because of loopholes and perverse portfolio decisions of the private sector.

5. The share of total tax collection made up by direct taxes on income and wealth should be significantly raised. In many Latin American countries, the first objective should be to return to the level of direct taxes observed during the precrisis period. Such a policy would improve not only the equity of the tax system but also its income elasticity. If the income elasticity of the tax structure is not very high, a self-sustained growth process would lead to a renewed fiscal imbalance via a fiscal deficit increase that could not be financed given the rationing of the credit markets.[7]

To summarize, the main objective of public sector reform should be to increase both public investment and public savings. Public investment should be increased not only to stop the deterioration of public infrastructure but also to "prime the pump," thereby reducing the probability that an economy will fall into a "bottom-of-the-well" equilibrium in the post-stabilization period. If public savings are not raised, the increment in public expenditures will entail an increase of the public deficit that could not be financed, given the rationing of external credit markets and the high degree of financial fragility that the domestic ones are undergoing.[8] Likewise, if the policy succeeded in restoring the investment rate, it would have beneficial consequences by weakening the restrictions on growth posed by the Smithian and Keynesian constraints. The latter could occur to the extent that the increase in public investment induced a deterioration in the already depressing state of the private sector's animal spirits.

Concluding Comments on Trade Reform, Debt, and Balance of Payments

A side from some rather vague remarks on the ways to attract direct foreign investments and reverse capital flows, the Washington Consensus remains completely silent on the crucial question of how to close the external gap in a way that is consistent with the objective of growth resumption. To accomplish this goal, a significant reduction of real transfers abroad — compatible with both the fiscal program and investment recovery — seems unavoidable. Moreover, the amount and time profile of the flows of funds involved should be known by debtor countries with much more certainty than is presently the case. As Tanzi puts it:

> ... it is clearly better for economic policy when policy makers know for sure that the servicing of the debt will require, say, a future

constant payment of 3 percent of GDP, so that they can adjust their policies accordingly, rather than knowing that there is a 50 percent probability that the payment will be 1 percent and a 50 percent that it will be 5 percent of GDP. Perhaps one of the greatest burdens associated with the debt crisis has been the creation of this uncertainty. Another has been the large amount of time that the policy makers had to allocate to this problem (Tanzi 1990, 25).

The issues raised by Tanzi stress the importance of achieving a solid, long-term agreement between debtor countries and the governments of creditor countries, multilateral agencies, and commercial banks. Regardless of the specifics of each case, this agreement's targets should not be established in terms of the current account performance but rather in terms of the evolution of real foreign indebtedness.[9] Moreover, such agreement should also include contingent provisions to deal with unexpected shocks in the terms of trade and other variables outside the control of debtor countries.

The Washington Consensus does stand emphatically for an outward-oriented growth strategy because it entails, among other things, a more efficient allocation of new investments and, therefore, higher growth. The desirability of a more outward-oriented growth strategy raises no controversy at present. The key question, however, remains how to accomplish it. Although this question admits of no easy answer, it certainly merits more detailed discussion.

In the first place, an outward-oriented growth strategy should not be considered just a strategy to increase exports. Without a matching increase in imports, given the present context of most Latin American countries, any improvement in export performance would mean only larger real transfers abroad with negative repercussions on investment and growth. Brazil in the 1980s, where the impressive performance of exports had no favorable effects on growth, constitutes a good case in point. Second, but no less important, reforms adopted to make the economy more open in the long run, must not impair stabilization in the short run. For policy makers, this poses a complex problem, especially regarding fiscal and exchange rate policies, which cannot be solved on *a priori* grounds.

Let us consider exchange rate policy first. According to long-term considerations, there is no doubt that economic policy should ensure that the real exchange rate be high and stable to promote export growth and provide the right signals for new investments. Stabilization requires, however, that the nominal exchange rate be used as an anchor for price and wage decisions and expectations. Therefore, during a certain period, domestic currency must appreciate in real terms, which seems to be the initial outcome of most stabilization attempts, both successful and unsuccessful.

Unfortunately, there are no clear-cut answers to this conflict, and it makes no sense to attempt to find general solutions applicable at any time or place. Given the many conflicting tasks that are simultaneously assigned to the exchange rate, and the great uncertainty experienced by Latin American economies, it seems prudent not to rely on a floating regime to do the job. This conclusion is justified on theoretical grounds both by the critique of "over-shooting" and by the empirical evidence registered in some Latin American countries of extremely volatile exchange rates under floating regimes. All this suggests that some direct control by the Central Bank over the evolution of the exchange rate, regardless of its specific nature, may be unavoidable.

Fiscal policy is also subject to similar tensions between the short and long run. With the long run in mind, the WC approach advocates suppressing all taxes on exports. Export taxes are a vital source of revenue for the public sector in many Latin American countries. Eliminating them without ensuring they will be replaced by other taxes capable of generating an equivalent amount of fiscal revenues can be extremely dangerous for both the fiscal balance and stabilization. Moreover, lack of tax policy predictability can have negative repercussions on export performance, which are at least as serious as those originating on export taxes. The recurrent, frustrated attempts to lift taxes permanently on grain exports in Argentina clearly illustrate this point.

There is a related question. As we have seen, rents stemming from natural resources in several Latin American countries constitute a relevant source of public revenues. In some cases, the state has direct command over rents because it has property rights on the resources. Mexico, Chile, and Colombia are good examples of this situation. Sometimes, however, although it is certainly not the best alternative, the only available way to socialize these rents is to impose taxes on primary exports. Argentina might be in this situation.

This raises a third, more general question, namely that of export promotion. The successful experience of East Asian NICs was based on a "pick-the-winners" strategy. Among other components — including the maintenance of an undervalued currency — this strategy relied on an active state role in selecting leading economic sectors and promoting their sales abroad. Brazil's impressive export performance since the 1970s and the success of Colombia in expanding its "minor" exports have followed a similar course. Even in Chile, export promotion was not entirely absent (Meller 1990; Ffrench-Davis et al. 1990).

Given the constraints that the current situation imposes on the use of tax exemptions and credit support, the prudent use of multiple exchange rates seems justified as a second-best solution. Recent failures of multiple exchange rate systems in some Latin American countries should, in fact, be attributed to destabilization and government mismanagement rather than to insur-mountable deficiencies of the system itself.

Multiple rates naturally call for some exchange controls. The failure of financial markets to spontaneously prevent the denationalization of savings without disruptive domestic consequences strengthens the need for exchange controls to limit capital movements. The inconvenience of liberalizing the capital account in the present context is even shared by some of the participants of the Washington Consensus (Williamson 1990).

Finally, there remains the issue of import liberalization. As noted above, one of the main goals of an outward-oriented growth strategy should be to increase imports at least as fast as exports. Trade reform is also required to eliminate anti-export biases and provide more adequate information for investment decisions. Most of the WC proposals on this subject are certainly valid, but they need some qualifications. Consider first the recommendations to eliminate all nontariff barriers, reduce the average level of tariff protection, and diminish sectoral differences in the tariff structure. Generally speaking, these are sound recommendations, especially when access to intermediate and capital goods imports at competitive international prices is at stake. Nevertheless, they deserve a few additional remarks. It should be noted, for example, that most Latin American countries have already gone a long way in the process of lifting nontariff barriers and rationalizing their tariff structures. It is worth recalling that the maintenance of some level of import protection is justified on at least two grounds. First, tariff receipts represent a major source of indispensable fiscal revenues. Second, it is accepted both theoretically and empirically that infant industries require some kind of import protection, although on a strictly temporary and decreasing basis (Krugman 1988; Williamson 1990).

Because of the comparative, static nature of their approach, however, the most critical omission in the WC proposals on trade liberalization concerns its dynamic aspects. This is no minor problem. The dramatic failure of Southern Cone liberalization attempts in the late 1970s can be attributed precisely to dynamic factors.[10] One of the main lessons of those experiences refers to the appropriate sequence of tariff reductions. If the basic goal of trade reform is to provide adequate incentives for improving resource allocation and investment decisions, liberalization should begin with the intermediate and capital goods sectors. Otherwise, as experience shows, it can lead to massive imports of final consumer goods with devastating consequences for the balance of payments and the level of economic activity. Needless to say, such an outcome can only have negative repercussions for "animal spirits" and investment.

There is also the critical issue of timing and opportunity for trade reform. The above-mentioned conflict between the short and long run reappears here. Trade reform is lasting, and policy makers should resist the temptation to use it for stabilization purposes. In fact, as also shown by experience, the combination of an abrupt liberalization and an overvalued domestic currency can severely impair expectations and become an explosive mix for both stabilization and growth objectives.

This is not to deny the beneficial influence that liberalization and other long-term reforms can have in consolidating stability. Rather, the point to be emphasized is that a relatively stable environment, and a high and stable real exchange rate, should be considered as basic prerequisites for successful liberalization. Also because of its long-term character, trade reform should proceed gradually. Gradualism is required to allow an orderly relocation of productive factors, thereby reducing uncertainty and enhancing investment prospects. This was the approach taken by Colombia, the Latin American country with the best macroeconomic performance throughout the 1980s.

Finally, given the importance of imperfect competition, intraindustry specialization, and economies of scale as determinants of current trends in international trade,[11] Latin American countries are well advised not to rely on market mechanisms and price signals as the only instruments of an outward-oriented growth strategy. In fact, according to several authors, price signals did not play such a central role for investment decisions in the successful development processes that followed this strategy in East Asia (Sachs 1987; Taylor 1988; Amsden 1989).

In this respect, the opportunities that regional integration can offer for growth recovery in Latin America should not be dismissed. The process of integration initiated by Argentina, Brazil, Paraguay, and Uruguay represents a step in the right direction, though major results cannot be expected from the MERCOSUR initiative before a more stable environment is achieved in the region.

Notes

1. Even the economic terminology referring to the situation and the needed reforms suffers from the effects of the crisis. According to Feinberg (1990, 22), "Washington did appropriate the language of structuralism but turned it on its head. Whereas in Latin America 'structural flaws' meant market failures and 'structural change' meant government action, in contemporary Washington it is government interventions that are structural distortions and liberalization and deregulation that are the corresponding necessary structural reforms."

2. John Williamson (1990, 7) defines "Washington" as "the political Washington of Congress and senior members of the administration and the technocratic Washington of the international financial institutions, the economic agencies of the U.S. government, the Federal Reserve Board, and the think tanks." According to Williamson, however, "Washington does not, of course, always practice what it preaches to foreigners."

3. See Stanley Fischer (1987) for an analysis of the main issues raised by the liberalization literature.

4. If this contention were true, the task of achieving growth would be much easier and the situation more hopeful, since Latin American countries would be able to restore growth in a world of rationed capital markets just by improving resource allocation.

5. See Max Corden (1990) for the case of Turkey and other successful stabilization experiences that received strong support from abroad.

6. Among these instruments are industrial promotion policies that created a growing number of tax revenue expenditure items in the budget, indiscriminate subsidies that were not targeted nor clearly stated in the budget, preferential credit at negative interest rates through the central bank aimed at socializing private losses, and onerous investment policies designed to finance projects of long maturity in both the public and private sectors.

7. As we have seen in the first section, the WC considers that an aggressive privatization policy can play a relevant role in fostering growth and balancing public sector accounts, in addition to expenditures and tax reforms. However, it must be taken into account from the point of view of macroeconomic consistency that there are restrictive conditions that the privatization process must fulfill in order to achieve such objectives. On privatization in Latin America, see Marcel (1989); and Fanelli and Frenkel (1990a).

8. In fact, these guidelines for public sector reform are aimed at exploiting to a maximum the beneficial consequences on the activity level of Haavelmo's theorem regarding the multiplier of the balanced budget.

9. The same reasons that justify the use of the operational deficit as a target for fiscal performance apply here.

10. See Corbo et al. (1986) and the extensive literature there cited.

11. See, for instance, Paul Krugman's (1988) discussion of the new theories on this subject.

References

Amsden, A. 1989. *Asia's Next Giant. South Korea and Late Industrialization.* New York: Oxford University Press.

Bhagwati, J. 1987. "Outward Orientation: Trade Issues." In *Growth-Oriented Adjustment Programs*, eds., Victor Corbo et al. Washington, D.C.: IMF and World Bank.

Corbo, V., J. de Melo, and J. Tybout. 1986. "What Went Wrong with the Recent Reforms in the Southern Cone?" *Economic Development and Cultural Change* 34 (3).

Corden, M. 1990. "Macroeconomic Policy and Growth: Some Lessons of Experience." Annual Conference on Development Economics. Washington, D.C.: World Bank.

Ffrench-Davis, R., P. Leiva, and R. Madrid. 1990. "Evaluación de la política comercial en Chile." UNCTAD, mimeo.

Fischer, S. 1987. "Economic Growth and Economic Policy." In *Growth-Oriented Adjustment Programs*, eds., Victor Corbo et al. Washington, D.C.: IMF and World Bank.

Fischer, S. 1990. "Comment." In *Latin American Adjustment: How Much Has Happened?* ed., J. Williamson. Washington, D.C., D.C.: Institute for International Economics.

Feinberg, R. 1990. "Comment." In *Latin American Adjustment: How Much Has Happened?* ed., J. Williamson. Washington, D.C.: Institute for International Economics.

Fischer, S. and I. Husain. 1990. "Managing the Debt Crisis in the 1990s." *Finance & Development*, June.

Frenkel, R., and G. Rozenwurcel. 1990. "Restricción externa y generación de recursos para el crecimiento en la América Latina." *El Trimestre Económico* 225, México.

Guitian, M. 1987. "Adjustment and Economic Growth: Their Fundamental Complementarity." In *Growth-Oriented Adjustment Programs*, eds., Victor Corbo et al. Washington, D.C.: International Monetary Fund and World Bank.

Kahn, M., P. Montiel, and H. Nadeem. 1986. "Adjustment with Growth: Relating the Analytical Approaches of the World Bank and the IMF." Washington, D.C.: World Bank. Discussion Paper (Development Policy Issues).

Krugman, P. 1988. "La nueva teoría del comercio internacional y los países menos desarrollados." *El Trimestre Económico* 217.

Meller, P. 1990. "Chile." In *Latin American Adjustment: How Much Has Happened?* ed., J. Williamson. Washington, D.C.: Institute for International Economics.

Michalopoulos, C. 1987. "World Bank Programs for Adjustment and Growth." In *Growth-Oriented Adjustment Programs*, eds., Victor Corbo et al. Washington, D.C.: International Monetary Fund and World Bank.

Sachs, J. 1987. "Trade and Exchange Rate Policies in Growth-Oriented Adjustment Programs." In *Growth-Oriented Adjustment Programs*, eds., Victor Corbo et al. Washington, D.C.: International Monetary Fund and World Bank.

Selowsky, M. 1990. "Stages in the Recovery of Latin America's Growth." *Finance and Development*, June.

Tanzi, V. 1989. "Fiscal Policy and Economic Reconstruction in Latin America." Working Paper. Washington, D.C.: IMF.

Taylor, L. 1988. "La apertura económica: Problemas hasta fines del siglo." *El Trimestre Económico* 217.

Williamson, J. 1990. "What Washington, D.C., Means by Policy Reform." In *Latin American Adjustment: How Much Has Happened?* ed., J. Williamson. Washington, D.C.: Institute for International Economics.

Chapter Five

Politics: A Key
for the Long Term
in South America

Marcelo Cavarozzi

Introduction

During the 1980s, most of South America made the transition from military authoritarianism to political democracy. At the same time, established patterns of state-society relations suffered radical transformations, especially in the case of newly industrializing countries.[1] This "second transition" was manifested in the decline of the state-centric matrix prevailing in the Southern Cone, Brazil, and Mexico during the half century that followed the international depression of 1929-1932 (Cavarozzi 1992).

The democratic transitions and crisis of the state-centric matrix gave rise to various interpretative perspectives that dominated sociological and economic analysis of Latin American societies, especially in the cases alluded to above. The first of these approaches focused on the short term and studied the dynamics of the transitions to political democracy in the 1980s and the strategies of the coalitions that led these transitions. The second approach, developed toward the end of the 1980s, placed greater emphasis on the long term. In particular, it focused on the processes of structural adjustment linked to the shrinkage of the state and the accompanying expansion of the influence of market logic on social behavior.

These interpretative focuses were developed autonomous to each other. The focus on transitions was elaborated from elements suggested in the

This chapter stems from a project directed jointly by the author and Manuel Antonio Garretón on "The Restructuring of Latin American Societies: Chile and Argentina," with the support of the John D. and Catherine T. MacArthur Foundation.

pioneering work of Guillermo O'Donnell and Phillipe Schmitter (1986), which proposed a framework for the comparative study of the installation and collapse of authoritarianism in South America and Southern Europe. Emphasis was placed on factors related to 1) the conditions immediately preceding the installation of authoritarian regimes in order to evaluate how to impede their regeneration and 2) the consequences of specific modalities of transition on the probability of consolidating political democracy. However, these "transition questions" do not cover all the relevant factors that influence the course and outcome of contemporary processes of political democratization.

Theories of structural adjustment, in turn, have tended to devote almost exclusive attention to economic aspects, concentrating, above all, on the themes of reducing state intervention in the economy and the parallel contraction of the role of the public sector in the accumulation process (Williamson 1990; Sachs 1985). The fact that both approaches have significant lacunae and are also conceptually divorced from each other has had various analytical consequences. A discussion of these consequences will lead me to suggest an alternative conceptualization of the political and economical processes in contemporary Latin America.

What are the most significant conceptual vacuums? At least three can be mentioned. First, the predominant theoretical perspectives have clouded the perception of the all-encompassing nature of the changes occurring in Latin America. The disarticulation and dismantling of the mechanisms of state intervention were part of a broader process of disintegration of the state-centric matrix. This disintegration involved both economic and political aspects. As already mentioned, the focus on structural adjustment neglected the political dimension of the process of change. However, the alternative focus on transition also failed to provide adequate answers because it concentrated, by definition, on the analysis of a short-term conjunctural process: the transition from one form of political regime to another — that is to say, from authoritarianism to democracy.

This contextual bias has hindered attention to longer term political processes. More specifically, it obscured perception of the political formula that had developed parallel to the economic component of the state-centric matrix. The central elements of the state-centric political formula were to a large degree linked to the difficulties inherent in the consolidation of a political regime, whether democratic or otherwise. As will be seen, this formula, which began to unravel in the 1970s, had a hybrid nature, although its final stage was dominated by military authoritarianism, especially in the case of South America.[2] The defining element of this political formula was (with the exception of Uruguay) an unresolved tension between democracy and authoritarianism.

Second, the replacement of the state-centric model with an alternative matrix organized around market logic is still far from complete even in those cases where the process has advanced most decisively, as in Chile, and to a lesser extent, in Argentina and Mexico. In any event, the change should be seen as consisting of overlapping elements of decline (linked to the disorganization of the state-centric matrix), on the one hand, and of elements of creation related to the reorganization of social behavior on the basis of a different set of principles, on the other. In general, analyses of the processes of decline have tended to favor the explicit policies for dismantling the regulatory and interventionist framework of the state, an impetus that was inspired by neoliberal postulates. In contrast, less attention was paid to nondeliberate aspects of the disarticulation of the previous matrix — to the transformation in the behavior of the sociopolitical actors, the causes of which were relatively independent of explicit policies.

Distinguishing between the dismantling and the disarticulation of the state-centric matrix will allow me to emphasize the importance of the sharp break with the past that took place beginning in 1982 with the advent of the debt crisis. In this regard, the comparison between new democracies and the authoritarian regimes that survived during the 1980s calls for a different perspective regarding the relative functionality of authoritarian regimes. I propose to question the hypothesis of the effectiveness of the foundational dictatorships as tools for promoting change toward a matrix organized around market logic. This hypothesis proclaims the presumed capacity of authoritarian regimes to overcome the resistance of sectors opposed to the change in behavior linked to the state-centric matrix. I believe it is more valuable to explore the possibility that the relative success of authoritarian regimes during the 1980s was related to their ability to ameliorate, and sometimes reverse, the inevitably negative effects of the processes of disorganization and adjustment experienced by Latin America, with the partial exception of Colombia. The perspective I suggest, therefore, emphasizes that the effectiveness of post-1982 authoritarian regimes was related to their capacity to attenuate the disorganization of behavior typical of processes of change rather than to their promotion of new patterns of behavior.

Third, the issue of political democracy remains tied to the authoritarianism-democracy dichotomy in most perspectives on the transitions. In turn, theories of structural adjustment tend to conceive of democratization as one of the components of a unilinear liberalization process. Within this framework, democratization is viewed as going hand-in-hand with deregulation of the economy, privatization, and the growing influence of the market. I propose to shift the focus of the discussion in another direction. In all of Latin America, from one end of the spectrum (where the emergence of a new matrix seems more evident, as in Chile or Mexico) to the other (that is, in those cases where disorganization and chaotic adjustment have predominated, of which Peru is the most extreme example), politics is changing as much for the elites as for the masses in relation to the patterns of social behavior sustained by the state-centric matrix. This change of behavior directly affects the meaning of democracy in present-day Latin American societies.

The Political Formula of the State-Centric Matrix

In his analysis of the literature on liberalism and the bourgeois order in Brazil, Wanderley Guilherme dos Santos reminded us that the market model implies a normative concept of state (dos Santos 1978, 32). Nevertheless, it is clear that in each capitalist society the specific contents of this concept vary and, consequently, the links between market and state are articulated in different ways. In general, in every capitalist society the behavior of the market takes account of, and becomes intelligible through, certain mechanisms by which social behavior internalizes the state, its actions, and often even the possibility of its intervention. In each capitalist society, however, the significance and specific effects of the state's "presence" in the market, whether direct or indirect, are quite different.

In post-1930 Latin America, both the implicit concept of the state and of its functions were significantly redefined. The most explicit component of this change was related to state intervention in the economy. As has been analyzed by several U.S. and Latin American economists, the nature of industrialization was modified (resulting from determined state support of the process), state regulation of markets — particularly labor and capital — was expanded, and the economy was restricted (among other reasons, as a result of state action). Similarly, most Latin American countries experienced the emergence of what Albert Hirschman termed the "social and political matrix of inflation" (Hirschman 1981). The partial exception to this rule was the "stabilizing development" experienced by Mexico during the 1950s and 1960s.

In reality, the regime of "moderate" inflation, with annual average rates that fluctuated between 25 and 60 percent, was related to a more general characteristic of the new matrix — to its political economy. The "inflationary tax" was one of various fiscal mechanisms generating resources for the financing of expenditures that assumed a crucial role in the new model, which was based on state promotion of development and the growth of the internal market. These mechanisms, however, were characterized by their high degree of instability and interchangeability, and by the difficulty in generating a significant degree of consensus among the different social and economic actors.[3]

As I have previously suggested, the significance of the fiscal mechanisms implemented since the 1930s, and above all in the postwar period, was not limited to the economic impact they had on different actors. These mechanisms also constituted fundamental elements of a specific way of conducting politics under the aegis of the state-centric matrix. This is one of the main reasons why I contend that the second aspect of the changes that took place since the 1930s was linked to the strictly political functions of the state — that is to say, to the way in which state institutions intervened in politics and affected the manner in which it was carried out. I will define these changes as components of a "statist model of politicization."[4]

The central characteristic of the Latin American state-centric matrix was not, as some have erroneously concluded, an elevated degree of *dirigismo*, especially if by this we mean state intervention in the economy. Adhering to a strict definition, the European economies that Claus Offe (1983) referred to (using the formula of the Keynesian welfare state) were also in that sense interventionist. Rather, the specific Latin American context was related to two other circumstances. The first was the fact that politics, which "affected the lifetime opportunities of practically the entire population," (Kohli 1990, 14) was primarily organized around the actions of the state. In this respect, the role played by the presidency and its executive agencies was quite exclusionary, as was that of certain decentralized institutions, especially in some cases such as Brazil and Chile. The second circumstance was that political action was channeled and organized around the executive to filter and eliminate strong democratizing elements, frequently by strictly electoral means or by direct relations established between leaders and the masses.

This process, however, did not prevent the executive from exercising extensive discretionary power and from imbuing participatory mechanisms with certain hierarchical and authoritarian elements. In conjunction with this tendency, Latin American legislatures tended to become subordinated appendages of executive power or, alternatively, barricades from which the most privileged economic and social sectors defended their prerogatives. Brazil and Chile were also the most significant examples of this second tendency.

The centrality of the executive was clearly related to the symmetrical weakness of the legislative branch, the party system, and the institutions of the judiciary. In some cases, such as Mexico, the relevance of these institutions, even when symbolic, was quite minimal. In contrast, the role of political parties was significant in the political systems of Chile and Uruguay, both as efficient, continuously functioning mechanisms for the selection of high officials and as a suitable arena for the confrontation of alternative political options. Nonetheless, even in the Chilean case, and to a certain extent in Uruguay after the end of the informal hegemony of the Colorado party in 1958, the fragility of the consensus achieved between the elites and the masses undermined the party system. This consensus, of course, was what had allowed the party systems to function stably as the central articulators of the political regime.

This pattern of statist politicization and the resulting weakness of the political regime was perhaps the fundamental characteristic of the Latin

American state-centric matrix. As suggested by Offe (1983), the politico-economic formula prevalent in Western Europe and other stable liberal democracies rests on two foundations: the welfare state and the party system. In liberal democracies, the party system serves to organize the mechanisms of political interaction among different actors who recur to different sources of power — whether economic, organizational, intellectual, clientelistic and kinship-based, or simply repressive. In multiparty democracies, political parties construct the linkages necessary for the implementation of political exchange. They do so because they are the main actors operating in the political arena — the only domain in which different sources of power can be translated into a common currency: the vote.

This is not to say that actors other than parties frequently operate in political and social spheres. Furthermore, it is clear that numerous and important transactions are conducted in arenas other than those reserved for political party interaction. Nevertheless, in multiparty democracies the vote expressed through the parties constitutes the common denominator that ultimately provides the mechanism needed for the execution of transactions involving actors having unequal resources that are otherwise not reducible to a common currency.

Since the decline of oligarchical regimes in Latin America, especially in the cases to which I have referred to, new methods of conducting politics have been introduced. These new modalities involved increased participation (resulting from the incorporation of previously excluded social sectors) as well as the emergence of more complex and pluralistic mechanisms of negotiation.

The weakness of political regimes, however, was compensated for by the fact that political interchange flowed primarily through executive-controlled channels. In one sense, then, Latin American states were strong: the societies in which they operated tended to be hyperpoliticized, and it was the state that made the final decisions on the most important economic and social controversies. In another sense, Latin American states were weak: neither democratic nor authoritarian mechanisms were fully consolidated, and an unstable combination of discretionary prerogatives (which were never completely legitimized) and blackmail (which was carried out by means of various modes of participation) constituted the essence of a political formula in which the state's capacity to enforce its own measures was considerably undermined.

Within this formula, the effectiveness of electoral participation by the masses was fundamentally related to its disruptive potential, not to the desire to contribute to the legitimation of decision-making mechanisms or to the will to promote a higher degree of accountability by public officials. Electoral participation, or even the mere threat that it would materialize, frequently became a tool of political blackmail used by almost everyone to undermine the authority of both civil and military regimes. Political representatives of the middle and lower classes, as well as of antidemocratic elites, at one time or another resorted to this tactic. As a result, the systematic expansion of participation did not contribute to the consolidation of governability within the model.

As Carlos Díaz Alejandro noted in his shrewd analysis of Latin America's contemporary economic history, one of the most concrete manifestations of the weakness of the political consensus has been a proportional increase of inflation since the end of the 1940s. Inflation constituted an implicit process of state intermediation that partially veiled the expropriatory and redistributive effects of public policies. In fact, inflation either replaced the consensus that had emerged as a result of explicit political interaction or, alternatively, served as a substitute for the acquiescence generated by effective authoritarian regimes.

In any event, two distinct politico-economic alternatives took shape during the following three decades. In Mexico and Brazil, the state was able to maintain a relatively high capacity of initiative in relation to societal actors. In both cases, the superior economic and political resources controlled by the state allowed it to sustain significant growth rates. In the Southern Cone, in contrast, social actors were able to "defend themselves" more effectively against the state's discretionary prerogatives, although to different degrees. Consequently, the boldest state initiatives were consistently blocked, regardless of their source. The principal corollary of this tendency was the onset of institutional paralysis, especially in the cases of Chile and Uruguay.

Nevertheless, a relative equilibrium was maintained within the state-centric matrix until the beginning of the 1970s. Then the classic mechanisms of the model began to show signs of exhaustion, especially in the Southern Cone. From 1971 to 1975, the implicit fiscal pact that had been in operation during the postwar period in Uruguay, Chile, and Argentina began a process of irreversible breakdown.[5]

In the three countries of the Southern Cone, there was an exacerbation of distributive conflicts, the most notable manifestations of which were the evolution from moderate inflation into a system of high inflation and a widening of the fiscal deficit.[6] Similarly, this process coincided with the intensification of the politico-ideological conflict linked to the confrontation of capitalism and socialism. In the three countries, the left consolidated itself as a powerful electoral option at the same time that leftist armed movements — which were more violent in Argentina and Uruguay than in Chile — began to emerge.

The Chilean socialist left consolidated its status as an electoral alternative at the national level and achieved victory in the presidential elections of 1970. In Uruguay and Argentina, in contrast, leftist parties or factions had more modest electoral projections and were depicted as fearful adversaries by military officers anxious to demonstrate the existence of communist subversion. In all three countries, military reaction to leftist assertion was relatively swift. Constitutional governments, regardless of their different politico-ideological configurations, were deposed by military coups that unleashed an unusual degree of repressive violence.

In the 1970s, Brazil and Mexico also manifested some elements of the crisis of the state-centric matrix — namely, an increase of inflation and fiscal deficits and, especially in Mexico, an incipient process of capital flight. However, the "overdetermination of policy" operated in a manner opposite to that of the Southern Cone, prolonging the longevity of the matrix.

The projects implemented by military dictatorships in the Southern Cone combined the objective of physically and politically eliminating the left and its perceived allies with the eradication of state intervention and the behaviors associated with it. In contrast, the authoritarian regimes in Brazil and Mexico implemented not only more moderate political strategies but also, in the case of Mexico, more inclusionary ones. Moreover, the governments of both Mexico and Brazil sought to reverse the incipient decline of the state-centric matrix by taking a new "leap forward." Hence, public investments became the driving force of a deepening of capitalist industrialization whose vitality, in Brazil's case, would extend into the following decade.

Despite the different and even opposite objectives of the dictatorships of the Southern Cone and of the development-oriented regimes of Brazil and Mexico, during the second half of the 1970s both resorted to a classic mechanism of the state-centric matrix. Proponents of the various schools of state-led development, as well as orthodox and anti-*dirigista* reformers, appealed to a financing mechanism that avoided the exacerbation of the zero-sum game: the procurement of foreign loans. Despite some novel features, such as their volume and the ease with which they could be obtained, these loans differed little from the traditional mechanisms of the state-centric matrix. The similarities included their instability, interchangeability, and the absence of strings attached to explicit political exchanges.

Thus, in the case of the Southern Cone military dictatorships, the 1975-1976 and 1981-1982 periods were characterized by a contradiction and also by an illusion that proved to be unfounded. The contradiction was obvious enough: it resided in the fact that the centrality of the state and related institutions of the executive was heightened precisely at a juncture in which the closing of the statist or *dirigiste* cycle was being postulated, at least rhetorically.

The illusion, in turn, was that of inaugurating an authoritarian millen-nium that would construct a new formula to replace the state-centric matrix's pattern of statist politicization. In other words, the objective was to eliminate with one blow the unresolved tensions between democracy and authoritarianism that had characterized the state-centric matrix. The frustration of this illusion coincided with the beginning of a new phase that was inaugurated by the onset of the debt crisis. After 1982, the specific projects of Latin American governments, whether authoritarian or democratic, mattered very little. Changed external conditions significantly reduced existing margins of maneuver and posed a new challenge to Latin American democratic regimes: avoiding the disorganization and chaotic adjustment associated with the exhaustion of the old model.

The Course of the 1980s

In the previous section I asserted that, during the second half of the 1970s, the cases of Brazil and Mexico contrasted with those of the Southern Cone. Brazilian and Mexican elites opted for the intensification of the process of state-led development in a framework of relative optimism. The renewed dynamism of the Mexican economy was achieved as a result of the initially successful efforts of the José López Portillo government to repair deteriorated state-business relations and by the euphoria caused by the initiation of operations of new oil fields located in southeastern Mexico. In Brazil, a process of gradual liberalization controlled from above by the military was initiated in the mid-1970s under the leadership of General Ernesto Geisel. At the same time, public investment was increased in the hopes of stimulating the creation and expansion of capital-intensive export industries of high technological content.

The new dictatorships of Argentina, Chile, and Uruguay, in contrast, sought to dismantle the machinery of state interventionism, and they supported the opening of the economy to foreign trade and to international capital markets. These goals required significant alterations in the behavior of internal actors accustomed to state tutelage. Therefore, the military resorted to formulas which combined economic incentives with penalties for the business sector. And although they were used more selectively, harsh repressive methods continued to be employed by these regimes to liquidate popular and leftist movements.

Despite this fundamental contrast, the neodevelopmentalist authoritarian regimes and the foundational dictatorships of the Southern Cone shared two attributes. The first was cited in the previous section: both resorted to state-centric mechanisms, especially in the form of foreign loans, to finance programs of industrial "deepening." Moreover, the manner of conducting politics was never divorced from the statist framework. In South America, existing despotic attributes were simply heightened, and attempts were made to eradicate the capacity for democratic blackmail that had been traditionally exercised by most social groups vis-à-vis the state.

It is worthwhile to emphasize the second shared attribute in order to understand the sharp break that occurred beginning in 1982. Both new-generation statists and orthodox reformers were inspired by external models and directives. However, the programs implemented at the end of the 1970s sprang from options that had been endogenously generated. It was indeed paradoxical that the phenomenon that made possible the prolongation of the state's relative autonomy in policy making — abundant and inexpensive external credit — contributed to the emergence of new and more severe patterns of dependence in the decade of the 1980s.

The mirage of inexpensive foreign financing dissipated when the global recession intensified after 1981. Real interest rates jumped from near zero to as much as 10 percent, and the flow of external funds was interrupted. The debt crisis became a watershed inaugurating a new era in Latin America. Beginning in 1982, the question was no longer whether or not to face the difficulties of adjustment, or whether it would be desirable to reduce the state. The question was now simply how to do it.

I have elsewhere examined how the debt crisis coincided with a convergence of the political trajectories of the five countries that comprise this analysis (Cavarozzi 1992). They all experienced periods of turbulence with severe macroeconomic imbalances and serious threats to the stability of the political regimes. In the four South American cases, the external shocks coincided with the postulation of democracy as an alternative political model. In the Southern Cone and Brazil, the replacement of authoritarianism, therefore, became one possible outcome of the crisis that occurred at the beginning of the 1980s. Consequently, the issue of democracy was immediately placed on the agenda of the principal political and social actors.

In Mexico, in contrast, no democratic opposition emerged that could realistically aspire to power, despite the erosion suffered by the regime of the Partido Revolucionario Institucional (PRI) during the transition from José López Portillo to Miguel de la Madrid. Because of the weakness of the opposition and the relative strength of the regime, the possibility that the effects of the crisis would result in an overflow of political activity outside established channels was much smaller than in the Southern Cone.

The factors that account for the contrast between the vulnerability of the South American military dictatorships and the relative strength of the Mexican regime will not be analyzed here. Rather, the post-1982 period will be examined in order to compare the performance of the five regimes in handling their economic and political problems during the 1980s, stressing the instances in which they reacted differently. Before doing so, however, I wish to reiterate a point mentioned in the introduction.

In the three countries of the Southern Cone, the decline of the state-centric matrix began in the first half of the 1970s. From 1973 to 1975, the dismantling of the previous model was induced from above in Chile, Uruguay, and Argentina. As a result of the exacerbation of traditional bottlenecks — mainly external and fiscal in nature — as well as acute political conflicts, the

behavior of social and political actors also became disorganized and autonomous relative to government policy objectives.

Although the erosion of traditional patterns of behavior continued, until
1982 none of the three countries achieved much success in generating
alternative patterns organized around market logic. This failure, produced in
part by the application of erroneous economic policies, resulted in serious
internal and external imbalances faced by the three countries in 1981 and
1982. It should be remembered that the serious setbacks suffered since 1980
by the financial systems of Chile and Argentina actually preceded the
explosion of the debt crisis. As I have already noted, at that point similar crises
were also experienced in Brazil and, especially, in Mexico.

The most important consequence of the 1982 crisis was the loss — or
at least severe diminution — of the state's capacity to control the economy
from above. Since the market, or rather the "invisible hand," had failed to
consolidate a new pattern of social behavior, the five countries and practically
all of Latin America faced a new threat: the possibility that reduced ability to
control the economy would dramatically erode order and public authority. All
of this heightened the risk that the decline of the state-centric matrix would
not result in the articulation of an alternative politico-economic model, but
rather in a process of accelerated and self-generating disorder.

Between 1983 and 1989, these risks materialized in Argentina and Brazil.
Chile and Mexico, on the other hand, managed to achieve equilibrations that,
although quite precarious in the latter case, nonetheless allowed a measure
of institutionalized channeling of social and economic behavior. Similarly,
Chile achieved high levels of GNP growth beginning in 1985. This pattern was
later replicated in Mexico at more modest levels. Uruguay occupied an
intermediate position: although closer to the situation of Argentina and Brazil
than that of Chile and Mexico, Uruguayan leaders managed to avoid the
extremes of chaotic adjustment and political dissolution that occurred in
Argentina and Brazil under Raúl Alfonsín and José Sarney.

The partially successful equilibration achieved by Chile and Mexico may
be attributed to three factors. First, the continuity (or regeneration) of relatively
strong state mechanisms. Second, the fact that the restructuring process was
not totally subordinated to restrictions associated to adjustment. And third, the
state's ability to redefine its role, which allowed it to co-direct (in association
with business) the restructuring process with a measure of effectiveness.[7]

The Chilean and Mexican experiences suggest that the process of
disintegration of the state-centric matrix, and its eventual replacement with
another model, has a paradoxical element that has often been ignored.
Success in the transition to an alternative model, characterized as much by
reduced levels of public sector participation in the gross national product as
by the dismantling of traditional regulatory mechanisms, may require the

active presence of a strong state. In its absence, vicious cycles of disorganization could prevail, leading to entropy and rupture of public order as well as the inability to reverse the pernicious phenomena of social marginality and economic decadence.

The risk of remaining trapped in a spiral of disorganization points to the convenience of distinguishing between two different dimensions of state action in the transition toward a model characterized by the primacy of the market. First, the balance between state and market is crucial. State regulation seems "structurally" necessary to guarantee adequate levels of investment in areas such as research and development, maintenance of the physical infrastructure, and education, as well as to assure that equity considerations are not entirely abandoned.

The second consideration is perhaps more conjunctural, although equally important. The presence of a state endowed with a certain autonomy and the capacity effectively to manage instruments of policy determination and implementation appears necessary to prevent the drift of transitions in the direction of chaotic adjustment and political disorganization.

The comparison of the two groups of countries suggests that the successful reconstruction of public authority (Chile), or its reinforcement (Mexico), was achieved in contexts of nondemocratic continuity. On the other hand, the transitions to democracy often coincided with chaotic adjustment or, in a few cases, with the achievement of a mediocre equilibrium "at the bottom of the well," as happened in Uruguay and also in Bolivia. In these last two cases, the maintenance of relatively low inflation rates and the reduction of the fiscal deficit for a period extending beyond two years failed to create the conditions necessary for the restoration of acceptable indices of economic development.

It may be rash to conclude that the economies of Chile and Mexico have "taken off," especially in the latter case. Beyond the issue of whether the present course stabilizes in these countries or not, however, any analysis of the decade of transitions to democracy in South America presents a bleak picture of the way that democratic institutions and successful economic restructuring interacted.

During the post-1982 period, surviving authoritarian regimes and new democracies found themselves confronted as much with the collapse of the old international order and the severe restrictions associated with the degree of indebtedness as with the experience of profound transformations in collective behavior. Both processes drastically eroded the capacity to exercise public authority. A comparison of these two groups of countries can lead us to a simplistic conclusion: that during the crucial 1982-1990 juncture, the surviving authoritarian regimes performed better due to their ability to discipline the different social sectors and administer "bitter pills" while the democracies lacked, or were not able to develop, these capabilities.

It would be a mistake to deny that authoritarian regimes proved to be more effective in administering the process of economic restructuring and avoiding the collapse of the principles of public authority. There is considerable truth, therefore, in the statement that the new civilian governments failed in their attempts to manage the crisis and the restructuring process through democratic institutions. Leaders such as Alfonsín, Sarney (as well as Hernán Siles Zuazo and Alan García), their parties, and the irresponsible opposition they confronted exhibited an utter incapacity to perceive the severity of the crisis fully.

It appears similarly evident that democratic governments, even when led by competent officials, require more time to (re)construct effective state institutions. Democracies cannot take the shortcuts available to despotic regimes and must rely on negotiation and compromise in order to achieve consensus on rules and, often, on substance. However, Latin Americans presently feel a sense of urgency often bordering on desperation. This is certainly not propitious for the effective functioning of representative mechanisms.

Although the administration of the crisis and the restructuring process by Latin American democracies has been largely unsuccessful, superficial conclusions should, nonetheless, be avoided. In those cases where institutional change occurred before the process of restructuring (as in countries where authoritarian regimes were replaced by representative democracies in the first half of the 1980s), the dynamic generated by this political change exacerbated the situation of near ungovernability that had been inherited from the dictatorships. The nondemocratic regimes that survived the turmoil of the beginning of the decade (and also the democratic successors, as in the case of Chile) enjoyed an "overtime" period that allowed them to take advantage of three important circumstances. First, they benefitted from a learning process regarding their own errors and those committed by other emerging democracies. Second, the democratic opposition they faced fully perceived the magnitude of the combination of factors that threatened governability in Latin America. And third, they profited from a change in the approach of international lending institutions, especially those associated with the U.S. government. This approach shifted from an exclusive obsession with the immediate repayment of the debt to the need to restore the long-term financial and economic viability of the countries of the region.

As a preliminary conclusion, I would like to emphasize a corollary that emerges from the discussion above. It has, inevitably, pessimistic overtones. In the 1982-1990 period, the surviving authoritarian regimes — Chile and Mexico — turned out to be better equipped than the new democracies to avoid the most extreme aspects of the processes of chaotic adjustment and disorganization of established social behavior experienced in Latin America. However, this should not lead us to extrapolate to other circumstances and historical contexts authoritarianism's greater effectiveness in managing the crisis and economic restructuring.

The South American military regimes (including that of Chile) exhibited a level of ineptitude similar to that of the democracies, and, indeed, the economic policy errors they committed were at least as serious. Similarly, one of the most important reasons for the relative success of authoritarianism is related to political continuity and its contrast to the turmoil caused by the transitions to democracy.

Finally, recent events — including the return of democracy and continuity of sustained economic growth in Chile — are redefining the conceptual parameters of what constitutes "economic success" and its relation to specific types of political regimes. Thus, it is worthwhile to question whether the types of regimes that proved most adequate for the purpose of avoiding chaotic adjustment and providing for a minimum destruction of state order (the challenge of the 1980s) are also the most effective for the purpose of restoring sustained economic growth and reversing deepening poverty and marginality (the challenge of the 1990s).

The Meaning of Democracy in Contemporary Latin America

This final section will address the theme of the "meaning" of democracy. My objective is to suggest a different conceptual approach regarding the process of democratization. This suggestion concerns important transformations in the way democracy functions in contemporary Latin American political systems and calls for a brief theoretical digression. Most analysts concur on the convenience of defining democracy as a type of political regime. By doing so, we avoid the confusion that ensues when one speaks of "real" or "substantive" democracy, which is conceived of as the opposite of "formal" or "procedural" democracy. However, narrowing the concept of democracy to a type of political regime does not help to understand the relationship between political democracy and broader patterns of social organization.

The issue of the meaning of democracy corresponds to a different analytical level than that embraced by the two approaches dominant in recent works. The first approach focuses on the analysis of the relation between democracy and social structure, and, more specifically, between democracy and capitalist development. The linkage between these two processes has been recently emphasized by Dietrich Rueschemeyer, Evelyne Stephens, and John Stephens (1992). According to these authors, democratization and the emergence and consolidation of democratic regimes depend on, or at least are influenced by, class structures and alliances, the state, and the configuration of transnational power structures.[8]

The basic proposition of Rueschemeyer, Stephens, and Stephens is that capitalist development promotes the emergence and consolidation of democratic regimes by debilitating the land-owning class, which, according to the authors, constitutes the main obstacle to democratization. Capitalist development also strengthens the middle and working classes, which are seen as the principal agents of democratization. The authors' comparative analysis generally substantiates their hypothesis, although it may be pointed out that in some Latin American countries (such as Argentina, Uruguay, the Center-South of Brazil, and certain regions of Mexico) the half-century of agricultural development prior to the First World War actually sustained the emergence of land-owning classes that, although antidemocratic, organized production along capitalist lines.[9]

A second type of reflection underlies the discussion of the different types of democracy. This approach is preoccupied with the "quality" of democratic regimes. The recent propositions formulated by Guillermo O'Donnell (1992 and Chapter 6 in this volume) and Francisco Weffort (1992) regarding "delegative democracy" fit within this framework of analysis. O'Donnell, in particular, maintains that the recent South American transitions are creating a peculiar variety of political democracy, especially in the cases of Brazil, Argentina, and Peru. According to this perspective, these "delegative democracies" combine representative mechanisms with the weakening of the infrastructural power of the state (Mann 1984).

These processes have especially negative effects on popular sectors, the most adversely affected social group. Here the erosion of the state's capacity to enforce the law coincides with the popular classes' disenchantment with the effectiveness of democratic mechanisms for alleviating their problems. This disenchantment translates into a political withdrawal that inclines them to "delegate" their grievances and demands to a new type of leader. These new leaders declare that participation within the framework of representative institutions, as well as "mobilizing" patterns of political action, are obsolete and unproductive.

However, beyond the novel contributions provided by these two approaches, there is another, neglected theme that I wish to explore: the fact that democratic practices and the functioning of democratic institutions have different connotations according to prevailing political arrangements. Two logics coexist in every modern capitalist society, whether in the core or the semiperiphery.

The first is related to competition for political power and the interests linked to its reproduction. The second is associated with the representation of class and citizen interests, one of the fundamental aspects of which is the inclusion, exclusion, or asymmetrical participation of political institutions. These two logics are not reducible to one another but rather are interrelated.

To understand the course of politics in any given society entails deciphering the historically determined nature of these interrelations. These interrelationships may be illustrated through a brief discussion of historical phases of Latin American democratization.

The first stage was that of *democratization of oligarchic regimes.* The sociological approach of Rueschemeyer, Stephens, and Stephens is particularly applicable to this stage because during this period politics was still, as it were, simple and unidimensional. The pressure of the middle and popular sectors, especially those linked to the push toward capitalist development and some segments of the peasantry, was directed toward their inclusion into the political "game" that had been hitherto confined solely to the social and economic elites and their representatives. Demands were essentially antioligarchic, including the clamor for universal suffrage, the elimination of fraudulent electoral practices, the acknowledgment and cessation of repression of middle and popular sector organizations (especially labor unions), and the universal application of the law.

Democratic pressures contributed decisively to the decline of oligarchic regimes and, thus, to the advent of a second phase. Nevertheless, this process did not lead to the establishment of relatively stable political democracies except in one case: that of Uruguay. The final result was rather a hybrid one, with the parallel growth and projection of both democratic and antidemocratic (or authoritarian) forces as essential elements, which I refer to as the *state-centric political formula.*

The tension between democratic and authoritarian forces impacted on the behavior of all relevant actors, ranging from the bourgeoisie to the middle and popular sectors. Moreover, this type of politicization, which I have defined as statist, tended to generate a complex and fragmented political class in which party politicians, government functionaries, interest group representatives, the military, and the intelligentsia coexisted conflictively. This heterogeneous configuration tended to favor extremely varied and even antithetical "mechanisms of representation."

These mechanisms included, among others, the vote, military demands and threats of intervention, influence within bureaucratic echelons, participation in corporate associations, participation in patron-client networks, street mobilization, and the pretended embodiment of national or class interests by individual leaders, ideologues, and the military. The multiplicity of mechanisms was not accidental, since each provided differential advantages to various segments of the political class in the competition for political power.

However, the basic difficulty of statist politicization was that it was not able to produce a stable equilibrium between the diverse modes of *representation* (of either social sectors or the general population) and the patterns of *negotiation* (within the political class). The lack of consensus regarding either a democratic or authoritarian formula had as a corollary the establishment of a structural complicity that was tacitly inherent in the maintenance of a hybrid political formula. Of course, this phenomenon did not exclude the tendency toward "specialization." Indeed, some actors — such as the old oligarchies, important segments of the urban bourgeoisie, and certainly the military — preferentially resorted to antidemocratic threats. However, these actors also often sabotaged the functioning of authoritarian mechanisms and regimes, thus contributing to a pendular return to the condition of fragile equilibrium.

At the same time, the middle and popular sectors, as well as their political and sectorial representatives, tended to specialize in the application of prodemocratic pressure largely based on blackmail. Consequently, adherence to democratic values was generally quite feeble, even in the case of the *democráticos*.[10]

The principal corollary that emerges from these observations is that the search for correlations or affinities between the post-1930 Latin American capitalist model, on the one hand, and democracy and authoritarianism, on the other, does not lead us down a fruitful path. Latin American politics was neither authoritarian nor democratic during the nearly half a century that followed the crisis of 1929-1932.

Therefore, the tendency to reduce the possibilities to a single Rueschemeyer-style dichotomy impoverishes the analysis. For the same reasons, the O'Donnellian "discovery" of an alleged affinity between delayed capitalist industrialization in the semiperiphery and bureaucratic authoritarianism generally confuses the conjunctural moment (that is, the authoritarian wave of the late 1960s and early 1970s) with the long term. In the long term, a hybrid political formula took root, which combined (sometimes in a context of stability and sometimes of instability) both democratic and nondemocratic elements.

The collapse or displacement of the military authoritarian regimes in the 1980s signalled the exhaustion of the state-centric matrix. Although the research on the South American transitions of this decade provides significant theoretical and empirical contributions, most studies generally ignore the fundamental fact that the installation of democratic regimes implied more than the simple removal from power of the military regimes. In addition, these transitions marked the exhaustion of the way of conducting politics that had predominated for almost half a century.[11]

At least in South America, then, the decade of the 1980s was characterized by the twin evolutions to which I have alluded: the end of the military regimes and the extinction of the hybrid formula that sustained both democratic and authoritarian regimes in an unstable equilibrium. The transitions that took place during this decade inaugurated a third phase, the definite characteristics of which are still difficult to identify precisely and whose implications for democracy remain hard to ascertain. Nevertheless, some conjecture regarding the tendencies emerging during the last few years may be advanced.

Depolitization and Social Decomposition

In principle, we may define the recently inaugurated phase by emphasizing those characteristics of the preceding phase that have been either significantly altered or have disappeared. It is possible to discern the overlapping of two processes that are not entirely independent: first, the relative decline in the preeminence of politics; and second, the decomposition of social patterns of behavior that had predominated for nearly half a century.[12] Although the statist politicization of the state-centric matrix weakened institutions and social rules, such rules pervaded almost all social behavior and provided it with coherence.

In other words, the state-centric matrix was characterized by hyperpoliticization. Social behavior, including that taking place within the sphere of "civil society," was preferentially oriented toward the state. For this reason, the exhaustion of the state-centric matrix political formula implied not only a displacement in the centrality of politics but also the disintegration of patterns of traditional behavior and the disarticulation of the identities of collective actors that had structured such behavior in the past.

The results of this process are inherently ambiguous since the traditional modalities of political action combine, as I have indicated, both participation and control from above, negotiation, and naked arbitrariness. In the state-centric formula, the integration of previously excluded sectors and the expansion of "spheres of equality" has a counterpoint in the weakness of institutionalized consensus and a systemic propensity toward the use of violence.[13] In any case, adverse combinations prevailed: governments that retained the monopoly of violence were not distinguished by their respect for constitutional precepts nor by their conviction regarding the desirability of a more or less universal enforcement of the law, and vice versa.

Beyond emphasizing what is disappearing — or in some cases, that which remains but is slowly disintegrating — it is appropriate to inquire how the vacuum created by depolitization and disintegration of past practices is currently being filled. Analysis of this issue requires caution. In every pivotal period of transformation, it is difficult to distinguish mere "transition phenomena" that no doubt will tend to exhaust themselves rapidly from other patterns of behavior that will prove to be more stable and that will probably produce new forms of collective action. At any rate, my intention here is simply to enumerate some existing tendencies without any analytical pretensions.

Abortive Return to the Past

In the 1980s, a series of phenomena implied the decomposition, though not complete extinction, of patterns of behavior associated with the state-centric matrix. First, defensive behaviors emerged and persisted, both in the economic as well as in the politico-cultural spheres, behaviors whose effectiveness was intimately associated with modalities of collective action typical of the state-centric matrix. For example, rigid demands aimed at forcing the state to reconstitute past tutelary and redistributive practices are manifestations of these behaviors.

In most cases, the possibility of favorable state responses to these demands has been undermined. Perhaps the sole exception to this rule, albeit a partial one, involves the case of Mexico. Therefore, past behaviors have generally lost meaning for members of the different social sectors. Formal and informal associations have, for the most part, become relatively empty shells reduced to the role of reproducing ritualistic practices increasingly disconnected from the daily concerns of the people who have undergone a process of privatization and atomization.[14]

A second example of behavioral decomposition manifested itself more specifically in the field of institutionalized party politics. It is related to an erroneous assumption held by many politicians and party militants in Latin America: the supposition that past, state-centric levels of popular political participation and politicization of daily life constituted "natural phenomena" that were not related to, or dependent on, the dominant type of political formula.

The initial acceptance of this premise during the 1980s caused many actors to assume that the task was simply one of expunging politics of its authoritarian and repressive components in order to reconstitute a politicized, participatory citizenry that would strengthen democratic institutions. This erroneous perspective was most often apparent on the left of the political spectrum, with the Brazilian Partidos dos Trabalhadores (PT) and the Peruvian Izquierda Unida being perhaps the most notable cases. Nevertheless, some leaders of traditional political parties (such as the Argentine Unión Cívica Radical) also harbored illusions about the inauguration of a new republican age based on popular participation and the disappearance of antidemocratic threats.

The mirage of (re)building representative and participatory democracy was reinforced by the fact that most of the transitions were characterized by peaceful antidictatorial mobilization and by considerable enthusiasm generated by political parties during the first democratic elections. Nevertheless, in practically every case, this enthusiasm proved short-lived. Most of the population, especially in the cases of Brazil, and Argentina, soon proceeded to accuse not only the democratic governments but also the political parties of responsibility for the decline of living standards, the deterioration of public services, and the disruption of daily lives associated with hyperinflation.

Minimalist Politics

The discrediting of the first postauthoritarian constitutional governments —as dramatically illustrated by the collapse of the Alfonsín and Sarney administrations — had extremely deleterious consequences for party systems, namely, the advent of a new generation of *caudillo* presidents who base their appeal on antipolitical rhetoric and attitudes. The new *caudillos* —exemplified by Carlos Menem, Fernando Collor de Mello, and Alberto Fujimori (prior to the April 1992 putsch) — do not represent a complete rupture with the personalist leadership style typical of the state-centric formula. The earlier version, represented by Juan Perón (1945-1955) and, to a lesser extent, Getúlio Vargas (1950-54) and Carlos Ibáñez del Campo (1952-1958), came to power as a result of relatively clean elections but tended to disregard political parties and to assert that they exercised popular representation above legislative institutions and democratic rules. This trait is shared by the minimalist *caudillos* of our age, who also present two important innovations over the populist leaders of past decades.

First, the new *caudillos* have established a complicity with the masses that reinforces the population's political apathy. After experiencing dramatic declines in their standard of living, as well as suffering the effects of hyperinflation, the popular sectors and important segments of the middle class long for someone who will "get things done" without requiring their participation beyond the act of voting. In fact, those political leaders who still direct appeals at the masses for the purpose of increasing popular participation and mobilization are received with skepticism and suspicion. The new *caudillos* are shrewdly attuned to this collective mood and promise to accomplish their objectives while arguing that political organization and mobilization are counterproductive. Moreover, the Menems and Fujimoris depict collective participation as an obstacle to the exercise of their functions and, indeed, as conducive to the return of corrupt and self-interested politicians.[15]

Secondarily, the new *caudillos* favor a style of leadership in which they attempt to maintain the initiative in an exclusionary fashion, thus permanently generating political innovations linked to an increasingly absorbing and exceedingly centralizing presidency.[16] "Political normalcy" and the gradual construction of institutionalized routines and the sluggish tempo associated with "checks and balances" have a negative connotation in the realm of minimalist politics. Normalcy has now given way to the frantic and constant fabrication of political events, often through the manipulation of information, and to the rapid mobilization of public opinion on any given issue.

Finally, the practices of presidents associated with the minimalist style of politics have rekindled and intensified a trait already present in the state-centric matrix: a significant degree of corruption. In addition to the weakness of mechanisms of politico-administrative accountability and the lack of checks and balances among the branches of government, there is now a substantial measure of new discretionary power afforded to the executive by the privatization of public enterprises.

As demonstrated by presidents Collor and Fujimori, the minimalist style of conducting politics can consume itself quite rapidly. In the case of Peru, the president, supported by the military, carried out an institutional rupture. The putsch enjoyed broad popular support but has inaugurated a new modality of *régimen de excepción*, the final consequences of which are difficult to foresee. In Brazil, the successful impeachment of President Collor de Mello revealed an unexpected vitality of democratic institutions, especially as pertains to the parties, Congress, and the judiciary. However, the institutionalized channeling of a crisis that resulted from an arbitrary and nearly insane style of presidential decision making will not resolve the problem of how these same institutions respond to the economy's ungovernability. The weakness of the Itamar Franco government created a political hiatus that appears quite dangerous in view of the general economic situation and an extremely high rate of inflation.

Argentina's Carlos Menem survives as the only example of a new *caudillo* who is able to maintain democratic institutions while attempting to consolidate a presidential legitimacy that marginalizes both congress and the parties. The Argentine president, however, faces two obstacles that in the past proved to be unsolvable within the existing political regime and the exigencies of the national economy. The most serious of these, that of succession, has plagued Argentine politics since the oligarchic era. Menem confronts the dilemma, as did many of his predecessors, of either effecting a legitimate transfer of power or attempting to prolong his presidential mandate without violating either the constitution or the precarious party system coexistence rules first established around 1983. This challenge is by no means minor to an organization such as the Peronist party, which has historically never experienced a democratic transfer of power, either internally or at the level of the political regime.

The second obstacle confronted by Menem is relatively contextual, although no less serious. This is the dilemma of how to achieve flexibility in the management of the economy — especially as pertains to monetary and foreign exchange policy — without eroding the precarious confidence generated among the business community by the so-called Cavallo plan. In sum, the Argentine political system, although not necessarily the democratic regime, presently hangs by the weakest of threads.

The cases of Peru, Argentina, and Brazil, postulated by O'Donnell as the clearest examples of delegative democracy, reinforce my reticence to utilize such an all-inclusive category to designate a new type of political regime (O'Donnell 1992 and this volume). I believe that neither Raúl Alfonsín nor José Sarney (less so Isabel Perón) can be successfully explained within this framework. In contrast, Carlos Menem, Fernando Collor de Mello, and Alberto Fujimori — until his *autogolpe* — more clearly approximate the profile of leaders who exercise top executive power in a context associated with delegative democracy. However, the fragility and transitional nature of the processes with which these leaders are associated suggests that we are witnessing "transition phenomena." If I am correct, the contemporary political context can best be portrayed as a combination of minimalist politics and an erosion of state power that has drastically reduced the state's capacity to exercise the monopoly of violence and to enforce the law in a relatively universal manner.

The Key to the Future:
A State Anchored in the Politics of Explicit Interaction

One of the central arguments of this chapter is that the Latin American state-centric matrix was not exclusively related to import-substitution industrialization or to the partial closing of the economy. This model was also linked to a political formula and the manner in which conflicts of interest and of values were resolved. In this formula, the state partially substituted for the market insofar as it made decisions involving transactions among private agents on the basis of political and administrative criteria.

At the same time, however, the state constituted itself as the anchor of a political regime organized in accordance to hierarchical and nonrepresentative principles that promoted the incorporation of previously excluded sectors. As a result, political democracy, although never completely abolished, was feeble in state-centric Latin America. Market behavior, for its part, never achieved total independence from patterns of state regulation that, as a general rule, neither adhered to the law nor emerged from explicit or institutionalized mechanisms of political interaction.

One of the corollaries of statist politicization in the previous model was the fact that each expansive episode of state intervention — a process I have characterized as a permanent "escape forward" — eroded the precarious foundation of the political regime as a functional entity. This tendency, which culminated explosively in the cases of Brazil and the Southern Cone, contributed to the emergence of another poorly understood phenomenon: the chronic weakness of an over-extended state. This state gradually postponed its fiscal and political crisis by successively creating mechanisms of reciprocal compensation that lacked a common "clearinghouse."

The military interlude of the 1970s attempted to resolve the bottlenecks of the state-centric formula through the imposition of despotic regimes (and their subsequent replacement with various forms of "tutelary" democracy) as well as through the eradication of the interventionist state. But the relevance of the Southern Cone dictatorships certainly does not stem from the achievement of these objectives. With the partial exception of Chile, the military dictatorships were unable to achieve a minimum stabilization of authoritarian rule. Moreover, their anti-state projects were often contradictory and reversible. On the other hand, the foundational authoritarian regimes of the 1970s *did* act as catalysts to the final crisis of the state-centric matrix, which erupted full blown during the next decade and which spread throughout the region.

Therefore, the principal legacy of the 1980s was collapse of the complex system of networks that linked the different social spheres, including 1) economic behaviors, 2) the pattern of integration into the international system, 3) the associative modalities of the diverse social sectors, and 4) the shared understanding of the "meaning" of politics, which hinged on the belief that everything should pass through a state-controlled network of "public" agencies and through state-dominated patterns of interaction internalized by "private" individuals and organizations. The loosening and rupture of these links eventually created a general process of disarticulation that, as in the case of Peru and, increasingly, Brazil, presently threatens the national integrity of some countries.

Thus, one of the alternative courses taking shape during the transitional interregnum resulting from the exhaustion of the state-centric matrix consists of a pattern of disarticulation and atrophy caused by the de-statization of Latin American societies. This assertion does not imply a disregard for the positive aspects of the present situation, which include a possibility of creating a market that, being relatively more independent from state intervention, may allow for a fuller assumption of the risks associated with entrepreneurial initiative. Reinforcement of the present trend toward the greater autonomy of civil society is also a distinct possibility, particularly given the disintegration of the various modalities of state tutelage that in the past shaped individual and group behavior. Last but not least, the erosion of hybrid political regimes reduces the risk of repeating repressive authoritarian episodes that have for so long afflicted state-centric Latin America.

Nevertheless, it would be erroneous to assume that the tendencies present in each of these spheres — the market, civil society, and the political regime — will "naturally" lead to the formation of societies characterized by improvements in general welfare, justice, and social harmony. As we have seen, the experiences of the last decade provide us with ample evidence of how 1) "more market" (and "less state") may imply more exploitation and marginalization, 2) "more civil society" (and, in a different sense, "less state") may involve increased atomization and anomie, and 3) "more political democracy" may produce not only increased apathy but also a devaluation of politics, which loses significance in terms of everyday life and the specific exigencies associated with problems affecting the majority of the population.

The challenge faced by Latin Americans in the 1990s consists of creating a politics capable of reconstituting, on a new foundation, a developmentalist state capable of propelling their societies beyond the limits of the state-centric matrix. The challenge, in other words, is to replace the exhausted logic of statism, not with a de-staticized society but with an alternative political logic. This new logic must emerge from broad-based negotiations within a representative democratic regime among the relevant social and political actors to define the role of the state and its limits. Unless some version of politico-religious fundamentalism were to triumph in Latin America, it is difficult to conceive of this new pattern of conducting politics as being anything other than democratic.

Notes

1. The process of configuring a new pattern of relations between state and society began in the 1930s in Argentina, Brazil, Mexico, Chile, and Uruguay.

2. The archetypical cases of the refoundational authoritarian regimes of the 1970s were the Chilean (1973), Uruguayan (1973), and Argentine (1976) military regimes. In a previous work, I agreed with the analysis made by Héctor Schamis (1991), who stresses the error of including the refoundational authoritarian regimes of the 1970s in the same category as the bureaucratic-authoritarian dictatorships that had emerged during the previous decade in Brazil and Argentina (Cavarozzi 1992). As opposed to other previous or contemporary military dictatorships, the three refoundational regimes aimed at a radical reform of the economy and politics of the state-centric matrix. Nevertheless, toward the end of the 1970s, Brazil and Peru, which had been originally exemplified a different genre of authoritarian regime, assumed some of the characteristics of the refoundational dictatorships.

3. "Instability" refers to cyclical movements in the implementation of fiscal mechanisms that determined permanent alterations in the benefits and losses affecting diverse actors. For its part, the interchangeability of fiscal mechanisms was related to their short life span. This was partly related to the depletion of specific resources available to the state, but the principal cause of this phenomenon was the learning process undertaken by the social actors, who modified their behavior in order to protect themselves from state financing mechanisms that were detrimental to their interests and in order to exert pressure in support of those who favored their objectives. The result, as I noted, was a lack of consensus regarding public policies.

4. This politicization pattern is similar to the one alluded to by Atul Kohli in his analysis of contemporary politics in India (Kohli 1990). Kohli describes it as "a politicization pattern that emerges when the state is able to affect the lifetime opportunities of many social groups and when this state is accessible by democratic means." In Latin America there were certainly multiple paths of access to the state, and these were not limited to democratic procedures.

5. Ricardo Carciofi (1990) has formulated one of the sharpest analyses of how the gradual disorganization of the state-centric model's fiscal mechanisms accelerated in the case of Argentina during the 1970s, culminating in the explosion of 1975-1976.

6. The high inflation systems of contemporary Latin America translated into a jump in average annual rates from two to three digits and the consistent use of indexing mechanisms.

7. In contemporary Latin America, one of the necessary ingredients for the reconstruction of dynamic economies is the presence of a development-oriented state, one neither confronted by an antagonistic bourgeoisie nor dominated by it. This is, in part, what Peter Evans (1992) refers to in his concept of "embedded autonomy." However, Evans warns of a "complication" that is especially relevant to Latin American

cases but which he, nonetheless, sidesteps in his discussion. His list of efficient developmentalist states is almost completely limited to East Asian exclusionary states. The obstacles to achieving an effective balance between autonomy and embeddedness are much more serious in situations where capitalists are not only embedded in the state but so are other social sectors. It is more difficult to achieve the equilibrium Evans refers to in those societies where politics are complex and less concerned embeddedness necessarily involves a much broader array of social actors, in contrast to the East Asian cases, in which the central issue has primarily revolved around relations between capitalists and an authoritarian state.

8. Although the treatment given by these authors to the role of the state and transnational power structures is not as solid as their keen analysis of class structure in Western Europe, Latin America, and the Caribbean, they nonetheless advance significantly beyond the classic work of Barrington Moore.

9. Note that the central preoccupation of Rueschemeyer, Stephens, and Stephens is sociological in nature. Their objective is to compare the impact of different class structures on the probability of emergence and consolidation of democratic regimes.

10. In any case, it is worthwhile to identify some significant differences among cases in this analysis. In Mexico, the political regime structured around PRI hegemony did not rely on a high degree of "specialization" regarding the type of pressure applied by the different actors. The broader consensus regarding the balance between democracy and authoritarianism to a large extent explains Mexican institutional stability. At the other end of the spectrum, Argentine and Brazilian social actors exhibited democratic and/or authoritarian tendencies in a much clearer fashion. The result was a pendular oscillation between democracies and essentially weak authoritarian regimes, with particularly spasmodic cycles in the case of Argentina. In Chile, on the other hand, the institutional stability of the 1932-1973 period was based on a permanent reform of the rules of the political game and the political exclusion of large sectors of the population until the 1960s. Only Uruguay was able to consolidate a relatively stable polyarchy, which was based on the formal or informal predominance of the Colorado party until 1958, and which itself collapsed between 1971 and 1973.

11. Although the authoritarian enclaves mentioned by Manuel Antonio Garretón (1994) have not wholly disappeared, and the possibility of future antidemocratic reversals cannot be ruled out, what is certain is that one of the sequels of the change in the course of democracy is the exhaustion of the particular authoritarian model imposed on South America for such a long period.

12. The ambiguous nature of the new processes was in different forms suggested to me by comments from Blanca Heredia, Antonio Camou, and René Millán. Obviously, I take responsibility for the reflections they inspired.

13. This propensity, in some cases, manifested itself primarily at the level of the global political system (these were the more unstable systems, such as Argentina and Brazil). In other cases, violence prevailed to a larger degree in the informal political interactions of diverse social spheres (perhaps the case of Mexico was in this sense the most extreme).

14. I have addressed this topic in a previous article (Cavarozzi 1992), in which I referred to trends of intra- and inter-organizational erosion.

15. In the minimalist style of politics, parties and their leaders are portrayed as pursuing narrow factional interests and even questionable individual benefits. Unfortunately, the spectacle displayed by most South American parties does not much differ from this self-serving assessment. Parties are plagued by factionalism and the most aberrant forms of clientelism. These tendencies reinforce assertions to the effect that it is best to bypass legislative institutions in the decision-making process.

16. This phenomenon is related to a redefinition of the role of the media, especially television, in Latin America.

References

Carciofi, Ricardo. 1990. "La disarticulación del pacto fiscal: Una interpretación sobre la evolución del sector público argentino en la década de los ochenta." *Documento de la CEPAL* 36.

Cavarozzi, Marcelo. 1992. "Beyond Transitions to Democracy in Latin America." *Journal of Latin American Studies* 24 (2).

Cavarozzi, Marcelo. 1978. "Elementos para una caracterización del capitalismo oligárquico." *Revista Mexicana de Sociología* XL (4).

Dos Santos, Wanderley Guilherme. 1978. *Ordem Burguesa e Liberalismo Político.* São Paulo: Duas Cidades.

Evans, Peter. 1992. "The State as Problem and Solution: Predation, Embedded Autonomy and Structural Change." In *The Politics of Adjustment: International Constraints, Distributive Justice, and the State*, eds. Stephan Haggard and Robert Kaufman. Princeton, N.J.: Princeton University Press.

Garretón, Manuel Antonio. 1994. "The Political Dimension of Processes of Transformation in Chile." In *Democracy, Markets, and Structural Reform in Contemporary Latin America: Argentina, Bolivia, Brazil, Chile, and Mexico*, eds. William C. Smith, Carlos H. Acuña, and Eduardo A. Gamarra. New Brunswick, N.J.: North-South Center/Transaction.

Hirschman, Albert. 1981. "The Social and Political Matrix of Inflation: Elaborations on the Latin American Experience." In *Essays in Trespassing: Economics to Politics and Beyond*, ed. Albert Hirschman. Cambridge: Cambridge University Press.

Kohli, Atul. 1990. *Democracy and Discontent: India's Growing Crisis of Governability.* Cambridge: Cambridge University Press.

Mann, Michael. 1984. "The Autonomous Power of the State." *Archives Européenes de Sociologie* XXV (2).

O'Donnell, Guillermo. 1992. "Democracia Delegativa?" *Cuadernos del CLAEH* 17.

O'Donnell, Guillermo, and Philippe Schmitter. 1986. *Tentative Conclusions about Uncertain Democracies.* Baltimore, Md.: The Johns Hopkins University Press.

O'Donnell, Guillermo, Philippe Schmitter, and Laurence Whitehead, eds. 1986. *Transitions From Authoritarian Rule.* Vols. I-IV. Baltimore, Md.: The Johns Hopkins University Press.

Offe, Claus. 1983. "Competitive Party Democracy and the Keynesian Welfare State." *Policy Studies* 15.

Rueschemeyer, Dietrich, Evelyne Huber Stephens, and John D. Stephens. 1992. *Capitalist Development and Democracy.* Chicago: University of Chicago Press.

Sachs, Jeffrey. 1985. "External Debt and Macroeconomic Performance in Latin America and East Asia." *Brookings Papers on Economic Activity* 2.

Schamis, Héctor. 1991. "Reconceptualizing Latin American Authoritarianism in the 1970s: From Bureaucratic-Authoritarianism to Neoconservatism." *Comparative Politics* 23 (2).

Weffort, Francisco. 1992. *Qual Democracia?* São Paulo: Companhia de Letras.

Williamson, John. 1990. *Latin American Adjustment: How Much Has Happened?* Washington, D.C.: Institute for International Economics.

Chapter Six

The State, Democratization, and Some Conceptual Problems
(A Latin American View with Glances at Some Post-Communist Countries)

Guillermo O'Donnell

The State and New Democracies

In the last two decades, the breakdown of various authoritarian systems has led to the emergence of a number of democracies or, more precisely, polyarchies, as defined in Robert Dahl's (1971) classic formulation. Several scholars have shown there are various types of polyarchies. Arend Lijphart (1968 and 1984) pioneered the effort, showing that polyarchies can differ in dimensions as important as whether access to and the exercise of public authority is based on majoritarian or consensual rules. But polyarchies share crucial characteristics: they are all representative, institutionalized democracies.

In contrast, most of the newly democratized countries are not moving toward a representative, institutionalized democratic regime, nor do they seem likely to do so in the foreseeable future. They are polyarchies of a different type — one which has not yet been theorized. This chapter is a preliminary attempt to contribute to that theoretical effort.[1] It is a warranted exercise for two reasons. First, a sufficient theory of polyarchy should encompass all existing (political) democracies, not just the representative, institutionalized ones. Second, since many of the new democracies have a peculiar political dynamic, one should not assume that their societal impacts will be similar to those of present *and* past representative, institutionalized polyarchies.[2]

Recent typologies of new democracies based on the characteristics of the preceding authoritarian regime, or on the modalities of transition, have limited power for predicting what happens following the installation of the first democratically elected government. Three countries are of central concern here — Argentina, Brazil, and Peru. Argentina experienced transition by collapse, while Brazil's transition may have been the most protracted and probably the most negotiated (although not formally pacted) transition known. Both were preceded by exclusionary bureaucratic-authoritarian regimes. Peru, on the other hand, experienced transition from an inclusionary populist variety of military-authoritarian regime. In spite of these differences, it seems clear that following the transition from authoritarianism in these countries (as well as in Ecuador, Bolivia, the Dominican Republic, the Philippines, all the democratizing or liberalizing East Asian and African countries, and most of the post-communist ones), they too share important characteristics, indicating some convergence toward a "non-institutionalized" political form.[3]

Apart from describing their political and economic misadventures, the existing literature has done little more than indicate which attributes — representativeness, institutionalization, and the like — these countries do *not* have. However valuable these contributions, they do not yield needed theoretical clues. Furthermore, the teleological characterization of emergent democracies according to the absence of certain attributes hinders conceptualization of the differences among emergent democracies. Other, more policy- and "elite"-oriented analyses offer useful advice for democratizing political leaders, but the practicability of such prescriptions is contingent on the contextual situation in which those leaders find themselves.

For the study of "normal" polyarchies, the conceptual baggage of political science may be satisfactory, but to analyze the present situation and the prospects for most new democracies in Asia, Africa, Latin America, and Europe, I am convinced we must go back and do some basic work in political and legal sociology. Even though this chapter will refer primarily to Argentina, Brazil, and Peru, many of the points made should have wider applicability. Intriguing similarities or convergence with cases outside this group will occasionally be noted.

The analysis that follows is premised on one point: states are interwoven in various complex ways with their respective societies. This embeddedness implies that the characteristics of each state and society greatly influence which type of democracy will be likely to consolidate and which will merely endure or eventually break down. However obvious they may be, we have not sufficiently pursued the implications of these statements for the *problématique* of democratization. One explanation for this failing is that we deal in concepts which, as formulated in most of the contemporary literature, are not very helpful for our subject. This is especially true of the concept of the "state."

The state should not be conflated with the state apparatus, with the public sector, or with the aggregate of public bureaucracies. The latter unquestionably are part of the state, but they are not all of it. The state is also a set of social relations that establishes and maintains a certain order via centralized coercive authority over a given territory. Relations are formalized in a legal system that is created and backed by the state. The legal system is a constitutive dimension of the state and of the order that it establishes.

This order is neither equal, nor socially impartial. Under both capitalism and bureaucratic socialism, the order underlies and reproduces asymmetrical power relationships. But it is nevertheless an order in that manifold social relationships are based upon stable (if not necessarily approved) norms and expectations.

In one of those moments when ordinary language expresses the power relationships in which language itself is embedded — when decisions are made at the political center (the "orders given") — those decisions usually "give order," in the sense that those commands are regularly obeyed. Acquiescence affirms and reproduces the existing social order. As Max Weber argued, social relations, including those of daily, preconscious acceptance of political authority, can be based on tradition, fear of punishment, pragmatic calculation, habituation, legitimacy, or the effectiveness of the law.

Effectiveness of the law consists of innumerable habituated behaviors that consciously or not are consistent with the prescriptions of the law.[4] Effectiveness is based on the widely held expectation, borne out by exemplary evidence, that such law will be enforced by a central empowered authority. This is the supporting texture of the order established and guaranteed by the contemporary nation-state. The law (including the habituation to which the expectation of its regular enforcement leads) is a constitutive element of the state; it is the "part" that provides the regular, underlying framework of the social order existing over a given territory.

In both the Continental and Anglo-Saxon traditions, the law is a codified dimension subject to the interpretations of professionalized knowledge. The law has its own organizational expressions, which are highly ritualized and institutionalized in contemporary democracies. Congress is understood to be the place where the debate and enactment of the primary laws of the land takes place, and the judiciary where conflicts of interest and arguments about the very meaning of the political community are tested and decided. As occurs with other aspects of the state, congress and the judiciary are perceivable embodiments of the broader phenomenon consisting of the social effectiveness of law.

Recognition of the law as a constitutive dimension of the state has been hindered by the approaches that have dominated Anglo-Saxon political science since the "behavioral revolution." Similarly, in spite of the contributions by Max Weber, Herman Heller, and others, approaches that prevailed in Europe were narrowly legalistic and have been based on a formalistic analysis of the written law, with scant attention to its sociological and political aspects. Both great traditions have been blind to the state as a complex reality embedded in its organizational, bureaucratic and legal dimensions.

Yet another dimension of the state is the ideological. The state (more precisely, the state apparatus) claims to be, and is normally believed to be, a state-for-the-nation. From explicit discourses up to the recurrent invocation of the symbolisms of nationhood, the state is the creator of the order discussed above. In all societies, that order is unequal, though from the apex of the state it may be claimed that the order is an equal one for everyone *qua* member of the nation. But this aspect of partial concealment (which is supported by the law, which structures the inequalities entailed by that order) does not preclude two fundamental realities.

First, this order is actually the supreme collective good. It furnishes generalized social predictability backed by eventually decisive actions of appropriate public bureaucracies. Second, even though it does not extend to other social relations, equality guaranteed to all citizens of the nation is crucial for the exercise of political rights entailed by a working democracy and, also, for the effectiveness of individual guarantees consecrated in the liberal tradition.

From this perspective, citizenship is not limited to the narrowly defined confines of the political. Citizenship is at stake, for example, when a party which perceives it has a legitimate grievance may not call upon a legally competent public agency to intervene and adjudicate the issue fairly. Even in the apparently more private realms of common law, the legal system puts the *public dimension* up for legal adjudication by a properly authorized agency of the state.

This inherently public dimension of private relationships (or, equivalently, this texturing by the state-as-law of those relationships) is violated when, for example, a peasant is *de facto* denied access to the judiciary in a complaint against the landowner. This "private" right must be seen as no less constitutive of citizenship than the "public" right of voting without coercion.

The crises in Argentina, Brazil, and Peru (as well as other countries in Latin America and elsewhere) affect more than the social and economic realms: each of these countries is suffering a profound crisis of state. The crisis of state exists along the three dimensions just discussed: the state as a collection of bureaucracies capable of discharging their duties with reasonable efficacy, the effectiveness of laws, and the plausibility of the claim that state agencies normally make decisions according to some conception of the public good.[5]

In contrast to the protracted crisis of state-centered and inward-oriented patterns of capital accumulation in these countries, other recently democratized or liberalizing ones have been able to evade similar crises due to specific circumstances that do not concern us here. In this group are Spain, Portugal, South Korea, Taiwan, and Chile, each of which emerged as an export-oriented economy actively integrated into world markets and relying on a lean but powerful and activist state apparatus.

Too often contemporary discussions of the state are obscured by the emphasis on the size and relative weight of the state apparatus. In most newly democratized countries, the state is indeed too large, resulting in numerous negative consequences. But in this context, the antonym of "big" is not "small" but rather "lean." Needed is a stream-lined, more effective set of public organizations which is capable of creating solid roots for democracy, addressing issues of social equity, and generating conditions for economic growth sufficient to sustain advances in both democracy and social equity.

A second factor too often overlooked concerns the strength or weakness of the state as a whole, including the state apparatus. Regardless of its size, a state apparatus may or may not effectively establish legality over its territory. The definition of a strong state is then not determined by the size of its bureaucracies but rather by its ability to establish such legality and to be perceived by its populace as engaged in more than the pursuit of particularistic interests. I argue below that current attempts at reducing the size and deficits of the state-as-bureaucracy are also destroying the state-as-law and undermining the ideological legitimation of the state. The many nefarious consequences of this process include threats to the long-run success of the economic policies that inspire state-shrinking attempts, not to mention to the institutionalization of democracy.

Current theories of the state often assume, as do current theories of democracy, that a high degree of homogeneity exists both in the territorial and functional scope of the state and the social order it supports. It is seldom asked (and even more rarely problematized) if such order, and the orders issued by the state apparatus, have similar effectiveness across the national territory and at every level of the stratified society.[6] The ideal of "equality before the law" has not been achieved fully in any country, as can be seen in the class biases universally found in the administration of justice. Scandinavian countries come quite close to full homogeneity, while the United States, both territorially and functionally, hovers close to the lower limit among contemporary institutionalized democracies.

In Latin America the countries of relatively high homogeneity (especially territorial) are the ones which have an older and more solid democratic tradition — Costa Rica, Chile, and Uruguay. Peru is the polar opposite. Bolivia and Ecuador are also close to extreme heterogeneity. Brazil and Mexico, in spite of decades of centralizing authoritarian rule, also are cases of high territorial and functional heterogeneity. Argentina lies somewhere along the middle of this continuum, together with Venezuela and Colombia — two fairly old but currently troubled democracies.

What happens when the effectiveness of law extends irregularly (if it does not disappear altogether) across territory and functions (including class, ethnicity, and gender relations)? What kind of state (and society) is this? What influence may these factors have on the type of democracy that might emerge?

I will limit myself to discussing some themes related to the crisis of the state in the three dimensions identified above. In these situations, ineffective states coexist with autonomous, territorially based spheres of power. States are unable to regulate social life effectively across their territories. Provinces or districts peripheral to the national center (which are usually hardest hit by economic crises and are already endowed with weaker bureaucracies than the center) create or reinforce systems of local power.

Peripheral power loci tend toward the extremes of personalistic rule — patrimonial, even sultanistic — open to all sorts of violent and arbitrary practices. In many emerging democracies, the effectiveness of a national order embodied in the law and the authority of the state fades away beyond the boundaries of urban centers. Even in those centers, functionally and territorially, the public dimension of the state often evaporates.

Urban areas are witnessing alarming increases in petty and organized crime, including drug trafficking; unlawful police interventions; the official use of torture and summary execution of suspects from poor or otherwise stigmatized sectors; the number of children abandoned to fend for themselves on the street; and the denial of basic rights to women and various minorities. More than evidence of a severe process of urban decay, these problems mark scant progress relative to the preceding authoritarian period. Most importantly, they indicate the increasing inability of the state to regulate effectively.[7]

Public spaces disappear, invaded by the desperate misery of many and replaced by the fear of using them. The insecurity reflected in the seclusion of rich neighborhoods and the ordeal of using public transportation shrinks public spaces and leads to a perverse kind of privatization that spills into other spheres. To be sure, these ills are not new, and some are more acute in one country than another. But unquestionably, they have worsened with the superimposition of a huge crisis on a feeble process of democratization.

Consider those regions where local powers (both those formally public as well as *de facto*) establish power circuits that operate according to rules which are inconsistent with, if not antagonistic to, the law that supposedly regulates the national territory. These are systems of private power (or, better, of privatized power, since some of the main actors hold state positions), where many rights and guarantees of democratic legality have no effectiveness. This phenomena extends to numerous private relationships which are usually decided, even by the judiciary of those regions, on the basis of the naked power asymmetries that exist among the parties.

These regions — which I am tempted to call "neofeudalized" — contain state organizations at the national, provincial, and municipal levels. But the obliteration of legality deprives regional power circuits, including state agencies, of the public, lawful dimension without which the national state and the order it supports vanish. The mistake of reifying the state may not be apparent when theorizing about homogeneous countries, but it becomes evident when the obliteration of the public dimension of state organizations makes them a part of power circuits that are perversely privatized.[8] Areas characterized by the evaporation of the state's public dimension are parts of the northeast and the entire Amazon region in Brazil, the highlands in Peru, and various provinces in the center and northwest of Argentina. In these places, the state has undergone an odd "reification" in the form of organizations that are, in fact, privatized, often sultanistic, circuits of power.

Although these characteristics of Latin America are well known, no attempt has been made to link them with the types of democracy that have emerged in Argentina, Brazil, Peru, and elsewhere. For that purpose, let us imagine a map in which the areas appearing in blue designate places where there is a high degree of state presence, both functionally and territorially (meaning the existence of reasonably effective bureaucracies and the effectiveness of properly sanctioned legality). The color green indicates a high degree of territorial penetration, but a significantly lower presence in functional/class terms. Finally, brown designates a very low level or absence of both dimensions. Thus, a map of Norway would be dominated by blue. The United States would show a combination of blue and green, with important brown spots in the South and in the large cities. Brazil and Peru would be mostly brown. Argentina would have relatively fewer brown regions, but a temporal map series would reveal brown areas to be on the increase.[9]

In brown areas, there are elections, governors, and national and state legislators. In many cases, these regions are heavily over-represented in the national legislatures. Even when nominally affiliated with national parties, parties operating in brown regions are no more than personalistic machines dependent on the privileges they can extract from national and local state agencies. Parties and local governments function on the basis of personalism, familism, prebendalism, clientelism, and the like. It is a world familiar to anthropologists which functions according to an elaborate, unwritten set of rules. In contrast to "traditional" societies, however, there are big, complex state bureaucracies within which extremely politicized and poorly paid bureaucrats obfuscate the very meaning of the term "corruption."

These circuits of power are re-presented at the center of national politics, beginning with the congress, the institution that, supposedly, is the source of nationally encompassing legality. In general, the interests defended by the "brown" legislators are quite limited: maintenance of the system of privatized domination that has elected them and the channelling of as many state resources as possible toward that system. Their votes are, thus, conservative and opportunistic. They depend on the exchange of "favors" with the executive and various state bureaucracies and, under weakened executives that need congressional support, they often gain control of the state agencies that furnish those resources. These conquests increase the fragmentation (and the deficits) of the state — the brown spots invade even the state's bureaucratic apex.

Furthermore, the game that these individuals play (in and out of congress) is facilitated by the lack of ideological content of their parties (which in itself is not necessarily bad). The opportunism and lack of party discipline — in situations where changing parties or creating new ones can be done at virtually no cost — makes an extreme *transformismo* the rule. Recent studies have noted the negative consequences of *transformismo* for the functioning of congress and the emergence of a reasonably stable party system, as well as for other aspects of the state (see Mainwaring 1990).

These consequences do not augur well for the institutionalization of democracy. For obvious reasons, the behavior of these politicians converges with the delegative, Caesaristic orientations of the executive, which is hostile to any form of horizontal accountability. Despite acute conflicts between legislators and the executive, the two combine forces to block the emergence of genuinely representative institutions.

In one sense, a "brown regime" can be considered representative in that it is consistent with the reality of countries whose patterns of political representation render their societies even more heterogenous. The problem is that this representativeness entails the introjection into the very center of power politics of authoritarianism — understood here as the denial of the public nature and of the effective legality of a democratic state and, hence, of citizenship.[10]

Our mapping exercise raises some important issues which are not developed here. What types of states are found in countries in which brown areas dominate? What kind of democratic regime, if any, can be established over such heterogeneity? To what extent may we apply theories of the state and democracy that assume far more homogeneity to our cases? Such questions have been central to the comparative endeavors of the social sciences. But they must now be revived and specified since the generalized perception of the universal victory of capitalism, and perhaps democracy, has led to their neglect. Failure to do so may lead us to repeat the mistakes of the 1960s, when many theories and comparisons consisted of the ethnocentric application of supposedly universally valid paradigms that ignored the structured variation to be found outside of the developed world. Today, mainstream economists suffer acutely from this bias, and sociologists and political scientists are hardly immune to its influence.

We should not forget that in a properly functioning democracy, legality is universalistic, and it can be successfully invoked by anyone, regardless of a person's position in society. Drawing on an old discussion, can the attributes "democratic" and "authoritarian" be applied to the state, or should they be exclusively reserved for the regime? The answer to this question, of course, depends on how we define state and regime.

With regard to regime, the definition proposed by Phillipe Schmitter and myself bears repeating: "the ensemble of patterns, explicit or not, that determines the forms and channels of access to principal governmental positions, the characteristics of the actors who are admitted and excluded from such access, and the resources [and] strategies that they can use to gain access" (O'Donnell and Schmitter 1986, 73). With some variations, this kind of definition is widely accepted. The definition of the state, however, is problematic. Against the prevailing view, my argument leads to the conclusion that attributes such as "democratic" or "authoritarian" do not only correspond to the regime but also to the state.

The logic of my position can be seen by reasoning *a contrario*. An authoritarian context has a fundamental characteristic: there is no legal system that guarantees the effectiveness of rights and that assures that individuals and groups can prevail against rulers, the state apparatus, and others at the top of the existing social or political hierarchy (or, if a legal system does exist, it lacks real effectiveness, or can be annulled *ad hoc*, or is subordinate to secret rules or to the whim of the rulers).

Authoritarianism is characterized by a truncated legality. Even in the case of institutionalized authoritarianism, the laws do not guarantee their enforcement against those in power. This affects a constitutive dimension of the state: the type of legality (which, in extreme cases, may entail absolute arbitrariness) that textures the particular order enforced over a territory. From this point of view, I do not see how we can avoid the conclusion that the state may also be authoritarian.

The converse also holds well. As long as a legal system includes the rights and guarantees of Western constitutionalism *and* public powers exist which are capable and willing to enforce (according to properly established procedures) such rights and guarantees even against other public powers, that state and the order it helps to implant and reproduce are democratic. Unlike the truncated legality of the authoritarian state, that of the democratic state, as Hans Kelsen argued in a somewhat different context, is complete. Democratic legality "closes" its own circuits by the universalistic application of its rules even against other state organizations. This feature is what differentiates the blue areas from the extensive and increasing brown regions of many new democracies.

Countries with large brown areas are schizophrenic democracies with a complex mix — both functionally and territorially — of important democratic and authoritarian traits. The state's democratic legality fades out along certain planes whose frontiers are defined by geography, class, ethnicity, or some combination of all three.

As a political form effective over a territory, democracy is necessarily connected with citizenship. Citizenship can exist only within the legality of a democratic state. Just because universal citizenship is an ideal which existing democracies only approximate does not mean the growing brown areas in many new democracies can be written off as irrelevant to theories of state and democracy. Nor should we assume that some inherent virtuous effect of political democracy or economic reform will eliminate those areas. The powerful way that authoritarian and democratic dimensions intermix in our cases demands reconceptualization of the very nature of the state and of the idiosyncracies of democracy (and regime) that exist there.

A state that is unable to enforce its legality supports low-intensity citizenship. In most brown areas of newly democratized countries, the *political* rights of polyarchy are respected. Typically, individuals are not subject to direct coercion when voting, and votes are counted fairly. In principle, individuals can form almost any sort of organization, they can express their opinions without censorship, and they can move about freely within and outside the national territory. These regions meet the attributes of polyarchy. This distinguishes between, say, Poland and Argentina, and Romania and Guatemala; whatever their constitutions say, the actual workings of political life disqualify the latter as polyarchies.

Among the countries that meet the criteria of polyarchy, different degrees and dimensions of democracy can be distinguished with references to equity and equality in various societal spheres or, equivalently, to social and economic democratization (O'Donnell and Schmitter 1986). Yet the concept of low-intensity citizenship does not refer to those (admittedly, very important) issues. Rather it refers specifically to the political sphere, to the *political* theory of democracy, or polyarchy.

As noted above, in brown areas of new democracies, specifically political conditions for the existence of polyarchy are usually met. But peasants, slum-dwellers, Indians, women, and others often are unable to receive fair treatment in the courts or to obtain from state agencies the services to which they are entitled or to be safe from police violence, and so forth. These restrictions are "extra-polyarchical" but still *politically* relevant. They reflect the extent of the effectiveness of the state-as-law, the abating of some rights and guarantees that, as much as voting without coercion, are constitutive of citizenship. A curious disjunction results: in many brown areas, the *democratic,* participatory rights of polyarchy are respected, but the liberal component of democracy is systematically violated. A situation in which one can vote freely and have one's vote counted fairly but cannot expect proper treatment from the police or the courts calls into serious question the liberal component of that democracy and severely curtails citizenship.[11] This disjunction is part and parcel of the mix of democratic and authoritarian components which characterizes these states.

The denial of liberal rights to (mostly but not exclusively) the poor or otherwise deprived sectors is analytically distinct from, and bears no necessary relation to, the question of the scope of social and economic democratization. Empirically, various forms of discrimination and extensive poverty and their correlate, extreme disparity in the distribution of (not only economic) resources, go hand-in-hand with low-intensity citizenship.[12]

Here lies the essence of the social conditions necessary for the exercise of citizenship: how can the weaker and the poorer be empowered in terms consistent with democratic legality and, thus, gain their full, democratic and liberal citizenship? Even a *political* definition of democracy (such as most contemporary authors recommend, and to which I adhere) must pose the question of the extent to which citizenship is really exercised in a given country. The issue here is not *per se* how much one regrets inequalities and would like to redress them. Rather, what is at stake are the consequences of those social conditions for the type of polyarchy and for the extent of citizenship found in each case.

A more concrete perspective on these issues requires us to examine, first, the crisis of the state and, second, a specific kind of economic crisis.

Aspects of the Crisis of the State

There is abundant evidence that the extraordinarily severe socioeconomic crisis suffered by most newly democratized countries furthers the spread of brown regions. This spread results not only from processes of social and economic disintegration but also from the profound crisis of the state as effective legality, as a set of bureaucracies, and as a legitimized agent of the common interest. Furthermore, this crisis arises from the strong antistatism of neoliberal ideas and policies,[13] especially evident in the commitment to diminish, at all costs, the size of state bureaucracies and deficits.

In the countries under consideration, various efforts are being used to balance fiscal accounts. Expenditures are tackled with privatizations and attempts to get rid of "excess" personnel, but lay-offs are impeded by laws which protect employee tenure and by strenuous union opposition which has proven costly for fragile governments. More effective in reducing deficits have been policies slashing the salaries of public employees.

In addition to diminishing salaries, there are indications of a severe degradation not only in the functioning of the public sector but in the very ideal of public service. Many capable officials have abandoned the public sector and those who remain find their status has dropped as sharply as their salaries. Prevailing antistatist ideologies view public employees with mistrust, and the news media as well as public lore are replete with anecdotes (too often true) of idleness, lack of competence, and corruption. If to be a state official was at one time a sign of high status, nowadays it is nearly the opposite.

Worse still is the change in expectations. Before the present crisis, to be a public official was to have a professional career with a predictable promotion path and a monthly income and fringe benefits that allowed a solid middle-class lifestyle, which usually included good housing and a university education for one's children. Except for some privileged pockets (such as the central banks), government careers no longer come close to meeting these expectations in countries undergoing crisis.

The conditions of public employment today are demoralizing. Specialized bureaucracies have been decapitated by the exodus of their most qualified employees, management is increasingly politicized, repeated "rationalizations" and "reorganizations" have failed, and physical plant decay has advanced dramatically. Picture the bleak circumstances of a typical functionary hammering away at a worn-out mechanical typewriter in an office where the paint and furniture have not been renovated for many years. These conditions provide fertile soil for a poorly motivated and unskilled bureaucracy, which, in turn, feeds the innumerable anecdotes that fuel the all-out assault on the state. Meanwhile, the political support needed for effecting a more balanced government policy toward its own apparatus is eroded.

Furthermore, under conditions of high and erratic inflation, state employees may lose 30, 40, and even 50 percent of their real incomes in the span of a month or two. Under these circumstances, employees naturally demand redress. They go on strike and demonstrate, at times violently. The result is frequent paralysis of essential public services. The consequences hit hardest in large cities, the center of power and politics. These protests contribute to the perception that democratic governments, and the politicians who run them, are unable (and for demagogic reasons, even unwilling) to prevent "chaos" and continuing economic deterioration.

The rational response of desperate state employees exacerbates the image of an unruly public bureaucracy far more interested in defending its "privileges" than in discharging its duties. Finally, impressionistic evidence indicates that strikes and other protests by public sector workers antagonize the popular sector and many middle-class segments. The anger of these groups, which are more dependent on public services than the more affluent, creates a cleavage that favors the antistatist offensive that conflates the necessary task of achieving a leaner state apparatus with the suicidal weakening of the state as a whole.

When coupled with shrinking personal incomes, dwindling career prospects, poor working conditions, and a hostile political environment, the countless interventions made by the state are propitious for the growth of corruption. In many bureaus, little gets done without graft: petty for the rich but taxing heavily on the poor. At the upper levels of the bureaucracy, corruption diverts huge sums of money, plundering scarce public resources. When corruption becomes a public scandal, it undermines trust not only in the state apparatus but also in the government that appears incapable of resolving the situation (if not of being an active participant in it).

Funding-starved governments seek temporary relief by increasing indirect taxes and the cost of public services. This strategy feeds inflation and has deleterious distributional consequences. Income and social security taxes are applied easily only to withholdings on the salaries of the formal sector of the economy, including public employees. The taxes imposed on the formally employed entail a burdensome tax rate, which very few pay, but which is nominally effective for the whole of the economy. (Considering that the formally employed are also the main contributors to social security, both employees and employers receive a powerful incentive to exit the formal sector.)

In periods of uncertain employment and falling salaries, the sharp deterioration of social services (both in Latin America and the post-communist countries) adds to the misfortunes of much of the population. This increases incentives for tax evasion and diminishes the cost of bribing. Generalized protest against "excessive taxes" occurs as the state's overall tax revenue diminishes. Direct taxes (those which a democratic government supposedly should emphasize) fall even more sharply. In sum, the long agony of the state-centered, import-substitution model of capital accumulation gives birth to a dinosaur incapable even of feeding itself, while current "solutions" lead toward an anemic entity no less able to support democracy, decent levels of social equity, and economic growth.

On Certain Economic Crises

I will discuss here a particular kind of economic crisis in which Argentina, Brazil, and Peru find themselves. This crisis is characterized by high and recurrent inflation[14] and hyperinflation punctuated by repeated attempts to control inflation and undertake "structural reforms" of the kind recommended by international lending organizations. Fortunately, this crisis currently assails a small set of countries, but several post-communist and African countries may be falling into this pattern. It can be postulated that the longer and deeper the crisis, the lower the confidence that the government will be able to solve it.

In the context of this crisis it becomes rational for everyone to act 1) at highly disaggregated levels, especially in relation to state agencies that may solve or alleviate the consequences of the crisis for a given firm or sector; 2) with extremely short time horizons; and 3) with assumptions that everyone else will do the same. A gigantic, national level Prisoner's Dilemma emerges when a profound and protracted economic crisis teaches each agent the following lessons:

- Inflation will continue to be high, and it is next to impossible to predict medium- or long-run fluctuations in inflation rates.

- Among such fluctuations, periods of extremely high or hyperinflation (monthly rates of, say, 50 percent and above) cannot be excluded.

- At some point, the government will enact some drastic intervention aimed at taming inflation, but such interventions are likely to fail.

- Expectations about the future of the economy are strongly pessimistic.

- Predictions about the future economic situation of each agent are contingent on shrewd and timely adaptation to the conditions imposed by the preceding points.

Although there is a dearth of studies at the appropriate microlevel, anyone who has lived under these circumstances knows that it is a harsh, nasty world. The dominant rational strategy is to do whatever is necessary to protect oneself against the losses threatened by high and erratic inflation. Remaining passive, or not having the resources for meeting the speed of inflation, guarantees heavy losses — for some, bankruptcy or abysmal poverty.

This is a world of *sauve qui peut*, and playing this game reinforces the very conditions under which it is played. The primary, basic phenomenon is generalized de-solidarization. Every rational agent acts at the level of disaggregation and with the time horizon deemed more efficacious in his/her defensive moves. To sacrifice short-term gains for the sake of longer-term ones makes no sense when the future situation cannot be predicted with any accuracy and abstaining from maximizing short-term gains may provoke heavy losses. Some agents, difficult to identify precisely from the data available, reap big profits. The ways to achieve success are many but skewed in favor of certain classes. One important way entails the plundering of the state apparatus.

For players of this game, broad, long-run economic policies, negotiated and implemented with the participation of highly aggregated interest associations, are not important. Since the government also has to dance to the rhythm of the crisis, its capacity to formulate those policies is very limited, and very often their implementation is canceled or captured by the disaggregated strategies just described. The surest way to defend oneself, and to eventually profit from the crisis, is to seek easy and rapid access to the state agencies that can deliver hoped-for resources. This is true basically but not exclusively for capitalists.

Privileges and favors are procured by the minimum-size coalition that is able to obtain the appropriate decisions by a given public agency. And those advantages must be obtained fast — if not, continuing inflation will eat them up. In this situation, the rational strategy consists of a double disaggregation: first, act alone or allied to the minimum possible sets of agents that can guarantee the desired outcome; second, colonize the state agencies that can provide sought-after benefits, avoiding more aggregated or public arenas that only complicate the attainment of the specific benefits expected. Various processes, such as the loosening of popular collective identities, the implosion of historically rooted parties, and the decreased importance of capitalist organizations, are expressions of the perverse collective consequences of rational defensive behavior.

Capitalists in Argentina, Brazil, and Peru have an important advantage. This is not a new game for them. Only the urgency, the stakes, and the level of disaggregation have increased. Capitalists in those countries, as well as elsewhere in Latin America, have a long history of living off the largesse of the state and in colonizing its agencies. They do not have to find many new counterparts inside the public bureaucracies or invent new ways to engage them in manifold forms of mutual corruption. The depth of the current crisis has accentuated these ills, demonstrated, for example, by the evidence of a great increase in corruption. Also, there is an enormous fragmentation of the state apparatus. Equivalently, state autonomy has declined sharply, not in relation to "a" capitalist class but in relation to the innumerable segments in which this class has disaggregated during the crisis. The problems noted above in the discussion of the crisis of the state are multiplied by these consequences of economic crisis, at the same time that the resulting disintegration of the state apparatus makes it even less capable of solving the crisis.

Each new spiral of the crisis is not identical with the preceding one. Actors learn. Those who were cunning enough to survive and even get ahead can buy at bargain prices assets held by the losers. The rapid concentration of capital in these countries reflects the gains of Darwinian survivors. Actors assume that since the previous stabilization efforts failed (and the government was further weakened), future efforts will also fail. Actors thus hedge their bets against the estimated high probability of future policy failure, which, of course, increases the likelihood of that same failure.

With each successive spiral, governments more desperately seek a way out of the crisis. However, the accompanying disintegration of the state apparatus, increasing fiscal deficits, hostile public opinion, harsh criticism from political party officials (including members of the governing party, who see themselves dragged into the abyss of the government's unpopularity), and the anticipatory hedging of powerful economic actors combine to thwart the success of the next policy attempt. The next stabilization attempt for an economy with increasing levels of immunization will be an intervention more radical than its predecessor. The stakes of the game become higher at every turn of the wheel.

The repeated policy failures contribute to the Darwinian selection process, at each turn made easier by the decreasing ability of the government to control the distributional consequences of its policies. Since many middle sectors are, in relative terms, affected most severely, cries protesting "the extinction of the middle class" are widespread and sometimes have antidemocratic overtones. In this situation, the government projects a curious image that combines omnipotence with naked impotence. Every attempt at solving the crisis is resonantly announced as the one that will finally succeed, thus justifying further sacrifices of the population. Simultaneously however, aside from the welcome relief of a temporary fall in inflation (usually at the cost of regressive economic contraction), it soon becomes evident that the government will not be able to implement other necessary policies. This is yet another factor shortening the time horizons and worsening the expectations that make the overall game so dynamic.

In these circumstances, society's image of itself is negative. One could collect thousands of expressions as evidence of the deep malaise and lack of solidarity induced by the ugly levels of opportunism, greed, and corruption. Furthermore, many of these antisocial behaviors entail blatant disregard for existing laws. As people observe that many violate the law and that the costs of doing so are often nil, the lesson learned further erodes the predictability of social relations. Widespread opportunism and lawlessness increase transaction costs of all sorts, and the texturing of society by the state-as-law weakens with each new spiral.

Bitter denunciations of the "moral crisis" follow. There are exhortations in the media and daily conversations for "restoring national unity," for the panacea of socioeconomic pacts (that under these conditions no rational actor would enter into in good faith), for "moralizing" public administration and business, and so forth. However welcome as indications of the resilience of basic values and public morality, pious exhortations ignore the locking in of social action into a colossal Prisoner's Dilemma.[15] More importantly, such utterances easily degenerate into a full-fledged condemnation of the democracy that performs poorly in so many respects.

The angry atomization of society is the other side of the coin of the crisis of the state, not only as a set of bureaucracies but also (and even more) as the lawful source of social predictability. The crisis leads to the erosion of the plausibility of the state as an authoritative agent of the country's interests. Rather, the state appears more and more as a burdensome apparatus allowing itself to be plundered by the powerful. The disintegration of the state apparatus and the decreasing effectiveness of the state-as-law make government incapable of implementing minimally complex policies.

It is no easy matter to decide which segments of the state deserve priority efforts at making them more effective. Nor is it easy to implement an industrial policy, or to decide the degree and sequencing of the financial and commercial opening of the economy, to agree on salaries and employment policies, and so on. Without this "restructuring," neither the current neoliberal policies nor alternative ones can hope to succeed.

In order for those policies not only to be formulated but also to be implemented, three conditions must be met. First, private and state agents must have at least the medium run as their time horizon. In the crisis described above, however, this condition is unlikely to be met. Government leaders have a short time horizon because the crisis forces them to focus on extinguishing fires that pop up everywhere, constantly jeopardizing their jobs.

Second, stabilization and, especially, structural reforms must be more than crude tools for whatever interests have access to them. The relevant state agencies must be able to gather and analyze complex information, be sufficiently motivated by the pursuit of some definition of the public interest, and see their role in creating such policies as a rewarding episode in their careers. As we have seen, except for some organizational pockets, these conditions are nowadays non-existent.

Third, some policies can be successfully implemented only if they go through complex negotiations with the various organized private actors that claim legitimate participation in the process. However, the extreme disaggregation of collective actors erodes the representativeness of most organized interests. Consequently, who can *really* speak for someone else in these countries? What *ego* can convince its *alter* that agreements will be honored by those he/she claims to represent? In this manner, the atomization of society mirrors and accentuates the disintegration of the state.[16]

How can these actors, behaving in extremely disaggregated, opportunistic and short-term ways, be represented politically? What can serve as anchors and links with the institutions (of interest representation and the specifically political ones, such as parties and congress) that texture the relationships between state and society in institutionalized democracies? What representativeness and, more broadly, which collective identities can survive these storms? The answers to these questions indicate very little, if any, progress is being made toward the achievement of institutions of representation and accountability.

On the contrary, the atomization of society and state, the spread of brown areas and their peculiar ways of promoting their interests, and the enormous urgency and complexity of the problems faced all feed the delegative, plebiscitary propensities of these democracies. From the pulverization of society into myriad rational/opportunistic actors and the anger about a situation that apparently nobody seems to be responsible for causing, there emerges a scapegoat: the state and the government. These common-sense conclusions lead to a perspective easily converted to simplistic antistatist ideologies. They also destroy the prestige of democratic government, its shaky institutions, and all its politicians.

Of course, the conclusions are grounded in reality. The failed policies, the blundering and vacillations, the impotent omnipotence, the evidence of corruption, and the dismal spectacles too often offered by politicians create the perfect excuse for the projective exculpation of society onto the manifold ills of state and government.

The least that can be said about these problems is that they do not facilitate progress toward a consolidated, institutionalized democracy. They also hinder the implementation of complex, long-term and multilateral negotiated policies that might take these countries beyond the crisis. And, finally, these problems powerfully interact with a tradition of Caesarist, anti-institutional politics, which exists in Latin America as well as other regions.

At this point, an overdue question must be posed: Can these downward spirals be interrupted? Or, more precisely, at what point and under what conditions might an interruption be possible? In posing this question, we must remember that our cases, Argentina, Brazil and Peru, suffer from a recurrent pattern of high inflation, punctuated by hyperinflation and failed stabilization programs.

Chile recently experienced similar problems but found a way out. With an effectiveness that Lenin would have admired, the policies of the Augusto Pinochet government eradicated most of what was left (after the Salvador Allende government) of the domestic-market, import-substitution-oriented bourgeoisie, which was too grateful for being rescued as a class to organize any concerted opposition. Of course, the Pinochet government also brutally repressed labor organizations and political parties that might have mounted an effective opposition to its policies. In this societal wasteland, huge social costs were incurred, and albeit with various changes and accidents, the neoliberal program was largely implemented.

Chile's new democratic government faces the still serious but less vexing problem of preserving low inflation, reasonable rates of economic growth, and favorable international opinion. The government must also ameliorate the inequalities that were accentuated by the preceding authoritarian regime. Nevertheless, the sober fact remains that the distributional consequences of more ambiguous and less harsh policies in countries such as Argentina, Brazil, and Peru have not been better than those under the Pinochet government. Furthermore, the resources presently available to the Chilean government for alleviating equity problems are relatively larger than those available to other Latin American nations. Finally, that Chile surmounted the spiral depicted in this chapter indicates that its state is in better shape for dealing with the equity and developmental issues it inherited.

Another such country may be Mexico, though inflation and its accompanying social dislocations never were as high as in Argentina, Brazil, and Peru. The Partido Revolucionario Institucional (PRI) provided a more effective instrument for policy implementation than anything available to our three cases. A third consideration is the geopolitical interests of the neighboring United States, which sometimes contribute to Mexico's painful and uncertain — but comparatively easier — navigation toward the achievement of long-run policy goals.

Bolivia is another country where the implementation of policies successful in taming inflation and liberalizing trade and finance (but not thus far in restoring growth and investment) was accompanied by a brutal repression scarcely consistent with democracy. Recent indications are that this pattern may also come to describe Argentina.

Focusing on the South American cases, what do Chile, Bolivia, and Argentina have in common? Quite simply, their crises — in Chile under authoritarian and in the other two under democratically elected governments —reached the very bottom. At their nadirs, these crises were characterized by 1) a state as a principle of order with only a slight hold on the behavior of most actors, as bureaucracy reaching extreme limits of disintegration and ineffectiveness, and at some point in time, a state unable to support the national currency; 2) a thoroughly defeated workers' movement, meaning one that it is no longer able to oppose neoliberal policies except by means of very disaggregated and short-lived protests; 3) a cannibalistic capitalist class from which have emerged winners who metamorphosized themselves into financially centered and outwardly oriented conglomerates (together with branches of commerce and professionals that cater to luxury consumption); and 4) a consensus that continued high and uncertain inflation is so intolerable that *any* solution is acceptable, even if it ratifies a more unequal world in which many forms of solidaristic sociability have been lost.

After society touches "bottom," draconian measures to control inflation and neoliberal restructuring efforts no longer confront powerful blocking coalitions. The more important fractions of the bourgeoisie are no longer antagonistic to those policies. The various expressions of popular and middle-class interests are weak and fractionalized, and the state employees who have survived their own ordeal are looking to improve their situation. The pulverization of society and of the state apparatus, together with the primordial urge to order the social world, thus eliminate the resistance that, unwittingly but effectively, fed the previous turns of the spiral.

In Chile this happened through the combined effects of the crisis unleashed under the *Unidad Popular* government and the repressive and determined policies of the Pinochet period. In Bolivia and Argentina, it is no small irony that, after hyperinflation, the end of the spiral came under presidents from parties and movements such as the Movimiento Nacionalist Revolucionario

(MNR) and *peronismo*. Probably, it was obligatory for such presidents, and only for them, to complete the defeat of the workers' movement.

And Brazil? Of the countries discussed, Brazil was the last to enter the crisis described here. Its larger domestic market and more dynamic economic performance created a more complex and industrialized economy than those of its neighbors, which cushioned it against the crisis. In a "paradox of success," Brazil's advantage may turn out to be a severe curse (O'Donnell 1992b). Brazil is populated with many powerful actors capable of blocking the more or less orthodox neoliberal policies that, nonetheless, have been and will be attempted again. In the absence of an alternative to continuing the spirals until hitting bottom, economic destruction in Brazil will greatly exceed that experienced by the countries mentioned above. Furthermore, in contrast to the Southern Cone countries, large segments of Brazil's population have nowhere lower to fall.

The Brazilian capacity of resistance would be all to the good if this alternative existed. But the only alternative on the table is recycling the same exhausted pattern of state-led capital accumulation. Granted, the players of this game can continue to plunder the dinosaur, but this will only accelerate the spiralling and produce perverse distributional consequences that cannot continue indefinitely.

A Partial Conclusion

Are there alternatives to the crises I have depicted? The Prisoner's Dilemma has a powerful dynamic: invocations of altruism and national unity — as well as policy proposals that assume wide solidarities and firm identities — will not do. If there is a solution, it probably lies in finding crucial arenas in which skilled action (particularly by the government) can lengthen time horizons and, consequently, the scope of solidarities of crucial actors. The best-known invention for such achievement is the strengthening of social and political institutions. Under the conditions depicted, this is indeed a difficult task.

In the contemporary world, the joyful celebration of the advent of democracy must be complemented with sober recognition of the immense (and, indeed, historically unusual) difficulties of institutionalizing and embedding democracy in these new contexts. As Haiti, Peru, and Thailand have shown, these experiments are fragile. Premature proclamations of the "end of history" aside, there are no immanent forces to guide the new democracies toward an institutionalized and representative form or to eliminate brown areas and manifold social ills that plague them. In the long run, new democracies may split between those that follow this felicitous course toward institutionalization and those that regress to all-out authoritarianism. But delegative democracies, weak horizontal accountability, schizophrenic states, brown areas, and low-intensity citizenship are part of the foreseeable future for many new democracies.

Notes

1. In addition to its somewhat sketchy character, this text has a major limitation: I do not deal directly with international and transnational factors, even though they often enter implicitly in my discussion. This chapter contains ideas that are only summarily developed. I am in the process of writing a book in which these and other ideas, and their empirical referents, are treated much more properly. I decided to publish the present text after the gentle insistence of various colleagues persuaded me that it would make sense to offer for discussion my views about themes and problems that I believe have been neglected at rather serious cost in current studies on democratization. I have limited citations to the barest minimum: the arguments I present here draw on various streams of literature and many valuable contributions to which my book will do proper justice.

2. One limitation of not dealing with international factors and only slightly with historical ones is that I do not discuss an assumption that sometimes creeps into literature: new democracies are "only" going through stages that institutionalized democracies passed through before.

3. In another work (O'Donnell, 1992a) I labelled these "delegative democracies," to contrast them with institutionalized (or, equivalently, consolidated or established or representative or, as we shall see, liberal) democracies. By the term "delegative," I point to a concept and practice of executive authority as electorally delegated the right to do whatever it sees fit for the country. I also argue that delegative democracies are inherently hostile to the patterns of representation normal in established democracies, to the creation and strengthening of political institutions and, especially, to what I term "horizontal accountability." By this I mean the day-by-day control of the validity and lawfulness of the actions of the executive by other public agencies, which are reasonably autonomous from the former. Furthermore, as we shall see, the liberal component of these democracies is very weak. Some authors tend to confuse delegative democracy with populism; both, of course, share various important features. But, in Latin America at least, the latter entailed a broadening (even if vertically controlled) of popular political participation and organization, and it coexisted with periods of dynamic expansion of the domestic economy. Instead, delegative democracy typically attempts to de-politicize the population, except for brief moments in which it demands its plebiscitary support, and it currently coexists with periods of severe economic crisis. While my previous text was basically a typological exercise, in the present one I look at some societal processes which seem closely related to the emergence and workings of delegative democracies.

4. I am using cautious language because I cannot deal here with the various nuances and qualifications that a more extended treatment of this matter would have to introduce. For a good discussion of these matters, see Cotterrell (1984).

5. Most post-communist countries suffer the additional, enormous problem that not even their geographical boundaries are beyond dispute and that various ethnic and religious cleavages prevent minimal degrees of allegiance to the respective states. In this sense, while several Latin American countries are undergoing processes of acute

erosion of an already existing nation-state, several post-communist ones are facing the even more vexing problem of beginning to build, under inauspicious economic and social circumstances, a nation-state.

6. "State penetration" was one of the "crises" conceptualized in the famous volumes in the 1960s on "political development" sponsored by the Social Science Research Council (see especially LaPalombara 1971). This same topic is central to Samuel Huntington (1968). But while these works are concerned with the expansion of any kind of central authority, my discussion here refers to the effectiveness of the type of legality that a democratic state is supposed to implant.

7. Of course, these are matters of degree. For example, the United States stands as a case where, in the past, some of these problems were pervasive —and they have not been entirely eliminated until today. But there now, as well as in England before, these problems motivated the creation of a rather effective, "apolitical," national civil service. In contrast, underlining some of the tragic effects of the crisis, the inverse is currently happening, namely the destruction of effective state bureaucracies and notions of public service.

8. One important symptom is the degree to which the drug trade thrives in these regions, often in coalition with local and national authorities. This convergence (and that of numerous other criminal activities) further accentuates the perverse privatization of these regions.

9. It should be mentioned that the measures of heterogeneity I am suggesting do not necessarily imply only one nationality under one state. (For example, the dominant color of Belgium is blue.) The disintegration of supranational empires, such as the Soviet Union and Yugoslavia, may or may not lead to states which are homogenous in the sense I specified here. For example, in Russia the erosion of public authority and the widespread disobedience of legislation means that even though this unit may be more "national" in the sense of containing a rather homogeneous population, in terms of the dimensions of stateness, it would indeed be dominated by brown. For a vivid description of the fast and extensive "browning" of today's Russia, see Reddaway (1993).

10. Consider the present political problems of Italy, which is arguably the most heterogenous of institutionalized democracies (with the exception of India, if that extremely heterogenous country can still be considered democratic). Italy is more homogenous than most of the countries I am discussing. Its problems are closely connected to brown areas and to the penetration of legal and illegal representatives of those areas in its national center. In the United States, whatever evaluation its Republican governments deserve, it is indisputable that in the past decade brown areas, particularly around large cities, grew frighteningly. These problems are also appearing in other rich countries, related to a series of global transformations, particularly in the economy. But in the present text, I want to stress factors, specific to certain countries, that greatly accentuate those problems. Again, and as always, comparisons are a matter of degree.

11. As Alan Ware (1992) puts it, "The claim of the liberal democracies to be *liberal* democracies rests on the claim that they have both well established and also accessible procedures for protecting the liberties of individual citizens."

12. The extensive poverty and inequality found in most of Latin America and the Third World is rooted in a long history, accentuated by the current crisis and economic

policies. It is different from the process of rapid growth in inequality taking place in post-communist countries. Whichever the pattern that will turn out to be more explosive, the latter points toward democracies which, almost at the very moment of their inauguration, suffer a sharp erosion in the intensity of citizenship.

13. By "neoliberal" policies I mean those advocated by international lending institutions and mainstream neoclassical theories. These policies recently have been experiencing some changes, presumably prompted by the very mixed record of their application. But a very strong — and indiscriminate —antistatist bias continues to be at their core. For a critique of these policies, see especially Adam Przeworski et al. (forthcoming). Even though I agree with the critique and am one of the cosigners of this book, I must clarify that I did not participate in the section of this volume containing that analysis. See also Przeworski (1992) and Bresser Pereira, Maravall, and Przeworski (Chapter 7 in this volume).

14. By this I mean periods of three years when monthly inflation averaged above 20 percent, with peaks of three-digit figures per month.

15. Although I cannot extend the argument here, it should be noticed that none of the conditions identified by the literature as conducive to cooperative solutions in the prisoners' dilemma hold in the situation I am depicting.

16. One should not forget the longer-term effects of the crisis (and of the indiscriminate antistatist ideology underlying current economic policies) on public goods crucial for sustaining economic growth. I refer in particular to education, health, and science and technology policies and to the modernization of physical infrastructure. These are grossly neglected, in spite of many warnings and complaints. To undertake policy reform in these areas, a reasonably lean and effective state apparatus is required.

References

Cotterrell, Roger. 1984. *The Sociology of Law: An Introduction*. London: Butterworths.

Dahl, Robert. 1971. *Polyarchy. Participation and Opposition*. New Haven, Conn.: Yale University Press.

Huntington, Samuel. 1968. *Political Order in Changing Societies*. New Haven, Conn.: Yale University Press.

LaPalombara, Joseph. 1971. "Penetration: A Crisis of Governmental Capacity." In *Crises and Sequences in Political Development*, eds. Leonard Binder, Lucian W. Pye, James S. Coleman, Sidney Verba, Joseph LaPalombara, and Myron Weiner. Princeton, N.J.: Princeton University Press.

Lijphart, Arend. 1968. "Consociational Democracy," *World Politics* 21 (January).

Lijphart, Arend. 1984. *Democracies. Patterns of Majoritarian and Consensus Government in Twenty-One Countries*. New Haven, Conn.: Yale University Press.

Mainwaring, Scott. 1990. "Politicians, Parties and Electoral Systems: Brazil in Comparative Perspective." Kellogg Institute Working Paper No. 141.

O'Donnell, Guillermo. 1992a. "Delegative Democracy?" Kellogg Institute Working Paper No. 172.

O'Donnell, Guillermo. 1992b. "Transitions, Continuities, and Paradoxes." In *Issues in Democratic Consolidation: The New South American Democracies in Comparative Perspective*, eds. Scott Mainwaring, Guillermo O'Donnell, and J. Samuel Valenzuela. Notre Dame, Ind.: University of Notre Dame Press.

O'Donnell, Guillermo, and Philippe Schmitter. 1986. *Transitions from Authoritarian Rule: Tentative Conclusions about Uncertain Democracies*. Baltimore: Johns Hopkins University Press.

Reddaway, Peter, 1993. "Russia on the Brink." *New York Review of Books* 28 (January).

Przeworski, Adam. 1992. "The Neoliberal Fallacy." *Journal of Democracy* 3 (3).

Przeworski, Adam, et al. Forthcoming. *Sustainable Democracy*.

Ware, Alan. 1992. "Liberal Democracy: One Form or Many?" *Political Studies* 40.

Chapter Seven

Economic Reforms in New Democracies: A Social-Democratic Approach

Luiz Carlos Bresser Pereira

José María Maravall

Adam Przeworski

Introduction

R ecipes for disaster seem quite clear. In recent years, whenever governments pursued left-wing economic programs, the result was inflation, fiscal crises, and balance-of-payment crises. Democratic governments that followed neoliberal tenets faced stagnation, increased poverty, political discontent, and debilitation of democracy. Peru under Alan García, Portugal during the first phase of the post-1974 regime, Greece under PASOK, as well as France during the first two years of Socialist rule provide evidence that a combination of economic stimulation with fiscal undiscipline generates economic crises. Argentina and Brazil, where several attempts at stabilization failed, as well as Poland and Bolivia, where stabilization was successful, show that the pursuit of "efficiency" can be counter-productive politically and economically.

Traditional postures which reject all attempts to stabilize, deregulate, and open the economy are untenable because of the social costs inherent in such programs once an overprotected, overregulated, oligopolistic economy enters the spiral of fiscal crisis. Procrastination, socially more tolerable and politically safer, only aggravates the crisis and prolongs deprivation. In turn, programs based on the promise of immediate improvement end in disaster.

Yet there is ample evidence that pursuit of the neoliberal ideological blueprint fares no better. When stability and efficiency become goals in themselves, government policies turn out to be economically either simply ineffective or counter-productive and politically explosive under democratic conditions. Stabilization attempts either fail or induce recessions so profound that they depress investment, undermine prospects for future growth, and generate social costs that make the continuation of reforms politically unpalatable in a democratic context. Moreover, the technocratic style in which these policies tend to be formulated and implemented undermines the consolidation of democratic institutions.

Hence, perhaps paradoxically, our conclusions make the case for left-wing governments to pursue a market-oriented program — that is, a pragmatic, "social-democratic" approach. This approach calls for reforms oriented toward growth, protection of material welfare, and full utilization of democratic institutions in the formulation and implementation of reform policies. Yet the specific recipe for such an approach is, unfortunately, less clear, precisely because there have been few successful experiences.

In the first part of this chapter, we argue that the success of reforms can be judged only in terms of resumed growth and consolidation of democracy, not in terms of any intermediate goals. We also identify the generic difficulty faced by new democracies attempting such reforms. In the second part, we review logical and empirical arguments concerning our three central hypotheses: 1) the reforms that constitute the currently standard recommendation — stabilization and liberalization — are necessary, but they are not sufficient to restore the capacity to grow unless they are accompanied by active state coordination of the allocation process; 2) since any reform package must consist of discrete steps taken over an extended period of time, political conditions for their continuation erode unless social policies protect those whose subsistence is threatened by the reforms; and 3) consolidation of democracy may be undermined unless representative institutions play a real role in shaping and implementing reform policies. In the final part, we summarize and develop our prescriptive views.

Our intent is not to provide comparable inductive evidence for each of the points. Given the paucity of historical experience, such an attempt is not feasible at the present. Nor is it possible to develop a blueprint for a policy that could be applied everywhere. Reform strategies must trade off conflicting objectives to meet constraints which are specific to each situation. Yet we do argue that several trade offs — notably between stabilization and growth, between social expenditures and growth, between social expenditures and the sustainability of reforms, and between political participation and the sustainability of reforms — are misconceived within the model that underlies the currently fashionable policy prescriptions.

Growth and Democracy as the Goal of Reforms

The recent wave of transitions to democracy began in Southern Europe in the mid-1970s, surged in Latin America in the mid-1980s, and swept

Eastern Europe, including the Soviet Union, in 1989-1990. These transitions often occurred when the respective economies faced serious difficulties.

In several countries, the collapse of authoritarian regimes was accompanied by economic crises, caused typically by the exhaustion of state-led and inward-oriented strategies of development. The state grew too much, regulated in excess, protected beyond reason. In Latin America, the state was onerous; in Eastern Europe, overwhelming. Special interests of bureaucrats, managers of large firms, and private businessmen replaced the public interest. Populist practices, combined with inward-oriented developmentalist strategies, led to fiscal undiscipline and public deficits. The consequence, besides increasing inefficiency in the entire economic system, was fiscal crisis: in many countries, the state was bankrupt. Hence, even though regimes varied in degrees of authoritarianism, the state became economically impotent.

Since transitions to democracy often coincide with economic crises, many new democracies face a double challenge: how to resume growth and consolidate nascent political institutions simultaneously? Moreover, the reforms necessary to restore growth inevitably engender a deterioration in the material well-being of many groups. Under such conditions, the consolidation of democratic institutions can be easily undermined. The question thus arises whether any reform strategy can lead both to resumed growth and to the strengthening of democracy.

Posing the question in this way does not assume that new democracies are less capable of managing economic crises than established democracies or authoritarian regimes. According to some arguments, the capacity of new democracies to undertake stabilization programs and to implement structural reforms is hampered by the vast expectation of economic improvements and by vulnerability to popular pressures and to interest-group influence. Electoral cycles and pluralist competition further undermine long-term planning in new democracies (Ames 1987; Stallings and Kaufman 1989; Marer 1991). Yet new democracies have imposed economic discipline in hard times. Comparative studies of economic reforms in the less-developed countries have shown no systematic differences among regimes in the choice of economic reform strategies (Nelson 1990) and in economic performance (Remmer 1986; Haggard et al. 1990). And even if it were true that authoritarian regimes are more capable of imposing and preserving economic reforms, we would not be willing to treat democracy as an instrumental value, judged by its consequences for economic performance. The question we pose is not how regimes affect the success of economic reforms but whether there are ways to resume growth under democratic conditions. The ultimate economic criterion for evaluating the success of reforms can be only whether a country resumes growth at stable, moderate levels of inflation.

Economic reforms comprise various mixtures of measures designed to stabilize the economy, steps oriented to change its structure, and, at times, sales of public assets. The central purpose of stabilization is to slow down inflation and improve the financial position of the state. The central goal of structural reforms is to increase the efficiency of resource allocation. The aim of privatization is less clear, since ostensible reasons for the sale of public assets are not always the true ones.[1] Yet even if all these measures are successful on their own terms, their effect on growth is not immediately apparent. While particular reform programs differ in scope and pace, stabilization and, in particular, structural reforms necessarily cause a temporary decline of consumption. To be sustained, stabilization must entail a transitional reduction of demand, due to a combination of reduced public spending, increased taxation, and high interest rates. Trade liberalization, antimonopoly measures, reductions of subsidies to industries and prices inevitably cause temporary unemployment of capital and labor. Privatization implies reorganization: again, a costly transition. Moreover, market-oriented reforms are often undertaken when the effects of the original shock are still present and while some important markets are still missing. Finally, architects of reforms make mistakes, and mistakes are costly. Hence, the effect of economic reforms on growth must be negative in the short run.[2] Indeed, for proponents of reforms, unemployment and firm closings constitute evidence that reforms are effective: if currently low unemployment fails to rise to between 8 and 10 percent this year, said the Czechoslovak economics minister, Vladimir Dlouhy, "It would be a sign that the reforms were not working" (*Financial Times* 1991). Reform programs are, thus, caught between the faith of those who foresee their ultimate effects and the skepticism of those who experience only their immediate consequences.

This is why interim evaluations of reform programs tend to be highly inconsistent and controversial. Given that market-oriented reforms inevitably entail a transitional decline in consumption, it is not apparent how to judge their success. There are three ways to think about "success." The first, followed by Joan Nelson (1990) and most of her collaborators, is to define it in terms of a continued implementation of reform measures, whatever they may be. These evaluators gave up on using economic criteria to measure the success of reforms and chose instead to explain "the degree to which policy decisions were carried out rather than economic outcomes of the measures taken." The second, implicit in most economic literature and in Stephan Haggard and Robert Kaufman (1992), is to conceptualize "success" in terms of stabilization and liberalization. The third, to which we adhere, is to remain skeptical until an economy exhibits growth under democratic conditions.

The first conception is untenable, since it is based on the assumption that whatever measures have been introduced must be appropriate. This conception admits no possibility of policy mistakes and — the point bears repetition — such mistakes are frequent and perhaps inevitable. The choice of anchor (the nominal quantity on which the stabilization program rests), the sequencing of deregulatory measures (capital account versus trade first), the method and timing of devaluations, the distribution of cuts of public expenditures are not obvious. There is no such thing as "the" sound economic blueprint, only alternative hypotheses to be tested in practice and at a cost. Indeed, the sequencing of reform strategies evokes sharp disagreements and, as the Chilean debacle of 1982 demonstrates, wrong decisions lead to costly mistakes.

The second conception is safer but still based on the conjecture that stability and competition are sufficient to generate growth, a conjecture we believe false. This posture assumes that partial steps eventually lead to growth and prosperity. Proponents of reforms argue as if they had a Last Judgment Archetype of the world — a general model of economic dynamics that allows evaluating ultimate consequences of all the partial steps. Yet this model is only a conjecture. Inflation may be arrested by a sufficient dose of recession, but the evidence that successful stabilization leads to restored growth is weak. Opening the economy and increasing exports may result in improved creditworthiness of a country, but the beneficiaries may be only the foreign creditors. The sale of public firms may fill state coffers, but the revenues may be stolen or squandered. Thus, the causal links between particular reform measures and their ultimate goal remain flimsy. As Karen Remmer (1986) reported with regard to the International Monetary Fund (IMF) Standby Programs, there is "only a moderate correlation between the implementation of IMF prescriptions and the achievement of desired economic results."

If the ostensible purpose of market-oriented reforms is to increase material welfare, then these reforms must be evaluated by their success in generating economic growth. Anything short of this criterion is just a restatement of the neoliberal hypothesis, not its test. Given that the reform process entails intertemporal trade-offs, conjectures about distant consequences cannot be avoided. Yet, unless we insist on thinking in terms of growth, we risk suffering a long period of tension and deprivation only to discover that the strategy which brought it about was erroneous. The argument that "the worse, the better" cannot be maintained indefinitely; at some point, things must get better. Resumed growth is the only reliable criterion of economic success.

While economic reforms have been pursued by some authoritarian regimes and by some well-established democracies, newly established democratic regimes face simultaneously an urgent need to overcome economic crisis and to consolidate their nascent institutions. Hence, the second criterion of successful reforms must be the consolidation of democracy. And if reforms are to proceed under democratic conditions, distributional conflicts must be institutionalized. All groups must channel their demands through democratic institutions and abjure other tactics. Regardless of how pressing their needs may be, political forces must be willing to subject their interests to the verdict of democratic institutions. They must be willing to accept defeats and to wait, confident that these institutions will offer opportunities the next time around. They must adopt the institutional calendar as the temporal horizon of their actions, thinking in terms of forthcoming elections, contract negotiations, or, at least, fiscal years. They must assume the stance put forth by John McGurk, the chairman of the British Labour Party, in 1919: "We are either constitutionalists or we are not constitutionalists. If we are constitutionalists, if we believe in the efficacy of the political weapon (and we do, or why do we have a Labour Party?), then it is both unwise and undemocratic because we fail to get a majority at the polls to turn around and demand that we should substitute industrial action" (cited by Miliband 1975, 69).

Regardless of their age, democracies persist whenever all the major political forces find that they can improve their situation if they channel their demands and their conflicts through democratic institutions. New democracies are more vulnerable because institutional issues often remain unresolved for a long period after the installation of a particular democratic system (Przeworski 1991). The choice of institutions is often problematic and conflictual when a dictatorship falls. Often the conflict about the institutional framework continues — as in the case of Poland — or institutions are adopted only as an interim solution. In order to put in place an institutional framework, a previous democratic constitution may be reinstated even if it did not work in the past, as in the case of Argentina. At other times, a foreign constitution may be grafted on, or a constitution may be elaborated that is expected in advance not to evoke compliance, as in the case of Brazil. These institutional frameworks are frequently inappropriate for the specific political and economic conditions. Moreover, as Russell Hardin (1987) has argued, habituation plays an important role in inducing political actors to stay within the existing institutional framework. Constitutions are often "contracts by convention."

Hence, democratic institutions can be consolidated only if they offer politically relevant groups incentives to process their demands within the institutional framework. But economic reforms inevitably engender at least a transitional decline in consumption. This is then the source of the dilemma faced by new democracies: how to create incentives for political forces to process their interests within democratic institutions when material conditions must decline for the foreseeable future.

Neoliberal Versus Social-Democratic Approach: Theory and Evidence

Our purpose is to investigate whether there is a space between these two constraints. We seek a strategy that would lead to resumed growth under democratic conditions. As everyone else who plunges into these muddy waters, we rely on historical experience, arguments from first principles, and conjectures.

If success means resuming growth under democratic conditions, the evidence for successful recipes is much thinner than it is for disasters. The case that establishes the possibility of success as we define it is Spain, which underwent a painful period of industrial reconversion and irreversibly consolidated democratic institutions. This experience is paralleled by Portugal after 1983, and perhaps also by Uruguay. Chile is growing under democratic conditions, but the reform process — undertaken by an exceptionally repressive military regime — was long and its economic and social costs were enormous. South Korea underwent a successful stabilization in 1981 with some slowdown of growth, but both before and after, it has grown with relative rapidity. Mexico, with its peculiar political regime, has been more attentive to social costs and may be on the brink of resumed growth, while not yet operating with democratic institutions. Finally, among Eastern European countries, Hungary, which proceeded prudently by building market institutions and a social welfare system before plunging into the liberalization stage, may prove successful. Yet these cases are so varied that it is not easy to determine to what extent their success has been due to policies versus circumstances. Spain did not need to stabilize, while inflation rates in Portugal, South Korea, Mexico, and Hungary have been quite moderate by the standards of Argentina, Bolivia, Brazil, Poland, or Yugoslavia. Foreign debt was an overriding consideration in the case of Argentina, Bolivia, Brazil, Mexico, Hungary, Poland, and Yugoslavia but not in Southern Europe. And the scope of reforms differed from country to country, combining differently those measures aimed at stabilization, liberalization, and industrial reconversion.

Hence, we do not pretend to have established the conditions for success. Historical experience is too thin to permit a solid empirical evaluation of the approach we propose.[3] Let us summarize and evaluate the evidence with regard to our three main hypotheses:

- Stabilization and liberalization are insufficient to generate growth unless targeted to redress fiscal crisis and to generate public savings.

- Without social policy to protect at least those whose subsistence is threatened by reforms, political conditions for the continuation of reforms erode.

- The technocratic style of policy making weakens nascent democratic institutions.

Before we examine these hypotheses, a comment is required concerning stabilization policies. Luiz Carlos Bresser Pereira (1993) argues that these policies often fail because they do not redress "fundamentals" but also because they misdiagnose the causes of inflation and because they induce unnecessary social costs. This analysis is now widely shared. On the one hand, as Guido Di Tella (1991, 397) emphasized, trying to stop inflation solely by controlling nominal quantities is absurd. By failing first to correct fundamentals, which include above all the fiscal crisis of the state, heterodox policies simply postpone fiscal adjustment. On the other hand, inflation is often inertial. And, as Michael Bruno (1991, 2) observes, given this inertial character, "the orthodox cure is necessary but not sufficient. The correction of fundamentals does not by itself remove inflationary inertia.... Supplementary direct intervention in the nominal process, such as a temporary freeze of wages, prices, and the exchange rate, can substantially reduce the initial cost of disinflation." Correcting the fundamentals includes restructuring the flows of government expenditures and revenues and reducing the stocks of foreign and domestic debt. Breaking the spiral of inflation calls for policies targeted at nominal quantities, including income policies. Without correcting the fundamentals, stabilization policies are likely to be ineffective; without heterodox policies, they will be also inefficient. Exclusive reliance on the reduction of demand to break inflation engenders unnecessarily high social costs.

To examine the effect of market-oriented reforms on growth, we need to distinguish three questions: 1. Why do stabilization and liberalization of foreign trade and domestic competition induce recessions? 2. Why do some stabilization programs undermine future growth? 3. Are stability and competition sufficient for a resumption of growth?

Stabilization programs tend to induce profound recessions, even when they are not accompanied by liberalization. The reason is at least twofold: 1) stabilization is usually achieved by reducing demand, and 2) interest rates tend to soar beyond the targeted level during stabilization. The mechanism leading to excessive interest rates depends on the anchor that is being used (Blanchard et al. 1991), but one common effect is that successful stabilization makes holding money more attractive and the increased demand for money cannot be met by increased monetary emission without rekindling inflation. In turn, reductions of subsidies to industries and to prices, reduction of import tariffs, and domestic antimonopoly measures sharply lower rates of return and cause unemployment of capital and labor (Przeworski 1991, Chapter 4). Among the cases of successful stabilization,[4] unemployment increased sharply in the following countries: in Bolivia it rose after 1985;[5] in Chile, it climbed from 9.7 percent in 1974 to 16.8 percent in 1976; in Israel, from 5.1 percent in 1984 to 7.1 percent in 1986; and in Poland, from zero in 1989 to over 10 percent in 1991. In South Korea, the capacity utilization rate fell from 77.5 percent in 1980 to 69.4 percent by 1983.

While high interest rates may be transitory, their effect lasts beyond the stabilization period. As Stanley Fischer (1991, 404-405) pointed out, "Investment will not resume until real interest rates reach a reasonable level, and prolonged periods of high real interest rates create financial crises and bankruptcies even for firms that would be viable at reasonable levels of interest rates." Or, in Jacob Frenkel's (1991, 403) words, "stabilization efforts are often associated with extremely high real rates of interest, which discourage investment and hamper growth." Indeed, to consider again successful cases of stabilization, in Bolivia, private investment declined from the already minuscule level of 3.8 percent of gross domestic product (GDP) in 1984 to 2.7 percent in 1985 and 2.5 percent four years later; in Chile, it fell from 8.7 percent of GDP in 1974 to 3.9 percent in 1975, and it surpassed the prestabilization level only three years later; in Israel, gross investment (private and public) fell by 10.6 percent in 1985, recuperated a year later, and began to decline again in 1988. Only in Mexico did private investment grow rapidly throughout the stabilization period.

The second reason stabilization programs often undermine prospects for future growth has been highlighted by Vito Tanzi (1989): expenditure cuts, necessary to cope with fiscal crises, do not discriminate between government consumption and public investment. After having cited several instances in which stabilization policies undermined capacity for growth, Tanzi (1990, 30) concluded: "In all these examples, the *supply* has been reduced, thus creating imbalances that, in time, have manifested themselves as excessive demand. In these cases, demand-management policies alone would have reduced the symptoms of these imbalances but would not have eliminated the causes. Thus, stabilization programs might succeed stabilization programs without bringing about a durable adjustment...." Indeed, investment projects are often politically easier to cut than government consumption services or public employment. Both public infrastructure investments and measures to induce private investment are reduced, thus diminishing future supply. Evidence from successful stabilization experiences is uniform: in Bolivia, public investment declined from 8.4 percent in 1984 to about 3 percent after 1985; in Chile, public investment fell from 12.5 percent in 1974 to 4.8 percent in 1983, and it rose again to 7.1 percent by 1985;[6] in Mexico, public investment had already declined by 13.4 percent in 1987, and it continued to decline afterwards; in Eastern Europe, with the exception of Hungary, public investment simply collapsed.

Today. neither the observation that stabilization entails a recession nor even that stabilization programs often undermine conditions for future growth is controversial. Indeed, the voices we cite emanate from the World Bank and the International Monetary Fund (IMF). Where we depart from the neoliberal consensus is with regard to the point central in Bresser Pereira's (1993) analysis. We argue that market-oriented reforms are not sufficient to generate conditions for growth.

Admittedly, the empirical evidence is inconclusive. In Bolivia, the total GDP declined during the year following stabilization and then grew anemically, while per capita product continued to fall through 1990. In Chile, GDP tumbled by 12.9 percent in 1975; growth resumed until the great crash of 1982, when GDP fell by 14.1 percent, and it resumed again after 1985. In Israel, GDP (of the business sector only) actually grew during stabilization but became stagnant three years later. In Mexico, signs of a recovery are evident, but per capita growth continues weak. In South Korea, growth slowed but continued to be high by comparative standards. And all over Eastern Europe, GDP continues to decline.

Systematic reviews of evidence generate mixed conclusions. John Williamson (1990, 406) showed that among ten Latin America countries which had pursued "full or partial" reforms, four were growing in 1988-1989, while six were stagnant or declining; among eleven countries which did not pursue reforms or undertook them only recently, one was growing and ten were stagnant or declining. This is a positive but not an overwhelming correlation. O.R. Blanchard et al. (1991, 61) reported that "Looking at the post-stabilization performance of countries that have stabilized, one concludes that, in most cases, economic growth has returned only gradually and unimpressively." Scattered data concerning private consumption show the same. Clearly, these patterns lend themselves to differing assessments, particularly when they are juxtaposed to the experience of countries which continue to suffer from fiscal crisis and high rates of inflation. Yet the issue here is not whether countries that underwent a successful stabilization perform better than countries where stabilization attempts have failed. The question is whether a successful stabilization, when combined with other market-oriented reforms, is sufficient to generate growth.

Given the paucity of evidence, it is useful to review theoretical arguments. The neoliberal assumption — "the Washington consensus" (Williamson, 1990) — which underlies the program of market-oriented reforms is that once stability and competition are achieved, growth will follow. Yet, perhaps surprisingly, this neoliberal posture has shaky foundations even in neoclassical economic theory.

Markets may successfully orient individual agents to allocate resources efficiently, but they are not sufficient to coordinate individual actions toward intertemporal efficiency and other normatively and politically desirable goals.[7] "Market orientation" is not sufficient to generate "market coordination" toward collective prosperity.

To justify this assertion would call for a lengthy excursion into economic theory. The bare bones of our argument are the following: Those who expect the market to coordinate economic activities toward intertemporally efficient allocations of resources argue as if they could justify the proposition that competitive markets are sufficient to generate efficiency, at least in the absence of public goods, externalities, or increasing returns. But this proposition is based on the assumption that markets are complete, that is, that there is a market for every contingent state of nature. But, following Kenneth Arrow (1964) and Bruce Greenwald and Joseph Stiglitz (1986), this assumption is no longer tenable. And when some markets are missing, labor markets, capital markets, and goods markets do not clear, and the resulting allocation can be improved upon.[8] As the debate concerning public goods has shown, the mere fact that "the market does not do it" does not imply that the state would do it better. We still need to rethink the role of the state in a decentralized economy in which some markets and some information are inevitably missing. Having reviewed the inefficiencies caused by different types of market incompleteness, David Newberry (1989) concluded that the scope of government intervention is limited. Yet the notion that, if only left alone, "the market" would efficiently coordinate the allocation of scarce resources, is purely hortatory. In Peter Murrell's (1991, 73) devastating critique of reforms based on the neoclassical model, he notes "blanket prescriptions ... surely do not deserve a place in the debates between economists."

Neoclassical economic theory has little to say about growth. Its preoccupations are mainly static. And anyone who has read Joseph Schumpeter knows that static efficiency is a poor criterion of welfare. Indeed, several studies show that the Soviet economy was more efficient in the static sense than that of the United States: it was more efficient precisely because it generated little technical innovation. Dynamic economies are not efficient in the static sense; they use a number of techniques, with different cost-benefit ratios. In turn, the issue of whether a competitive market generates dynamic efficiency is already more complex. The theory of economic growth which emerged from neoclassical economics — the Solow-Swan model of exogenous growth — argued that competitive equilibrium is efficient but leads to stagnation of income in the absence of exogenous population growth and exogenous technical change. Recent models do provide an endogenous explanation of economic growth, but in these theories the competitive equilibrium is no longer efficient (Lucas 1988; Romer 1990; Becker, Murphy, and Tamura 1990).[9] The "engines of growth" in these models are externalities, whether in education, skills, or technology. And competitive markets, in which firms do not capture full return to their endowments, undersupply the factors that generate such externalities.

We need not get mired in the discussion of neoclassical economics to conclude that this theory's present state does not support the conclusion that stability and competition are sufficient to generate growth. Whether one takes the theory of incomplete markets, with their informational asymmetries, or the theory of endogenous growth, with constant returns to a single factor and dynamic externalities, or the theory of non-Walrasian trade, one will discover (still neoclassical) arguments that a certain degree of state intervention is necessary for growth. The neoliberal posture does not rest on any solid theoretical bases: to cite Stiglitz (1991, 12), "Adam Smith's invisible hand may be more like the Emperor's new clothes: invisible because it is not there."

Hence, in spite of the paucity of recent evidence, we consider that our first point is well supported: stability and competition are not sufficient for growth.

Economic reforms are inevitably a protracted process, and they necessarily induce a temporary reduction of consumption for a large segment of the population. Even if stabilization and liberalization programs are designed with a view toward resumed growth and even if the state adopts appropriate development strategies, the period between stabilization and resumption of growth is inevitably long. Sebastián Edwards and Augustín Edwards (1991, 219) estimate eight to ten years as an expected lag. In the meantime, per capita consumption will decline or stagnate, and some incomes will be pushed below the threshold of absolute poverty.

The typical argument of economists — that the economic blueprint is "sound" and only irresponsible "populists" undermine it — is just bad economics. A sound economic strategy is a strategy that addresses itself explicitly to the issue of whether reforms will be supported as costs set in. At the least, reforms must be credible (Calvo 1989). It must be in the best interest of politicians to pursue the measures they have announced, once they obtain support for these measures.[10] And credibility is not only a matter of economics: if policies are politically unsustainable, economic actors will not treat them as credible. But the difficulty is more profound. How can politicians persuade people to have confidence in a reform process that temporarily induces increased material deprivation?

If people are to make intertemporal trade-offs, if they are to accept a transitional reduction of consumption and to be impervious to "populist" appeals, they must have confidence that their temporary sacrifices will lead to an eventual improvement of material conditions. Policy style, about which more is said below, is an important factor in shaping this confidence. But even more important is that the imminent danger not threaten their livelihood. People whose physical survival is imperiled cannot think about the future: they have no intertemporal trade-offs to make.

Citizens of new democracies expect to be granted social as well as political rights. "Social citizenship" — in T.H. Marshall's (1964, 76) words, "a kind of basic human equality associated with the concept of full membership of a Community" — requires that security and opportunity be shared by all. Social policies respond to these demands through the provision of health and education and through income maintenance. This is limited when new democracies venture down the path of economic reforms: this is why short-term effects of stabilization and liberalization threaten the basic livelihood of those most adversely affected by moves toward a market economy. The question is whether these steps will be continued as a verdict of the democratic process.

Our evidence is extremely limited. We have one case, Spain, where social expenditures were considerably extended as industrial reconversion proceeded. In the case of Poland, they were drastically cut as the country simultaneously undertook stabilization and liberalization. Intermediate cases, such as Bolivia, developed, with foreign assistance, a narrowly targeted program of employment for the miners who lost jobs as a result of closing the mines. And Mexico, in a similar vein, developed a program of food subsidies for the groups most adversely affected by stabilization. The distinctive feature of Spain is that social policy was broad in scope — it comprised health, education, and income maintenance, and it entailed qualitative changes in the system of self-government and delivery — and that this policy was accompanied by an active labor-market intervention. Poland provides the clearest contrast: the pre-existing system of social services disintegrated, social expenditures were drastically reduced, survival was left principally to charity, and labor-market policy was limited to a compensation. The political effect was that in Spain the Socialist Party, which led the reform process, continued to win elections without a serious social upheaval. In Bolivia, parties supporting the continuation of reforms won a majority in the 1989 presidential elections; while in Poland, parties advocating that reforms be continued won about 20 percent of the vote in the October 1991 parliamentary elections. Yet, since the initial conditions and the challenges facing these three countries were quite different, it is hard to treat even these cases as paired comparisons.

Spanish social policy was sufficiently extensive that it could be conceptualized by the government and perceived by the population as progressing toward "social citizenship": a guarantee of reasonably adequate and equal welfare protection for all members of the political community. This policy was financed by a significant increase in fiscal revenues, originating from progressive taxation and distributed through a decentralized system of regional self-government. As José María Maravall (1993) demonstrates, the Spanish experience of "social citizenship" was distinctly tied to the consolidation of political democracy: in spite of widespread unemployment, people learned that political democracy brings social rights. As a result, one striking feature of Spanish public opinion data is the gradual disassociation between the evaluations of the economic situation and of political institutions.

Broad social policy may be unfeasible in countries with acute fiscal crises. Although welfare services in these countries are far from sufficient, they may have to be selectively reduced. Yet, from the purely economic point of view, such reductions will again undermine the capacity to grow. The central lesson of the endogenous-growth theories and, indeed, one of a few robust statistical findings concerning the determinants of growth is the importance of education, whether measured in terms of school enrollment rates or indices such as literacy (Meyer et al. 1979; Marsh 1988; Levine and Renelt 1991; Persson and Tabellini 1991). Primary education for women has particularly high returns in terms of per capita growth (World Bank 1991). And while no similar statistical studies seem to be available with regard to health expenditures, the 1991 *World Bank Development Report* (1991, 53-55) cites extensive evidence about the relationship of productivity to increased effects from health programs. Hence, stabilizations that occur at the cost of reducing expenditures on education and health are likely to be counterproductive with regard to growth.[11]

Short of guaranteeing social citizenship to everyone regardless of individual labor market status, there are three ways to secure basic incomes: maintain full employment, assure everyone of a minimum income, and insure against unemployment. Command economies relied on the first method; market economies on different combinations of all three, often with incomplete coverage. The safety net of welfare services has always been rudimentary and fragmentary in less-developed market economies, while it disintegrated along with central planning in the command economies.

Economic reforms cause unemployment, which is a new phenomenon among the command economies and an increasingly widespread one where markets had previously allocated jobs. When unemployment rises, basic income protection becomes the paramount concern of large segments of the population. These segments are several times larger than the number of those actually unemployed at any particular moment. Active labor-market and income-insurance policies are thus substitutes: without a net of social protection and without income insurance, a loss of employment means the loss of livelihood. This is a cost no one can tolerate even in the short run.

In the face of mounting unemployment, an active labor-market policy is, thus, essential to reduce not only economic but also social costs of reforms. The neoliberal posture is based on the assumption that once the economy is deregulated and privatized and, thereby, the conditions for competition created, markets will emerge and their operation cause resources to be reallocated across sectors and activities. Yet, markets do not "emerge" out of competition: they must be created by policy. Even if unemployment is only frictional or structural, an elaborate and costly system of institutions is required to orient the newly unemployed toward new opportunities.[12] Without a well-functioning labor market, resources will not be reallocated across sectors. Yet even when basic markets are present, the reallocation of resources needed to make some economies efficient may be too massive to take place without extensive state involvement. Poland provides an example, albeit an extreme one. If Polish agriculture is to become as efficient as that of Western Europe, the number of people dependent on agriculture would have to be reduced by at least 70 million, or about 20 percent of the population. A transformation of this magnitude cannot take place overnight, and all the OECD countries strongly support agriculture to avoid social and political effects of dislocation that competition would entail.

To the extent that widespread unemployment persists for extended periods, many people find themselves without a livelihood, and others live with the constant fear of unemployment.[13] And people who experience or feel threatened by unemployment are those most likely to oppose reforms. If their livelihood is not protected at least minimally by narrowly targeted income-insurance policies, resistance may assume explosive forms.

The political impact of market-oriented reforms may depend on 1) the initial income distribution, 2) the distributional effect of reforms themselves, and 3) the scope of social policies.

The effect of the initial income inequality is not obvious (Przeworski 1991). Consider two countries, one as unequal as Brazil — where the top quintile earns twenty-seven times more than the bottom one — and one as equal as the former Soviet Union, assuming the average income in both countries hovers slightly above poverty. Now, suppose that, as a result of reforms, average income temporarily declines without any change in distribution. Then the proportion of newly poor will be small in the income-unequal country, while in the income-equal country everyone might find himself in poverty. This seems to be the experience of Russia, where currently about 90 percent of the population is estimated to be below the poverty line. If the newly poor constitute the group most vociferously resisting reforms, then reforms are more likely to succeed politically in the initially less egalitarian country.

Our knowledge of the distributional effects of reforms is limited. On *a priori* grounds, it is expected that unemployment will hit less-skilled workers in some sectors and public employees, while the real value of pensions and other transfers will decline. The phenomenon of the *declassement* of the middle class — reductions in income that change class position, as when, for example, people are forced to move from an apartment to a *favela* — can be expected to be most explosive politically, while less educated, older, and socially isolated groups may be unable to express their reactions politically.

Social policies face the familiar dilemma between political effects and economic costs. On one hand, universalistic policies are politically more popular precisely because they are universalistic. But they are expensive, and when the level of provision is not sufficient to be effectively universal, access to social services must be rationed through administrative procedures that often deteriorate into clientelism and patronage. On the other hand, targeted, means-tested policies are cheaper but politically unpopular, since they are often perceived as gifts to those who do not want to work. Because universalistic policies entail higher taxes, policies that go a long way toward, but stop short of, universalism are optimal in generating political support.

Admittedly, our evidence that absence of social protection, whether in the form of broad social policy or targeted income-insurance schemes, is transformed into effective political opposition to reforms is again very thin: it relies on the juxtaposition of Spain and Poland.[14] Yet the Polish case —the only country where we were able to study the political dynamic at the microlevel — seems most suggestive (Przeworski 1993). In Poland, unemployment turned people against reforms and overwhelmed the beneficial effects that had been anticipated.[15] If market-oriented reforms fail in Poland for political reasons — and this possibility is real — it will be because unemployment was introduced without a social safety net. But we are aware that the causal chain leading from individual discontent to organized reactions and from organized reactions to the abandonment of reforms is contingent and complex. Reforms may well continue against popular resistance, even under democratic institutions.

This point brings us to our third and final hypothesis: technocratic policy style weakens nascent democratic institutions. The generic dilemma facing governments that embark on the path of reform is that broad consultation with diverse political forces may lead to inertia, while reforms imposed from above may be impossible to implement in the face of political resistance and economic uncertainty. Faced with this dilemma, governments can adopt four different policy styles:

1. If convinced of the need for immediate reforms, persuaded about the technical soundness of the economic blueprint, and equipped with decree powers, the executive may force reform measures on society. This "decretism" is so widespread that it seems almost inherent in the neoliberal approach. An overwhelming proportion of legal acts concerning the economy in Argentina, Brazil, and Peru consists of presidential decrees. The decrees need not, and often do not, correspond to programs advocated by victorious candidates. From Víctor Paz Estenssoro and Jaime Paz Zamora in Bolivia to Alberto Fujimori in Peru, recent years witnessed several cases of leaders who embraced the content and the style of reforms against which they had vigorously campaigned.

2. When the executive has no decree powers but enjoys a majority in the legislature, the same technocratic style appears as "mandatism." As Margaret Thatcher often observed, she told the people what she would do if elected. They voted for her, and thus she had a mandate to do what she believed appropriate; in the next election, the people could decide whether this is what they really wanted. This style is technocratic since, beyond the electoral campaign, it entails no

consultation with opposing political forces in the parliament and no negotiation with forces outside it, either in policy formulation or implementation.

3. "Parliamentarism" is a policy style which can result either from a deliberate decision by the majority to consult and negotiate with opposing forces in the legislature or, frequently, from the fact that proportional representation fails to generate majorities, thus making coalitions and compromise inevitable. While the government enjoys some autonomy, it consults and negotiates at various stages airing publicly policy options and conflicting views. Political support is thus organized as policies are being formulated and implemented; indeed, when no party has a majority, policies can only be pursued given the approval of a coalition.

4. Finally, "corporatism," or perhaps better "concertation," is a policy style which extends consultation and negotiation beyond the parliamentary actors to unions, employers' associations, or other interest groups.

Our hypothesis is that policy styles matter. Three considerations are pertinent, however. First, consultation and concertation may improve the technical quality of reform programs. We realize that this is an unorthodox view, since the usual argument is that negotiating the economic program undermines its logical coherence. Yet this assumes that the program is coherent and free from mistakes to begin with. We have already seen that this is a questionable assumption. Neither the logical consistency of any particular reform strategy nor the design of specific measures are obvious even to professional economists and, in fact, many important decisions are made in a haphazard way when they are hidden from public scrutiny.[15] Moreover, professional economists advise opposing political parties and even unions: their voices can serve to warn about impending mistakes. We believe that the Hungarian reform strategy, which prepared for social costs, is more likely to succeed than the Polish one, which did not. The reason Hungarians opted for this strategy is that politicians and economists, within and outside the government, disagreed about the appropriate sequence and pace of reforms.

Secondly, discussion and negotiation may serve to build political bases of support for particular reform strategies. If a program is forged in negotiations involving diverse political forces, it will be easier for these forces to support. Such a program may retard the pace of reforms and may eliminate the element of surprise necessary for some stabilization measures, such as freezes, price deregulations, or capital levies. Yet — to argue again against accepted wisdom — such a program may be more, not less, credible, because it creates political conditions for the continuation of reforms. Contrary to frequent announcements by technocrats that they will proceed regardless of political pressures upon them, decrees are often simply ineffective, precisely because economic agents anticipate that particular policies are politically unsustainable.

Finally, if one cares about democracy, one must take the political criterion as autonomous. Policy styles matter because they have an effect of channeling political conflicts and of teaching political actors where the real locus of power lies. The Polish experience is eloquent. Most decisions were made outside the framework of representative institutions and people quickly learned this. Repeated surveys show that people do not perceive the locus of power to be in the properly constituted institutions. Consultation and negotiation among representative organizations within the framework of representative institutions are necessary to channel political conflicts. If decisions are made elsewhere, representative institutions wilt; they do not necessarily crumble. Experience thus far demonstrates that regular elections can take place and civil rights can be observed even in systems in which the executive, suspended above the representative organizations and unchecked by other branches of the government, makes repeated recourse to decrees (O'Donnell 1992). But anyone concerned with the quality of democracy will view such a political system as greatly impoverished. And, the experiment is not yet over: the question remains open whether democratic institutions can survive when decrees announce miracles that fail and are followed by demands for further sacrifice.

Hence, we find that subjecting reform strategy to the competitive interplay of political forces is superior on all three points: it improves policy, it builds support for the continuation of reforms, and it helps consolidate democratic institutions. We do not see a trade-off between public discussion and the soundness of economic plans. Yet our advocacy of this policy style must be tempered in several important ways.

First, even if a government is eager to consult and negotiate, it cannot be assumed that it will find willing partners. The dominant strategy of the opposition may be to let the government make its mistakes, so that it becomes unpopular and loses elections. Sharing as a minor partner the responsibility for a socially costly program may turn out to be politically detrimental. The Portuguese Social Democrats bet on this strategy and experienced spectacular electoral success, but the Peronist Party and Argentine unions repeatedly rejected overtures from the Radical government. Moreover, excessive consensus also threatens democracy: opposition political forces are needed to monitor the government from an adversarial position.

Secondly, since the combination of left-wing partisan control with institutionalized concertation with unions and employers' associations generally creates superior economic performance in the OECD countries, a question emerges whether this policy style would not also be successful in the case of new democracies. Yet this question is largely irrelevant, since the organizational preconditions for such a policy style are absent in the countries we consider. Having reviewed union membership in eighteen newly democratic countries, Davide Grassi (1991) found that the largest degree of unionization among them is about 35 percent and that union density is positively related to wage militancy. Norbert Lechner (1985) and Adam Przeworski (1991) discussed other reasons why concertation with extra-parliamentary actors is not a feasible option in less developed countries. Indeed, since in many new democracies employers' associations enjoy a disproportionate political influence through informal channels and tend to oppose vigorously some essential elements of reform — notably trade liberalization and tax increases — concertation may result in undermining reforms.

Another way to pose the issue of policy style is to ask whether a "strong" or a "weak" government is more likely to see reforms through to the end. State strength, however, is an ambiguous notion. Some governments that appear strong because they issue decrees (without previously building the political bases of support) end up simply ineffective, the experience of Fernando Collor de Mello being a prime example. In turn, minority governments, which must build coalitions before they can launch a reform program, may become highly successful, as was the case with Portugal's socialist-social-democratic government. To be more precise, we must distinguish between constitutional constraints that bind all governments and the conjunctural outcomes of elections, which determine the majority or minority status of particular office holders. A government may be "weak" in the sense of not being constitutionally enabled to make certain decisions (because it must go through the legislative process, because legislation is subject to judicial review, or because some decisions are reserved for autonomous institutions, such as the Central Bank), or the government may be "weak" because it is politically unable to legislate without first persuading its own party or without building a coalition of several parties.

We have argued in favor of institutional structures that compel governments to discuss and negotiate while formulating and implementing policies. We see decree power as ineffectual economically and dangerous politically, and we see both political and institutional constraints as tempering technocratic proclivities.

Yet, as José María Maravall (1993) demonstrates, policy styles are not uniquely determined either by institutional framework or by majority status of a government, and given the paucity of successful cases, empirical evidence appears inconclusive. Moreover, we do not deny that governments cannot spend all their time consulting and negotiating: they must have the power to govern.[17] Nor do we underestimate the danger of self-serving, narrowly based opposition to reforms. Several sectors of society — notably, firms that enjoy oligopolistic rents, the bourgeoisie that resist fiscal pressure, employees in the public sector, low-skilled workers in the private sector, groups which traditionally enjoyed entrenched privileges, and peasants of Eastern Europe —may see their interests hurt as the result of reforms. Separately or in often strange alliances, they resist reforms. Yet the idea that reforms can escape resistance or be conducted so swiftly that groups will not have time to organize and be heard or that the program must be concluded before "political fatigue" sets in is infeasible. This technocratic posture is counterproductive to continued reforms and risky for democracy.

Indeed, a central reason opposition to reforms often assumes the form of defending short-term, particularistic interests is that these reforms are not a product of political interplay among representative organizations on the terrain of the representative institutions. Proponents of reforms should not fear democratic institutions: while we understand little about the micro-foundations of individual postures with regard to reform programs, there is overwhelming evidence that such programs enjoy widespread support initially, even when it is recognized that they will induce hardships. The Balcerowicz plan in Poland, the Collor I plan in Brazil, the Cavallo plan in Argentina, and even the Fujimori program in Peru enjoyed overwhelming support in public-opinion polls. If the representative system were allowed to process conflicts about reforms, it is likely that only reasonable differences of opinions and responsible conflicts of interests would emerge, not as a threat to the idea of reform as such but only to its specific blueprint. By stifling public discussion, the specter of "populist reaction" serves mainly to defend particular groups of technocrats against alternative conceptions and competing teams.

Yet since the neoliberal strategy entails significant social costs, reforms tend to be initiated from above and launched by surprise, independent of public opinion and without the participation of organized political forces. Reforms tend to be adopted by decree or rammed through legislatures without modifications that would reflect diversity of interests and opinions. The political style of implementation tends to be autocratic: governments seek to demobilize their supporters rather than compromise the reform program through public consultation. In the end, society is taught that it can vote but not choose; legislatures are trained to think that they have no role to play in policy elaboration; nascent political parties, trade unions, and other organizations are taught that their voices do not count. Hence, the autocratic policy style characteristic of the so-called "Washington Consensus" reforms tends to undermine representative institutions, to personalize politics, and to generate a climate in which politics becomes reduced to quick fixes or to a search for redemption. Even if neoliberal reform packages make good economics, they are likely to generate voodoo politics. Either the executive, impatient with the political process, decides to ram reforms through by closing other branches of the government, as in Peru, or the opposition to reforms assumes an extra-parliamentary form, as in Venezuela. Both of these reactions are a predictable effect of technocratic policy style.

These consequences are not inevitable. Indeed, the reason the "stop-go reform" pattern sets in is that democracy is incomplete to begin with. In a country with constitutional provisions that force the executive to seek legislative approval for policies before they are launched, with effective representative institutions, and with widespread political participation, government initiates reforms dependent on the support it musters. Reforms emerge from consultations channeled through the representative institutions. The Spanish Socialist government did proceed in this fashion and succeeded with widespread support in conducting the country through a painful program of industrial reconversion.[18] It is precisely the strength of democratic institutions, not exhortations by technocrats, which reduces political space for the pursuit of immediate particularistic interests — that is, for populism. Populism is an endogenous product of technocratic policy styles.

A Social-Democratic Approach to Market-Oriented Reforms

With consideration to all the caveats required by the paucity of evidence, we are ready to summarize our analysis in a more prescriptive fashion. We support reforms aimed at stabilization, defined principally as a reduction of fiscal crisis with all its attendant consequences, because we see such reforms as inevitable once an economy enters an inflationary spiral. Moreover, we believe that an increased reliance on national and international markets to allocate resources is required to enhance efficiency in economies that are monopolistic, overregulated, and overprotected.[19] We do not believe that such reforms can be pursued without a temporary decline of consumption, a rise in unemployment, or other social costs. Yet we have been critical of the standard neoliberal recipes since we believe that they are faulty in three fundamental ways: they induce economic stagnation, they incur unnecessarily large social costs, and they weaken nascent democratic institutions. This is why we seek to offer an alternative, "social-democratic," approach to market-oriented reforms.

This approach consists of three recommendations. First, social policy must be elaborated and put in place as stabilization or liberalization are launched. Secondly, the entire reform package must be efficient, in the sense of minimizing social costs, and must be designed with a view toward resumed growth. Finally, reform programs should be formulated and implemented as a result of political interplay of representative organizations within the framework of the representative institutions.

While in many countries the economic crisis is too acute to allow for the development of a universally oriented welfare system — as Spain was able to do — both labor-market institutions and basic-income protection schemes must be put in place simultaneously with reforms that cause unemployment and reduce consumption.

A social policy designed to protect everyone from the most dire effects must be an intrinsic part of any reform strategy that seeks continued political support under democratic conditions. Spain underwent a decade of unemployment hovering at about 16 percent and approaching 22 percent in 1985. During this time, the government repeatedly won elections, thanks to broad political support due somewhat to the absence of credible political alternatives but also to a considerable expansion of social policies. Social expenditure increased from 9.9 percent of GDP in 1975 to 17.8 percent in 1989. This expansion reduced the risk of reforms for groups most drastically hurt by the reform process, and it convinced people that the extension of social citizenship is a credible promise of democracy.

Labor-market institutions must be appropriate for the distribution and the duration of unemployment. In countries with a large informal sector, they must facilitate access to the formal labor market or petty entrepreneurship. They must comprise an information system, perhaps a subsidized credit system to promote self-employment, and, where the housing market is thin, a relocation system. Income protection must be sufficient to cover basic needs and to facilitate job search and retraining, without creating incentives to remain idle.

There is overwhelming evidence (Nelson 1990) that stabilization efforts are normally undertaken as a result of a fiscal crisis of the state. By "fiscal crisis" we mean not only that the public deficit is chronic or the public debt excessive but that the state loses the capacity to finance its debt in non-inflationary terms. The erosion of public savings deprives the state of the capacity to pursue any development strategy. Public savings are essential to stimulate investment and to allocate it more efficiently, to promote technological development, to protect the environment, and to pursue social policies.

Stabilization policies should be efficient in the sense of minimizing transitional costs, and must be highly attentive to the effect on growth. Expenditure cuts must discriminate between consumption and investment. In the spirit of Tanzi (1989), minimal public investment targets should be exempt from cuts and, following Mario Blejer and Adrienne Cheasty (1989), selective instruments that raise the rate of return to private investment should be preserved. Moreover, given the overwhelming evidence about the productive role of education, educational expenditures and preventive health programs should be treated as intrinsic aspects of public investment.

To put it bluntly, while public bureaucracies should be streamlined wherever they are excessive and public programs should be eliminated or reorganized when they are inefficient in delivering urgently needed services, stabilization should rely on a reduction of current consumption but not of investment, and this reduction should be targeted, via the tax system or a one-shot capital levy, at those who can afford it. This includes foreign creditors: in most countries, resumed growth is not feasible without a significant reduction of the external as well as the internal debt.

Tax reform which enforces compliance, broadens the income base, and significantly increases effective rates of collection must be an intrinsic ingredient of the reform package. Tax reform constitutes evidence that the distribution of burdens is equitable, but the immediate economic purpose is to raise state revenues instead of cutting expenditures that support future growth. We are unimpressed by arguments about the marginal deadweight cost of taxation. Empirical evidence is, at best, mixed[20] and present tax rates in most new democracies are abominably low, much lower than in the OECD countries (Cheibub 1991). Most resistance to taxation reflects a collective-action problem on the part of the bourgeoisie: while there is evidence that a financially healthy state, capable of pursuing consistent policies, would induce higher rates of return to private investment, firms and their stockholders, nevertheless, seek to escape their burden.[21] A recent study by the World Bank (1991, 82) shows that the rate of return to private investment projects rises from 10.7 percent when fiscal deficit is greater than 8 percent of GDP to 14.3 percent when the deficit is less than 4 percent. Hence, there is room for a Pareto-improving increase of state revenues: the rate of private after-tax return can go up as the effective tax rate is raised. To cite Blejer and Cheasty (1999, 46), "A tax system which is uniform and predictable, and which is associated with prudent macroeconomic management, may make higher rates more acceptable than they would be in a tax system with many exemptions that is associated with a fiscal position perceived to be unsustainable in the longer run."[22]

If growth is to be resumed, the goal of reform measures must be not only to reduce inflation and to increase competition but also to restore the capacity of the state to mobilize savings and to pursue development-oriented policies. Judicious and carefully targeted state intervention in allocating resources across sectors and activities is necessary to resume growth. Having examined the characteristics of financial markets in most developing countries, Blejer and Cheasty (1989) concluded that these markets do not efficiently allocate investments.[23] The state must acquire the capacity to mobilize savings. According to Blejer and Cheasty (1989, 45-47), the government should "aim to set its total tax revenues and its total expenditures (both current and capital) at levels that would yield an overall surplus, which could then be made available, on a competitive and nonconcessionary basis, to the private sector as well as to public enterprises. This would provide the government with a powerful and flexible tool that would facilitate ... the efficient allocation of investment." Moreover, they argue, "the government could increase domestic savings by undertaking actions which increase the perceived rate of return on private sector investments. One way of doing this would be to invest directly in projects which would result in positive externalities to the private sector."

We have nothing original to say about the content of state intervention: it is generally recognized that the state should engage in infrastructure investments, which is not supplied efficiently by private agents, and that it should pursue measures that increase the rate of return to private projects. This role includes a selective industrial policy that would comprise preferential credit rates for high-technology industries, in which the market rate of return is much lower than the social rate; for projects that suffer from high costs of entry, substantial economies of scale, or steep learning curves; and for projects which have potential spillovers across firms due to externalities and asymmetries of information between suppliers and buyers (Grossman 1990). The danger that the very capacity of the state to engage in productive activities and to favor private projects differentially would cause rent-seeking is real. The question of how to organize state institutions so that they would engage in activities that are socially beneficial and would abstain from responding to private interests remains central. Yet unless the state directly undertakes some investments and induces the private sector to undertake others, stabilization or liberalization will not lead to resumed growth.

If these arguments are valid, economic growth requires a significant and sizeable role for the state. Barro (1990) showed that the present utility of future consumption or, equivalently under a Cobb-Douglas production function, the rate of growth are maximized when the share of the public productive sector in output equals the marginal elasticity of public capital. Ronald Findlay (1990) presented a similar result with regard to public employment. Barro used 25 percent as a rough guess for the optimal size of the public capital stock, and Cheibub (1991) found statistically that this number is somewhere around 20 percent, depending whether one includes education and defense. Hence, some intermediate role of public investment and employment —very far from 100 percent but also far from zero — is optimal for economic growth.

Finally, reform programs must be processed through representative institutions. We have argued that the democratic process can improve the technical quality of reform policies and can furnish the bases for continued support for reform. Yet democracy is an autonomous value, for which many people bore sacrifices when they struggled against authoritarian regimes. The quality of the democratic process, perhaps less tangible than material welfare, affects the everyday lives of individuals: it empowers them as members of a political community or deprives them of that power. And if democracy is to be consolidated — that is, if all political forces are to learn to channel their demands and organize their conflicts within the framework of democratic institutions — these institutions must play a real role in the shaping and the implementation of policies that influence their life conditions.

Hence, our "social-democratic" approach to market-oriented reforms calls for orienting reforms toward growth, for protecting material welfare against the transitional costs of reforms, and for making full use of democratic institutions in the formulation and implementation of reform policies. We realize that each of these recommendations involves costs. Industrial policies, social policies, and political compromises cost money,[24] and trade-offs are inevitable. We do not offer blueprints: the design of specific reform strategies must reflect local constraints, and the trade-offs must be determined by the democratic process. We do argue, however, that in order to be successful, reforms must explicitly aim at growth, income security, and democracy.

Notes

---

1. While the ostensible purpose of privatization is to enhance efficiency or to increase fiscal discipline (Lipton and Sachs 1990), a more likely reason is often the desperate need to fill state coffers or to attract new investment.

2. For a detailed argument that market-oriented reforms necessarily cause a transitional decline of consumption, see Przeworski (1991, Chapter 4) and Blanchard et al. (1991, 10-11).

3. Several research projects seek to explain inductively the "success" of economic reforms. Clearly, the feasibility of such undertakings depends on the definition of the dependent variable. Karen Remmer (1986) studied the compliance with targets set by IMF standby agreements — a sufficiently large sample to permit inductive inferences. But if the implicit definition of the dependent variable is success viewed as resumed growth, then no rigorous quasi-experimental inferences are feasible. The Nelson et al. (1990) strategy of redefining success in terms of continuation of whatever reform measures is based on the false assumption that such measures are uniquely related to the ultimate goal. In turn, if success is defined in terms of resumed growth, there is just not enough historical evidence to permit inductive inferences. Thus, for example, the debates whether authoritarian or democratic regimes are more likely to undertake and persevere with reforms which engender growth are based on four successful cases — authoritarian Chile and South Korea, democratic Spain and Portugal — and innumerable cases of failure. This is why we did not try to set up a quasi-experimental research design: controlled comparisons of case studies are not yet feasible, if one takes growth under democracy as the *explanandum*.

4. With the exception of Eastern Europe and South Korea, the data cited here are derived from articles in Bruno et al. 1991. For Korea, see Rhee (1987). For Eastern Europe, see Przeworski (1991).

5. The exact figures are disputed; see Morales (1991).

6. Note that Edwards and Edwards (1991, 215) attributes the resumption of growth in Chile after 1985 to increased public investment.

7. On the static bias of the neoclassical theory, see Fanelli, Frenkel, and Rozenwurcel (1990).

8. As Newbery and Stiglitz (1981, 209) put it, "With an incomplete set of markets, the marginal rate of substitution of different individuals between different states of nature will differ; farmers (or producers, in general), in choosing their production technique, look only at the price distribution and their own marginal rates of substitution, which may differ markedly from those of other farmers and consumers. When they all do this, equilibrium which results may not be Pareto efficient; there is some alternative choice of technique and redistribution of income which could make all individuals better off."

9. The "engines of growth" in these models are non-decreasing returns to some accumulable factor of production — typically, knowledge of some sort — and externalities. If the returns to this factor can be captured by the market, there will be some monopoly power, as in Romer's (1990) model. If they are not, the competitive equilibrium will be inefficient, since the market will undersupply the factors that give rise to externalities. See Ehrlich (1990).

10. Suppose that at time t=0, a government promises to do A at time t=2 if it wins the election at time t=1. A strategy is credible if A is the maximizing strategy of the government at t=1. If a government says "reelect us and we will reduce unemployment," while it is clear that anyone who is elected must reduce public spending, the strategy will not be credible.

11. More generally, but surprisingly, recent statistical evidence demonstrates that growth is faster in countries which enjoy a more equal distribution of income. The 1991 *World Development Report* (1991, 137) presents startling data to this effect, while Persson and Tabellini (1991) offer regression analyses for two distinct periods.

12. Sebastián Edwards (1990) seems to be the only person who emphasizes the importance of active labor-market policy as an intrinsic element of a reform package, arguing that labor-market institutions should be created before stabilization-liberalization.

13. It is worth noting that increases in unemployment that invariably accompany market-oriented reforms are not necessarily accompanied by a fall in real wages for those who continue employed. Wage rates in the private sector rose sharply after stabilization in Great Britain under Thatcher, in Spain, as well as in Bolivia after 1985, and in Chile after 1975, while in all these countries the rate of unemployment hovered in double digits. Only in Eastern Europe did wage rates fall sharply as the economies stabilized. This is a puzzling phenomenon: see the discussion of Bolivia in Bruno et al. (1991). One explanation is that stabilization followed a drastic fall of wages, another one is that the exchange rate was overvalued, and the third is that unemployment had a highly structural character.

14. In an interesting study, Grassi (1991) found that among 18 new democracies wage militancy is negatively related to government spending, while it has no relation either to unemployment or investment. Hence, it seems that workers are willing to trade social spending for private wages.

15. According to Morales (1991, 29), unemployment was also the central issue which preoccupied voters in the Bolivian electoral campaign of May 1989. Note that we are not arguing that the mere presence of unemployment will cause people to turn against reforms and governments that pursue them, but only that this will occur if the unemployed have few prospects of finding another job and no income security. In Spain, for example, 58 percent of employed workers voted for the PSOE in the elections of 1986 and so did 57 percent of unemployed.

16. Zélia Cardoso de Mello, the former Brazilian Minister of Finance, recounts that to decide the amount of funds that should be the subject of a capital levy, she wrote three round numbers and pulled one of them out of a hat during a social gathering. See Sabino (1991).

17. Moreover, institutional constraints operate effectively only if they are supported by political conditions: institutions do not function in a vacuum. Influenced by the political culture of the United States, some neoliberal economists call for

constitutional restraint as the solution to the issue of credibility. Bernholz (1991, 50), for example, argues that instead of "prematurely" developing a welfare state, Bolivia should constitutionally restrain the power of government. In his view, "the discretionary power of the administration and of parliament have to be circumscribed.... An independent central bank that can refuse to extend credit to the government, constitutional limits on budget deficits and on maximum marginal tax rates, provisions against hidden expropriation without adequate compensation, and an independent judiciary are some of the institutional requirements necessary. Any violation of these rules should be prosecuted in the courts, and changes in the corresponding constitutional rules should require, say, a two-thirds majority in parliament." This kind of a program seems to be motivated by the idea that what we cannot get in the United States, we can introduce at least in Bolivia. But this idea cannot work in either country.

18. Note that when the Italian Communist Party decided in 1976 to support the austerity policy of the government, it processed one million workers through night school courses that explained the economic necessity of austerity.

19. All throughout this chapter, we have said little about privatization because we think that it is largely motivated by the need to improve the short-term financial position of the state rather than by long-term efficiency considerations.

20. Contrary to frequent assertions, the statistical evidence that taxes lower private investment is at best mixed. Saunders and Klau (1985) did not find any effects for the OECD countries, but Swank (1991) did. Blejer and Cheasty (1989) did not find it for the less-developed countries.

21. In the mid 1980s, taxes on income, profit, and capital gains amounted to 4.9 percent of government revenue in Argentina and to 67.4 percent in Japan; the average for Argentina, Bolivia, Brazil, Chile, Mexico, Peru, and Uruguay was 13.7 percent, while for 10 industrial market economies it was 40.0 percent. These calculations are based on Teitel (1991, 138).

22. For microlevel evidence based on interviews with Argentine businessmen, see López (1991).

23. They cite three reasons: 1) the capital market is undiversified and fragmented, 2) financial returns to savings and/or investment are insufficient, and 3) financial assets bear uncompensated risks.

24. To cite just one number, according to Morgan-Stanley Bank (*Financial Times*, December 19, 1990), the cost of social policies that would maintain minimal protection in Eastern Europe over the next five years is between US$270 and US$370 billion.

References

Ames, Barry. 1987. *Political Survival: Politicians and Public Policy in Latin America.* Berkeley: University of California Press.

Arrow, Kenneth J. 1964. "The Role of Securities in the Optimal Allocation of Risk Bearing." *Review of Economic Studies.*

Barro, Robert J. 1990. "Government Spending in a Simple Model of Endogenous Growth." *Journal of Political Economy.* 98(5).

Becker, Gary S., Kevin M. Murphy, and Robert Tamura. 1990. "Human Capital, Fertility, and Economic Growth." *Journal of Political Economy* 98.

Bernholz, Peter. 1991. "Comments." In *Lessons of Economic Stabilization and Its Aftermath,* eds. Michael Bruno, et al. Cambridge, Mass.: The MIT Press.

Blanchard, O.R., et al. 1991. *Reform in Eastern Europe.* Cambridge, Mass.: MIT Press.

Blejer, Mario I., and Adrienne Cheasty. 1989. "Fiscal Policy and Mobilization of Savings for Growth." In *Fiscal Policy, Stabilization, and Growth in Developing Countries,* eds. Mario I. Blejer and Ke-young Chu. Washington, D.C.: International Monetary Fund.

Bresser Pereira, Luiz Carlos. 1993. "Economic Reforms and Economic Growth: Efficiency and Politics in Latin America." In *Economic Reforms in New Democracies,* eds. Luiz Carlos Bresser Pereira, José María Maravall, and Adam Przeworski. New York: Cambridge University Press.

Bruno, Michael. 1991. "Introduction and Overview." In *Lessons of Economic Stabilization and Its Aftermath,* eds., Michael Bruno, et al. Cambridge, Mass.: The MIT Press.

Bruno, Michael, et al. eds. 1991. *Lessons of Economic Stabilization and Its Aftermath.* Cambridge, Mass.: The MIT Press.

Calvo, Guillermo A. 1989. "Incredible Reforms." In *Debt, Stabilization and Development. Essays in Memory of Carlos Díaz-Alejandro,* eds., Guillermo Calvo, et al. London: Basil Blackwell.

Cheibub, José Antônio. 1991. "Taxation in Latin America: A Preliminary Report." University of Chicago, Department of Political Science. July.

Di Tella, Guido. 1991. "Comment on the Panel Discussion." In *Lessons of Economic Stabilization and Its Aftermath,* eds., Michael Bruno, et al. Cambridge, Mass.: The MIT Press.

Edwards, Sebastian. 1990. "The Sequencing of Economic Reform: Analytical Issues and Lessons from Latin American Experiences." *The World Economy* 13.

Edwards, Sebastián and Augustín C. Edwards. 1991. *Monetarism and Liberalization: The Chilean Experiment.* Cambridge: Ballinger.

Ehrlich, Isaac. 1990. "The Problem of Development: Introduction." *Journal of Political Economy* 98.

Fanelli, José María, Roberto Frenkel, and Guillermo Rozenwurcel. 1990. "Growth and Structural Reform in Latin America: Where We Stand." Report prepared for UNCTAD. Buenos Aires: CEDES.

Financial Times. 1990. December 19.

Financial Times. 1991. February 6.

Findlay, Ronald. 1990. "The New Political Economy: Its Explanatory Power for the LDCs." *Economics and Politics* 2.

Fischer, Stanley. 1991. Comment on the Panel Discussion. In *Lessons of Economic Stabilization and Its Aftermath,* eds., Michael Bruno, et al. Cambridge, Mass.: The MIT Press.

Frenkel, Jacob. 1991. In *Lessons of Economic Stabilization and its Aftermath,* eds., Michael Bruno, et al. Cambridge, Mass.: The MIT Press.

Grassi, Davide. 1991. "Economic and Organizational Determinants of Wage Restraint in New Democracies." Manuscript. University of Chicago.

Greenwald, Bruce, and Joseph E. Stiglitz. 1986. "Externalities in Economies with Imperfect Information and Incomplete Markets." *Quarterly Journal of Economics* 90.

Grossman, Gene M. 1990. "Promoting New Industrial Activities: A Survey of Recent Arguments and Evidence." *OECD Economic Studies* 14.

Haggard, Stephan, and Robert Kaufman. 1989. "The Politics of Stabilization and Structural Adjustment." In *Developing Country Debt and the World Economy,* ed. Jeffrey D. Sachs. Chicago: University of Chicago Press.

Haggard, Stephan, and Robert Kaufman. 1992. "Economic Adjustment and the Prospects for Democracy." Paper presented at the workshop "States, Markets, and Democracy," University of São Paulo. July.

Haggard Stephan, Robert Kaufman, Karim Shariff, and Steven B. Webb. 1990. "Politics, Inflation and Stabilization in Middle-Income Countries." Manuscript. World Bank.

Hardin, Russell. 1987. "Why a Constitution?" Manuscript. University of Chicago.

Levine, Ross, and David Renelt. 1991. "A Sensitivity Analysis of Cross-Country Growth Regressions." World Bank Working Paper, WPS 609.

Lipton, David, and Jeffrey Sachs. 1990. "Creating a Market Economy in Eastern Europe: The Case of Poland." *Brookings Papers on Economic Activity.*

López, Juan. 1991. "Political Determinants of Private Investment in Argentina: Field Work Impressions." Manuscript. University of Chicago.

Lucas, Robert E., Jr. 1988. "On the Mechanics of Economic Development." *Journal of Monetary Economics* 22.

Maravall, José María. 1993. "Politics and Policy: The Experience of Economic Reforms in Southern Europe." In *Economic Reforms in New Democracies,* eds. Luiz Carlos Bresser Pereira, José María Maravall, and Adam Przeworski. New York: Cambridge University Press.

Marer, Paul. 1991. "The Transition to a Market Economy in Central and Eastern Europe." *The OECD Observer* 169 (April-May).

Marsh, Robert M. 1988. "Sociological Explanations of Economic Growth." *Studies in Comparative International Research* 13.

Marshall, T. H. 1964. *Class, Citizenship and Social Development*. New York: Doubleday.

Meyer, John W., Michael T. Hannan, Richard Rubinson, and George M. Thomas. 1979. "National Economic Development 1950-70: Social and Political Factors." In *National Development and the World System*, eds. John W. Myer and Michael Hannan. Chicago: University of Chicago Press.

Miliband, Ralph. 1975. *Parliamentary Socialism: A Study in the Politics of Labour*. 2nd edition. London: Merlin Press.

Morales, Juan Antonio. 1991. "The Transition from Stabilization to Sustained Growth in Bolivia." In *Lessons of Economic Stabilization and Its Aftermath*, eds. Michael Bruno, et al. Cambridge, Mass.: The MIT Press.

Murrell, Peter. 1991. "Can Neoclassical Economics Underpin the Reform of Centrally Planned Economies?" *Journal of Economic Perspectives* 5.

Nelson, Joan, ed. 1990. *Economic Crisis and Policy Choice: The Politics of Adjustment in the Third World*. Princeton, N.J.: Princeton University Press.

Newbery, David M. 1989. "Missing Markets: Consequences and Remedies." In *The Economics of Missing Markets, Information and Games*, ed. Frank Hahn. Oxford: Clarendon Press.

Newbery, David, and Joseph Stiglitz. 1981. *The Theory of Commodity Price Stabilization*. Oxford: Oxford University Press.

O'Donnell, Guillermo. 1992. "Delegative Democracy?" Kellogg Institute Working Paper No. 172.

Persson, Torsten, and Guido Tabellini. 1991. "Is Inequality Harmful for Growth? Theory and Evidence." Working Paper No. 91-155. Department of Economics, University of California, Berkeley.

Przeworski, Adam. 1991. *Democracy and the Market. Political and Economic Reforms in Eastern Europe and Latin America*. New York: Cambridge University Press.

Przeworski, Adam. 1993. "Economic Reforms, Public Opinion and Political Institutions: Poland in the Eastern European Perspective." In *Economic Reforms in New Democracies*, eds. Luiz Carlos Bresser Pereira, José María Maravall, and Adam Przeworski. New York: Cambridge University Press.

Remmer, Karen L. 1986. "The Politics of Economic Stabilization: IMF Standby Programs in Latin America, 1954-1984." *Comparative Politics* 19 (1).

Remmer, Karen. 1990. "Democracy and Economic Crisis: The Latin American Experience." *World Politics* 42 (3).

Rhee, Sungsup. 1987. "Policy Reforms of the Eighties and Industrial Adjustments in Korean Economy." KDI Working Paper No. 8708. Seoul: Korea Development Institute.

Romer, Paul M. 1990. "Endogenous Technical Change." *Journal of Political Economy* 98.

Sabino, Fernando. 1991. *Zélia, Uma Paixão*. Rio de Janeiro: Editora Record.

Saunders, Peter, and Friedrich Klau. 1985. *The Role of the Public Sector: Causes and Consequences*. OECD Economic Studies 4. Paris: OECD.

Stallings, Barbara, and Robert Kaufman. 1989. "Debt and Democracy in the 1980s: The Latin American Experience." In *Debt and Democracy in Latin America*, eds. Barbara Stallings and Robert Kaufman. Boulder, Colo.: Westview Press.

Stiglitz, Joseph A. 1991. "Wither Socialism? Perspectives from the Economics of Information." Manuscript.

Swank, Duane. 1992. "Politics and Structural Dependency of the State in Democratic Capitalist Nations." *American Political Science Review 86.*

Tanzi, Vito. 1989. "Fiscal Policy, Stabilization and Growth." In *Fiscal Policy, Stabilization, and Growth in Developing Countries*, eds. Mario I. Blejer and Ke-young Chu. Washington: International Monetary Fund.

Teitel, Simón. 1991. "Comments." In *Lessons of Economic Stabilization and Its Aftermath*, eds. Michael Bruno, et al. Cambridge, Mass.: The MIT Press.

Weede, Erich. 1983. "The Impact of Democracy on Economic Growth: Some Evidence from Cross-National Analysis." *Kyklos 36.*

Williamson, John. 1990. "What Washington Means by Policy Reform" and "The Progress of Policy Reform in Latin America." In *Latin American Adjustment*, ed. John Williamson. Washington, D.C.: Institute of International Economics.

World Bank. 1991. *World Development Report 1991.* Washington, DC: World Bank.

Index

Production Notes

This book was printed on 60 lb. Cougar Natural text stock with a 10 point CIS cover stock.

The text of this volume was set in Garamond for the North-South Center's Publications Department, using Aldus Pagemaker 5.0, on a Macintosh Centris 650 computer. It was designed and formatted by Stephanie True Moss.

The cover was created by Mary M. Mapes using Quark XPress 3.2 for the composition and color separation. Cover photo by The Miami Herald.

This book was copy edited by Jayne M. Weisblatt, Vanessa Gray, Erik Bridoux, and Mariela Córdoba.

This was printed in the United States of America by Thomson-Shore, Inc., of Dexter, Michigan.